ALASTAIR SAWDAY'S

Special

places to stay

British Hotels, Inns and Other Places

Edited by Tom Bell

Typesetting, Conversion & Repro:	Avonset, Bath
Maps:	Maps in Minutes, Cornwall
Printing:	Midas Book Printers, UK
Design:	Caroline King & Springboard Design, Bristol
UK Distribution:	Portfolio, Greenford, Middlesex
US Distribution:	The Globe Pequot Press, Guilford, Connecticut

First published in October 2000

Alastair Sawday Publishing Co. Ltd
The Home Farm, Barrow Gurney, Bristol BS48 3RW

The Globe Pequot Press
P. O. Box 480
Guilford, Connecticut 06437
USA

Second edition 2000

Copyright © October 2000 Alastair Sawday Publishing Co. Ltd

ISBN 1-901970-11-6 in the UK

ISBN 0-7627-0771-2 in the US

Printed in Slovenia

Alastair Sawday's

Special
places to stay

British Hotels, Inns and Other Places

"He who does not travel does not know the value of men."
- *Moorish proverb*

The
Globe
Pequot
press

Guilford
Connecticut, USA

Alastair Sawday Publishing
Bristol, UK

Contents

Introduction	9-16		
General map	17		
Maps	18-30		

South of England	**Page**	**Entries**	**Map**
Channel Islands	32	1	1
Cornwall	33-45	2-14	1
Devon	46-59	15-28	1, 2
Somerset	60-67	29-36	2
Bath & N.E. Somerset	68-70	37-39	2
Bristol	71	40	2
Dorset	72-74	41-43	2
Wiltshire	75-77	44-46	2
Berkshire	78	47	3
Hampshire	79-82	48-51	3
Isle of Wight	83-86	52-55	3
Sussex	87-95	56-64	3, 4
Kent	96-101	65-70	4
London	102-105	71-74	3

Centre of England			
Suffolk	107-113	75-81	4, 7
Norfolk	114-117	82-85	7
Nottinghamshire	118	86	6
Rutland	119	87	6
Cambridgeshire	120	88	3
Northamptonshire	121	89	3
Oxfordshire	122-131	90-99	3
Gloucestershire	132-142	100-110	2, 3
Herefordshire	143-144	111-112	2
Worcestershire	145	113	3
Warwickshire	146-147	114-115	3

Contents

	Page	Entries	Map
Shropshire	148-150	116-118	6
Cheshire	151-152	119-120	5, 6
Staffordshire	153-154	121-122	6
Derbyshire	155-156	123-124	6

North of England

Greater Manchester	158	125	6
Lancashire	159	126	6
Yorkshire	160-171	127-138	6
Cumbria	172-184	139-151	5, 6, 9, 10
Co. Durham	185	152	6
Northumberland	186	153	10

Scotland 188-221 154-187 8, 9, 10, 11, 12

Wales 223-238 188-203 1, 2, 5, 6

Quick reference indices	239-241
Company History	242
Little Earth Book	243
Other titles in the series	244
Order forms	245-246
Report form	247
Index - by hotel name	249-251
Index - by place name	252-254
Exchange rate table	255
Explanation of Symbols	256

Acknowledgements

Having pushed this particular square rock up a steep hill last year Tom Bell was prepared to push it up again this year. Either he is mad or he is just plain dedicated. He is probably both.

For to create a book like this is no mean task. It requires resilience, a stubborn streak, passion, an indestructible sense of humour and a genuine liking for people. But above all it demands a sense of perspective. Thus, after an easy day visiting exquisite hotels one should not dismiss the last one for not being 100% perfect. Similarly, after a tough day among Britain's worst one should not fall too easily into the arms of the next half-way decent place. Tom, luckily, has a powerful sense of what goes to make a good hotel, inn or 'other place'. He is unseduced by frippery and 'hauteur' - two elements still very much alive among Britain's hotel community. He can spot a snob at 50 paces, and a warmly authentic human being at 100.

So this book is Tom's work. He has received some warm, authentic, human reassurance from time to time, but he needs little help, and, more importantly, he never complains. I think he has, with this second edition, created what will soon be recognised as the simply the BEST book on Britain's hotels and inns. In so doing he will have done a lot of people a huge service.

Alastair Sawday

Series Editor:......................Alastair Sawday

Editor:...............................Tom Bell

Production Manager:..........Julia Richardson

Managing Editor:...............Jackie King

Accounts:........................... Bridget Bishop, Sheila Clifton, Sandra Hasell, Jenny Purdy

All things web:................... Russell Wilkinson

PR/Marketing:...................Jayne Warren

Symbols:............................Mark Brierley

Additional photographs:..... Quentin Craven, Lancashire Life magazine

Introduction

I have just returned from a glorious holiday in the Italian lakes, staying in hotels and inns that feature in our Italian book. It was good to be reminded that such a humble thing as a hotel can serve as far more than just a place to lay your head. One hotel high in the mountains above Lake Como left me feeling more human, more conscious of the humanity of others and more grateful for the sheer kindness of my host than I had thought possible in a 'mere' hotel.

It is this special quality in our hotels and 'other places' that makes this book special. We seek it out. We will go to great lengths to meet it. We feel more and more like the photo-hunters of rare beasts and endangered species, obsessed with news of a recent sighting. It is not easy.

I don't need to elaborate on the theme - 'most hotels are awful'. Most readers know it, and have experienced the true awfulness of hotels. It may have been in an old-fashioned English seaside hotel that is run by rules and disapproving landladies. Or you may have had a McDonalds-type experience, where every room is served up with identical smiles and pre-packaged language, where your breakfast sausage (manufactured where?) sits awkwardly in a predetermined position next to the tomato. Less dramatically, you may have been to a beautiful hotel whose owners failed to match the house, or to stay with marvellous people whose house was less marvellous.

We have avoided them all and focused only on the places which will - in their own way - enrich you. Many of them are original; all are highly individual. There are some other very good guides out there, but this one is something special - for we are relentless in our determination only to tell you about places we really like. Here they are.

Alastair Sawday

Introduction

This guide is a collection of extremely diverse places. It is for the adventurous, for old romantics and the open-minded. It is for those who wish to leave motorways far behind and travel to the middle of nowhere; for people who wish to connect with other people; for those of you who crave alternatives.

Above all, it destroys the myth that all British hotels are prohibitively expensive. The big groups and the corporate chains remain paid-up members of 'rip-off' Britain. They harness their buying power at the expense of the producer, cut corners and standards, then charge exorbitantly for their mediocrity.

This book is the antidote. It celebrates an endangered species - the indefatigably independent hotel owner, innkeeper and restaurateur. They all spend their days doing whatever it takes to make their places shine. It is hard work, much harder than you'd expect and far less glamorous than our dreams would have us believe. The hours are long, the margins are tight. The government does much to encourage their collapse. Business rates go up, budgets are squeezed by unrealistic employment laws and Brussels demands adherence to mind-boggling, time-consuming bureaucracy.

Somehow most survive to fight another day. In doing so they keep alive a tradition that is fading all too rapidly: they entertain us on our travels. They welcome us with generosity; they cook with passion and imagination; they fill our glasses with flowing wine and local ales; they allow us the time and space to recharge our batteries. All in all, it is no mean feat. We salute them.

How do we choose our Special Places

We search for the best of everything and write a book without fixed boundaries. If we discover a place where the art of convivial hospitality is being practised with flair, good humour and commitment, we want to include it. We evaluate each place on its own merits, not by comparison. We visit every property; value for money, atmosphere and aesthetics are key considerations. We like people who do their own thing, though idiosyncrasy is no excuse for poor standards. Good views are more important than bellboys, a good walk more appealing than a fitness centre. I shall refrain from listing the multitude of sins that have been visited on hotels by the chains and big groups, but if your idea of a weekend away is to check into the Birmingham Post House, then this book is not for you.

Subscription

You should know, however, that all owners pay a fee to be included in this book. It is an expensive book to produce. It is not, however, a directory;

Introduction

hotels cannot buy their way in - the payment is a fee, not a bribe! We also keep editorial control over what we write. The words are ours and ours alone.

What to expect

Hotels

About half this book is made up of hotels. They range from the small and sweet to the grand and gracious. A good way to know what to expect is to study both price and the number of rooms together. A small country house with between 7 and 12 rooms will be fairly tranquil; one with 20+ rooms will have more of a buzz. A hotel where rooms cost over £120 is likely to be grand. Inversely, if prices start at £60, you can expect less formality. The fewer rooms, the more personal it will be. Under ten rooms with room prices over £150 and you'll get something very special indeed. Room prices often vary quite a lot within a hotel. They often equate to the size and grandness of the bedroom; the huge Queen Anne four-poster may have sea views, but the small twin will have the same linen, be just as clean and you can enjoy the same reception rooms downstairs.

Inns

There are three types of inn: the smart inn, part-hotel, where you can expect a high level of formality, luxury and service (rooms: £80-£140); the dining pub, where a bar remains, but the restaurant is the magnet (rooms: £50-£90); and the traditional inn: bedrooms may either be simple (comfortable, clean, warm - you can book without fear) and have a lower price; or extremely stylish (antiques, four-posters) and have a higher price. Standards will be high, the value for money assured (rooms: £40-£80). Inns often have great range: a smart restaurant, a local's bar and somewhere for your mother-in-law. The food they serve is excellent, with menus to suit all appetites and pockets. Do remember, however, that bars may stay open late. If you are a light sleeper, ask about noise. If you want an early night, the room above the bar is not for you.

Restaurants with rooms

There are about 40 in this book. They are starting to blossom all over the country and this is great news. They offer very good value for money and the standard of service they give is unparalleled in Britain. There is often a Mediterranean feel about these places, the service informal, informative, passionate. They are always owner-run (and owner-cooked) - this is not a job, but a way of life - and while the food is exceptionally good, it is not just about the food; it also matters who you eat it with. They are stylish, on the rise, and will, in time, change the gastronomic landscape of the country.

Introduction

Other places?

Because the odd place crops up that defies pigeon-holing, but is too good to miss: a retreat centre, an organic farm, Pullman railway carriages, a couple of arts clubs, a cliff-topping castle... We like the term as it gives us some latitude to be adventurous, to take the occasional risk, to be a little different.

How to use this book

Map

Each property is flagged with its entry number on a map at the front of the book. The maps are for flagging purposes only. If you try navigating with them, you will get lost. We would recommend the WH Smith/AA road map of Britain; it is exceptionally clear and easy to use.

Rooms

All bedrooms have en suite bathrooms or shower rooms unless otherwise stated. When a room is not en suite, we let you know if it has a shared bathroom or a private one. It is always worth checking when you book.

Prices

The price listed is for two people sharing and includes breakfast unless stated. Room prices can range widely. The bottom price usually denotes the least expensive room in low season, the highest price, the most expensive room in high season. Less expensive inns and restaurants with rooms have very little price fluctuation throughout the year; hotels, though - especially the bigger ones - often have very good bargains between October and March. It is worth asking.

Room prices for single people are listed separately. This is a thorny issue. Single people nearly always pay more on a per person basis. Most owners charge a supplement for single occupancy of a double room, which is understandable. Some do not, which is generous. Others give you a small single room and charge nearly as much they would a double room for two people; this seems unfair.

Some places - usually extremely remote places and some restaurants-with-rooms - offer dinner, bed and breakfast rates only. The price, listed per person (e.g. dinner, B&B £65 p.p.), includes a three-course evening meal. Many places offer both room-only and dinner, B&B rates; the latter usually save you a few pounds. It may mean that you do not eat off the à la carte menu (if there is one), or that there is a supplement to pay if you do; please check when booking (see 'dinner' below).

Introduction

Special break' deals are often available at much-reduced prices. These are for two nights or more and usually get cheaper the longer you stay. These breaks are always sold on a dinner, B&B basis. It is not uncommon in this book to find dinner, B&B for £45-£60 a night per person, two nights minimum. Prices mid-week, off-season can be even lower. It is always worth enquiring.

Many hotels only accept two-night bookings at weekends (a handful, three-night only on Bank Holiday weekends). Weekends bring valuable revenue to small hotels, weekdays tend not to. An empty room on a Saturday night can be a big loss. It is worth noting that if you want to book a room for one night at the weekend two months in advance, you will nearly always be refused. However, if you leave it until the last minute and a room is available, you will nearly always be successful.

Practical Matters

Deposits

Most hotels require a deposit to secure a room. If you cancel you are likely to lose part, or all, of it. Check the exact terms when you book and have the hotel confirm the agreement in writing.

Meals

Breakfast - A full cooked breakfast is usually included; if not, the price is stated. Occasionally, only continental breakfast is available; this, too, is stated. Continental breakfasts are substantial, never just a bit of bread and jam. Breakfast times are given. 'Flexible' means 'whenever you like'.

Dinner - The standard of food coming out of the kitchens in this book is exceptional; 95% of places offer evening meals. When an exact price is listed (e.g. 3 courses, £25), it refers to a table d'hôte menu (usually five choices to start with, five main courses and five puddings). Table d'hôte menus help keep the standard of food high as it gives more control to the chef. A plain steak is often available, too. When a ranging price is listed (e.g. 3 courses, £25-£35), it refers to both a table d'hôte menu and an à la carte menu, sometimes just the latter. When a wide-ranging price is listed (e.g. dinner, £5-£25), it refers to a restaurant where you can have anything from a salad or a bowl of pasta (£5) to a three-course à la carte meal (£25). This is most common at inns. If you are allergic to certain food, state your preferences when you book; the owners will make sure you are looked after. Occasionally, there are no-choice menus. We try to make this clear in the text and most owners ask about food allergies when taking bookings. It never hurts to check. Restaurants often close one or two evenings a week. Again, we try to report this, but it is worth asking.

Introduction

Vegetarian food - Let people know you are vegetarian when you book. Chefs enjoy the challenge of creating interesting vegetarian menus, but need time to plan; some will even run their ideas past you. The same rule applies for special diets: the more notice you give, the more certain you can be of getting what you want.

Problems, problems...

If you encounter problems, please try to raise the issue with a member of staff while something can be done. If you feel you are getting nowhere, ask to speak to the owner or manager; they can often solve your problem at a stroke. Do remember that you are paying to be looked after and if the hot water isn't hot or your chicken isn't cooked, well... it should be! It is also worth remembering that while you may be a little embarrassed to make a complaint, the owner or manager has dealt with them before and is primed (one hopes) to deal with yours swiftly and efficiently. Owners often say 'if only I'd known'. Do give them the chance to sort it out. If, on the other hand, you try, and get nowhere, or if you experience downright rudeness, please let us know.

Tipping

Tipping is not, or should not be, expected though you may wish to reward exceptional service or kindness.

Hotel telephones

We strongly advise against the use of in-room telephones. The charges usually astronomical. Ask for exact per minute prices first.

Credit and debit cards

MasterCard and Visa are universally welcome; American Express is sometimes accepted, Diners Card hardly ever. Debit cards, such as Switch, are now widely accepted and some inns even offer 'cash-back'. Check when booking. A few places take cash and cheques only; the 'piggy bank' symbol will tell you which ones.

Smoking

Nearly all dining rooms and restaurants are 'non-smoking'. The odd one allows smoking when people have finished eating, but it is just that - the odd one. Some places are entirely 'non-smoking'. Inns are less likely to have smoking restrictions, but their restaurants usually do. Most bedrooms are non-smoking, a hard rule to enforce.

Children

Over three-quarters of the places in this book are child-friendly, but the

Introduction

presence of well-behaved parents is required. Often, baby-sitting can be arranged with advance notice. Children's suppers may also be available, while some places may not allow children in the restaurant after, say, 7pm. Child-friendly does not necessarily mean there is much for children to do, or that a hotel is child-proof or entirely safe. Some hotels will only accept children over a certain age; we give restrictions in the text.

Pets

The 'pets welcome' symbol is for well-behaved pets only, generally dogs. The symbol is given if pets are allowed in bedrooms, but that may be it - not sitting room, dining room, swimming pool. There may be a supplement to pay. Pet-friendly hotels usually keep only a few rooms for pets. They require you to control your pet at all times and if you cannot, they may ask you to leave. Please be extremely considerate. Always let the hotel know you are bringing your pet. If you do not, Fido may have to sleep in the car.

Arrival and departure times

These vary, but on the whole your room should be ready by 4pm and you will be asked to leave it by about 11am. Many hotels are happy for you to linger... as long as you don't do so in your room.

Black holes

We try to cover the country as comprehensively and evenly as possible, yet we never include places that fall short of our standards just to offer coverage in a particular area. This book is about staying in special places, not any old place.

Quick reference indices

At the back of the book we have given at-a-glance information to help direct you to houses perfect for you if you prefer to eat organic or homegrown food, stay somewhere with a swimming-pool or are looking for places with rooms under £40 per person. We can also direct you to houses that have ground-floor bedrooms, which are good for people of limited mobility .

Scotland

Talk to a west-coast hotelier about the BBC's weather reporting and you will be met by tormented cries and the odd nervous twitch; the inaccuracy is staggering. Outside it's a sunny 27˚C while on the telly it's a cloudy 16˚C and all of us who might follow the summer sun north stay in hibernation down south. Scotland gets a lot of sun in summer; May and September are particularly good months to visit.

Introduction

Environment

We seek to reduce our impact on the environment where possible by:

- Planting trees to compensate for our carbon emissions (as calculated by Edinburgh University); we are officially a carbon-neutral publishing company.

- Re-using paper, recycling stationery, tins, bottles, etc.

- Printing all our books on paper from sustainable sources.

- Encouraging staff use of bicycles (they're given free) and encouraging car-sharing.

- Celebrating the use of organic, home and locally produced food.

- Publishing books that support, in however small a way, the rural economy and small-scale businesses.

- Encouraging many owners to follow recommendations of the Energy Efficiency Centre to make their homes more environmentally friendly.

The Web

Our web site at www.sawdays.co.uk now has a huge collection of Special Places across Europe: hotels, inns and B&Bs in Paris, France, Spain, Portugal, Italy, Ireland and Britain. They are only a click away.

Disclaimer

We make no claims to pure objectivity in judging our special places to stay. They are here because we like them. Our opinions and tastes are ours alone and this book is a statement of them; we hope that you will share them.

And Finally

Your comments are vital to us and keep us up to date - please keep them coming. There is a report form at the back of the book; good or bad, let us know. If you know and love a place that we have not included, please let us know. You will receive a free book if we include it in the next edition.

Tom Bell

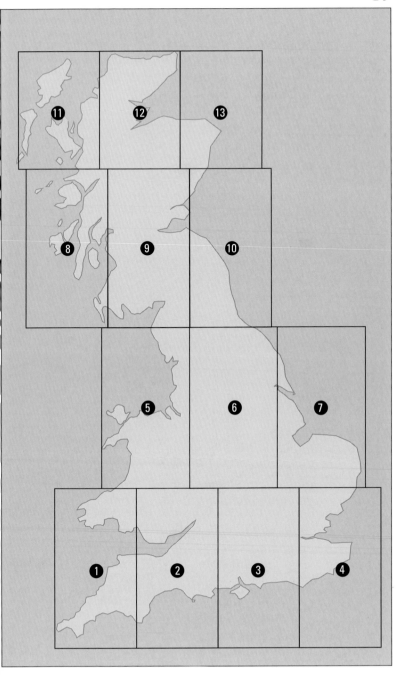

Guide to our map page numbers

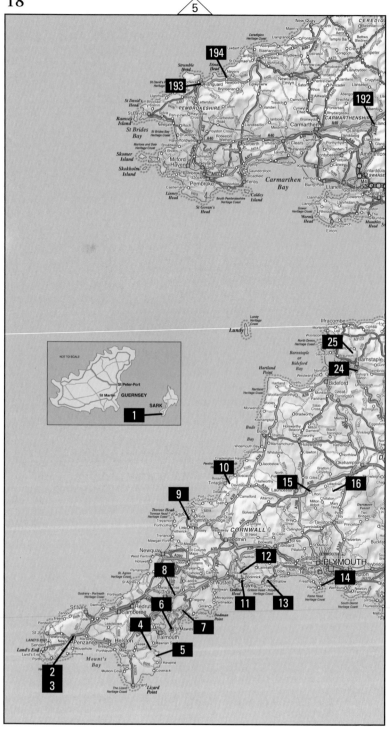

Map 1

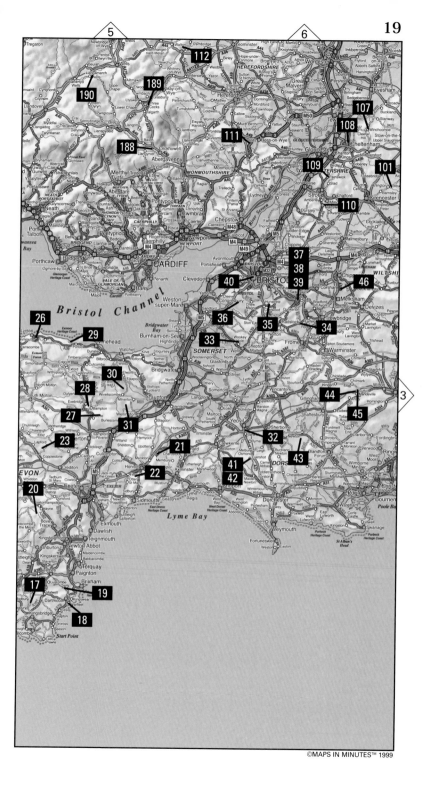

Map 2

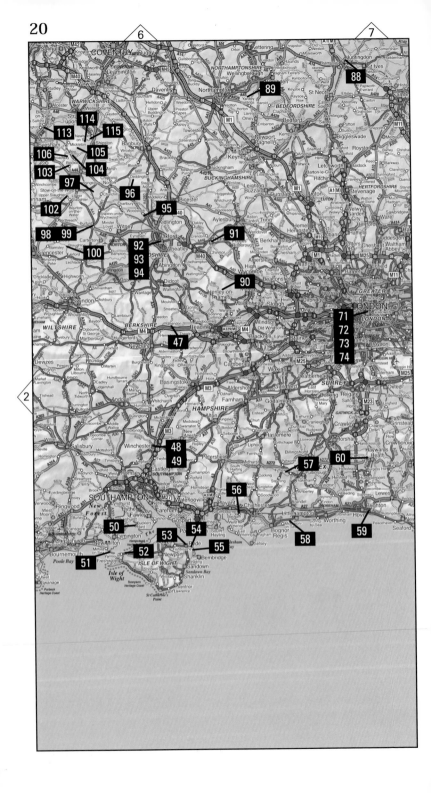

Map 3

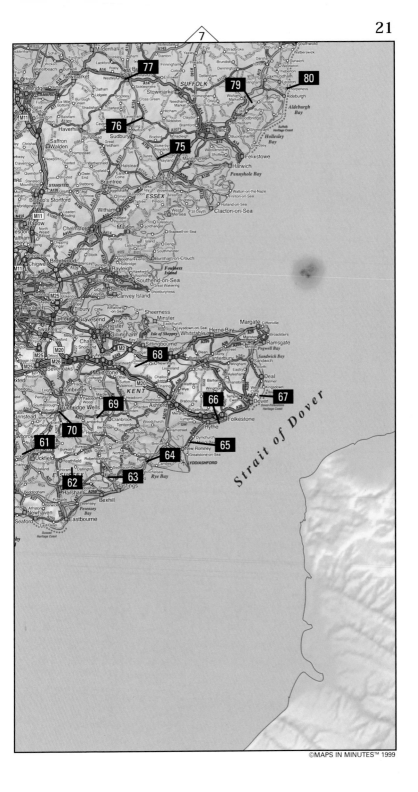

Map 4

©MAPS IN MINUTES™ 1999

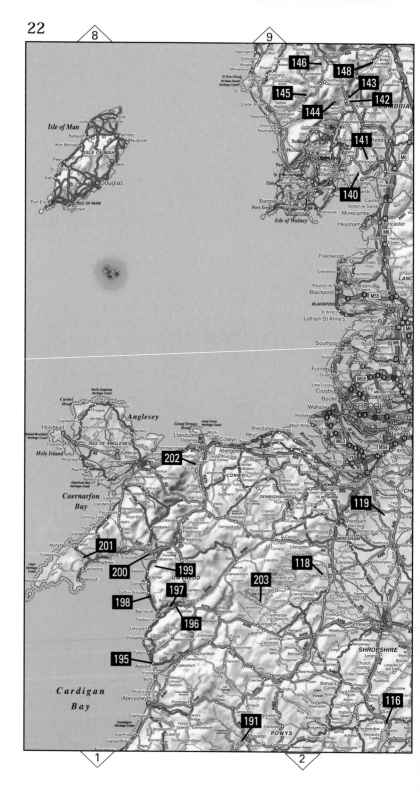

Map 5

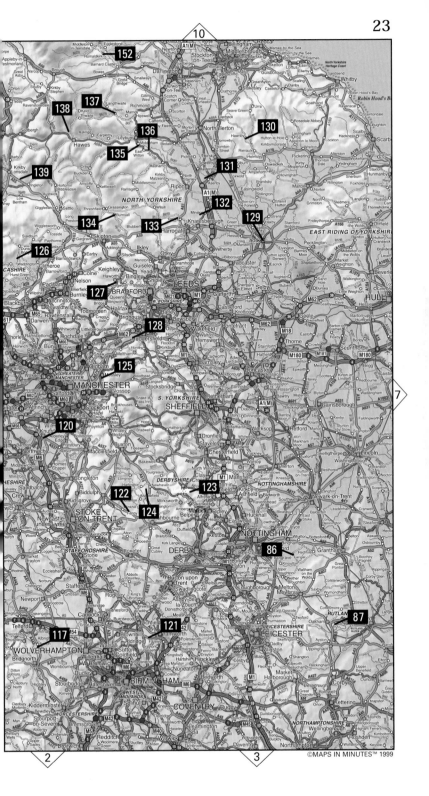

Map 6

©MAPS IN MINUTES™ 1999

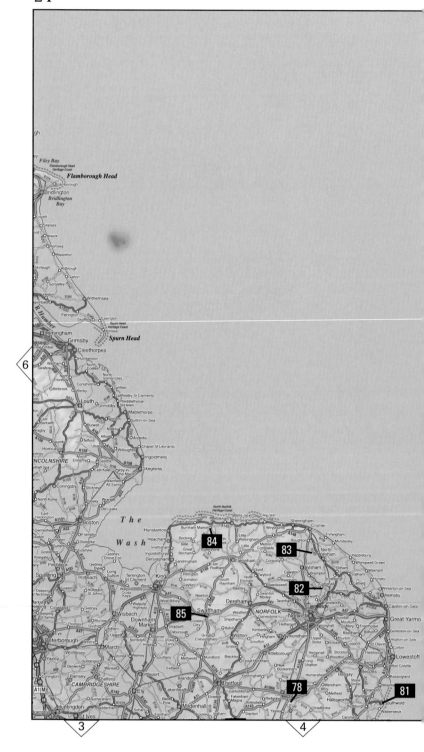

Map 7

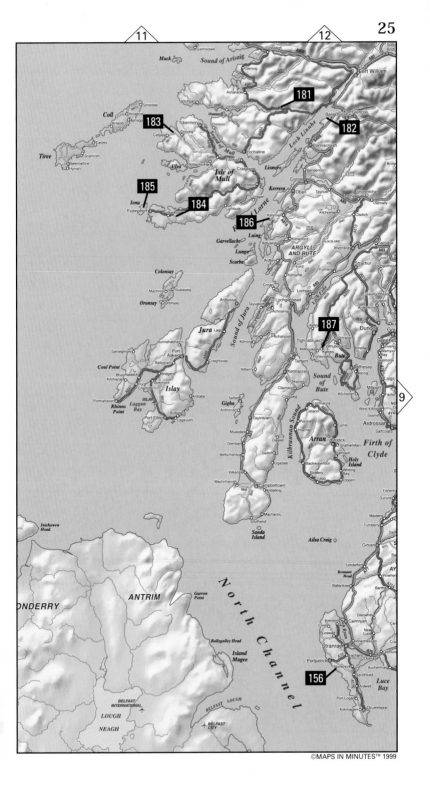

©MAPS IN MINUTES™ 1999

Map 8

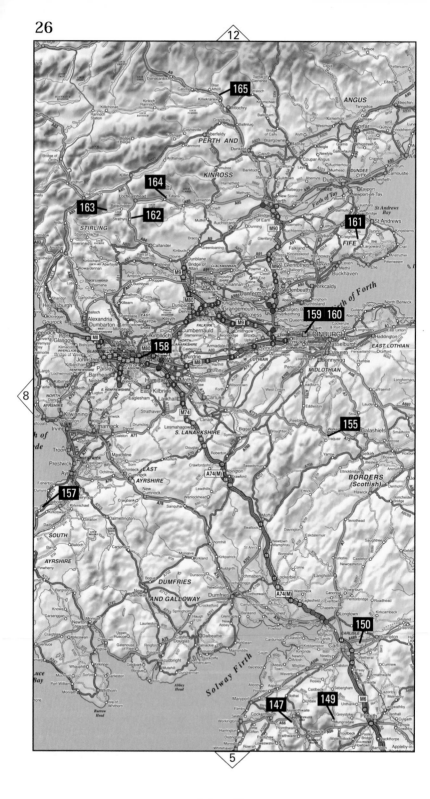

Map 9

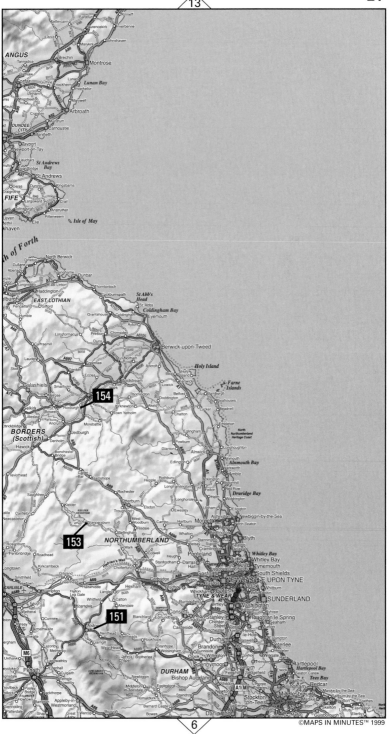

Map 10

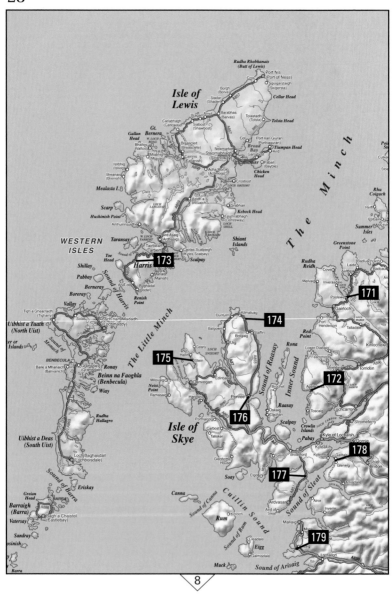

Map 11

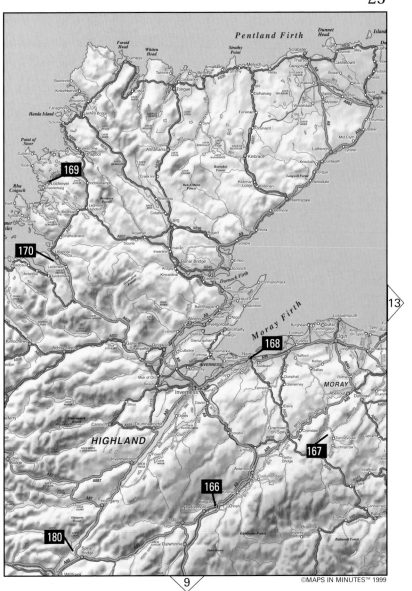

Map 12

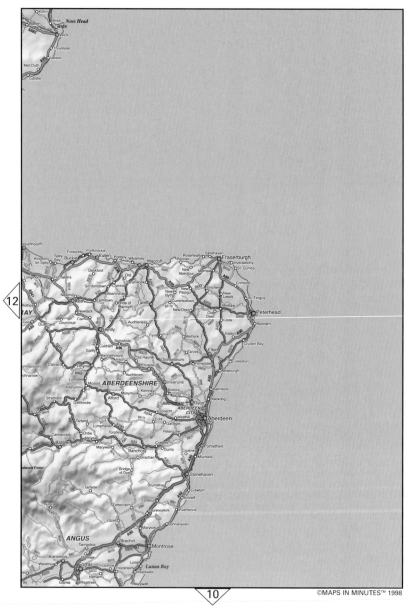

©MAPS IN MINUTES™ 1998

Map 13

The South of England

Channel Islands
Cornwall
Devon
Somerset
Bath and N.E. Somerset
Dorset
Wiltshire
Berkshire
Hampshire
Isle of Wight
Sussex
Kent
London

"Eat dessert first,
Life is uncertain"
– Anonymous

La Sablonnerie

Little Sark
Sark
Via Guernsey
GY9 0SD

Tel: 01481 832061
Fax: 01481 832408

Elizabeth Perrée

If you tell Elizabeth which ferry you're arriving on, she'll send down her horse and carriage to meet you. "Small, sweet world of wave-encompassed wonder", wrote Swinburne of Sark. The tiny community of 500 people lives under a spell, governed feudally and sharing this magic island with horses, sheep, cattle, carpets of wild flowers and birds. There are wild cliff walks, thick woodland, sandy coves, wonderful deep rock pools, aquamarine seas. No cars, only bikes, horse and carriage and the odd tractor. In the hotel — a 400-year-old farmhouse — there is no TV, no radio, no trouser press... just a dreamy peace, kindness, starched cotton sheets, woollen blankets and food to die for. The Perrées still farm and, as a result, the hotel is almost self-sufficient; you also get home-baked bread and lobsters straight from the sea. Elizabeth is Sercquaise — her mother's family were part of the 1565 colonisation — and she knows her land well enough to lead you to the island's secrets.

Rooms: 22: 6 twins, 5 doubles, 6 family and 1 suite; 2 twins and 2 doubles sharing 2 bathrooms.
Room price: £95-£123; suite £155. Dinner, B&B £59.50-£75.50 p.p.
Breakfast: Flexible.
Meals: Dinner, 5 courses, £30.
Closed: 2nd Monday in October until Wednesday before Easter.

Directions: Take ferry to Sark and ask!

Penzance Arts Club

Chapel House
Chapel Street, Penzance
Cornwall
TR18 4AQ

Tel: 01736 363761
Fax: 01736 363761
E-mail: pac@pzac.demon.co.uk
Web: www.chycor.co.uk/arts-club

Belinda Rushworth-Lund

Amusing, quirky and original... the Arts club has brought a little fun to old Penzance. Belinda has created an easy-going but vital cultural centre where you can fall into bed after a night of poetry and jazz in the bar, or after an evening of fish in the gaily-coloured restaurant. The bar is a feast of ideas and art, with paintings all over the walls and a mix of comfortable and attractive furniture, marble open fireplaces, driftwood, wooden floors and a most handsome wooden table. The little garden and balcony off the bar have fine views over the harbour. The bedrooms (attractive, colourful and surprisingly comfortable) are as charmingly flamboyant as the bar is raffish. There is elegance too, for the house was once the Portuguese embassy in more prosperous Penzance days. Not luxurious — the touches of scruffiness don't matter at all — but terrific value and one of the most engagingly individual places in this book. Rather than 'exclusive' (how we lament the word), this is 'inclusive' — a must for the open-minded.

Rooms: 4: 1 double and 3
twin/family/doubles, all en suite shower
and sharing wc.
Room price: £50-£60; singles £35-£40.
Breakfast: Flexible.
Meals: Tapas from £3. Lunch and dinner,
3 courses, £15-£20. Restaurant closed
Sundays (and Mondays in winter).
Closed: Never.

Directions: In Penzance, drive along
harbourside with sea on your left. Opposite the docks, turn right into Quay St (by the Dolphin pub). Up hill and house on right opposite St. Mary's church.

Map no: 1

Entry no: 2

The Summer House Restaurant with Room

Cornwall Terrace
Penzance
Cornwall
TR18 4HL

Tel: 01736 363744
Fax: 01736 360959
E-mail: summerhouse@dial.pipex.com
Web: www.summerhouse-cornwall.com

Linda and Ciro Zaino

Don't rush through; stay awhile — this is fun, and you'll get so well fed. After trawling through the hotels of Britain to find ones to include in this book, The Summer House was a glittering catch. It is stylish, imaginative, bustling, informal, colourful... a happy marriage of sunshine yellows, strong Tuscan shades and wooden floors. Squashy sofas rub shoulders with pieces of pure Gothic carving, a glass wall floods the house with light, and the walls show local artists. The restaurant continues the Mediterranean theme, its elegant room spilling out into the walled garden alive with terracotta pots and palm trees. Food is a vital part of the hotel — *le patron mange ici* (even the brochure is well written!). Ciro loves simple food and fresh ingredients; here they are wonderfully fresh, especially the lovingly displayed, inevitable fish. The bedrooms have an eclectic mix of family pieces and beautiful 'collectables', and are as colourful and gay as the hotel itself. Linda and Ciro run it with huge energy and enthusiasm. It is a place where guests talk to each other. *Children over 12 welcome.*

Rooms: 5: 2 doubles and 3 twin/doubles.
Room price: £55-£75; singles from £40.
Breakfast: Until 9.30am.
Meals: Dinner, 3 courses, £18.50-£22.50. Restaurant closed Mondays. Packed lunches from £6.
Closed: Occasionally in January.

Directions: With the sea on your left, drive along the harbourside, past the Jubilee open-air bathing pool. Turn right immediately after the Queens Hotel and the house is 30 metres up on the left.

Entry no: 3

Map no: 1

Tregildry Hotel

Gillan
Manaccan
Cornwall
TR12 6HG

Tel: 01326 231378
Fax: 01326 231561
E-mail: trgildry@globalnet.co.uk
Web: www.tregildryhotel.co.uk

Lynne and Huw Phillips

Take your pick — Gillan Creek, the Helford River, Falmouth Bay, and the Roseland Peninsula — the view here is comprehensively watery. At the bottom of the hill, the road ends and there are great views across the creek to St. Anthony's Church. At low tide hidden stepping stones will take you there, but be warned; they are slippery. Back up the hill, Tregildry makes the most of the view. Lynne and Huw rescued the place from neglect and gave the big downstairs rooms lots of windows. They are now smart, light and airy, full of squishy sofas and rattan armchairs, with piles of magazines, bursting bookshelves and Mediterranean colours. Wonderful food in the restaurant (Cornish crab cakes, spicy tiger prawns, rack of lamb) and a different table each evening so you don't miss the view, though pre-dinner drinks under parasols on the terrace insure against this (there are sun loungers, too). Bedrooms have a soft, clean country feel: fresh flowers, more rattan furniture, pinks, yellows and greens; all but two have seaward views. A track leads down to the coastal path and the cove below.

Rooms: 10: 7 doubles and 3 twins.
Room price: Dinner, B&B £70-£75 p.p.; singles £70-£85.
Breakfast: 8.30-9.30am.
Meals: Light lunches by arrangement. Dinner, 4 courses, included in price.
Closed: 1 November — 1 March.

Directions: South from Helston on A3083, past naval base on left, then left on B3293 for St. Keverne. After 3 miles, left to Manaccan. In village follow signs for Gillan. Signed down hill and right in Gillan.

Map no: 1

Entry no: 4

Trengilly Wartha Inn

Nancenoy, Constantine
Falmouth
Cornwall
TR11 5RP

Tel: 01326 340332
Fax: 01326 340332
E-mail: trengilly@compuserve.com

Michael and Helen Maguire and Nigel and Isabel Logan

It's hard to believe that the Helford river is navigable up to this point, simply because it's quite hard to navigate a car up the narrow, steep lanes — this is a deeply rural hideaway. It's worth the effort. Trengilly has won all the awards a pub can win: 'Best Free House of the Year', 'Pub of the Year', 'Best Dining Pub in Cornwall', and it really is everything you'd want from a country inn. The ales are honourable, the settles are wooden and the bar meals good. In summer, the garden fills — the locals *all* come here; and there's a jazzy restaurant — pastel blues and pale yellows — and a no-smoking conservatory, too. The hotel sitting room is as cosy as you could wish for with lots of books, cricket and political biographies, and an open fire. The bedrooms, all bar one with valley views, have simple old pine beds, some Laura Ashley, others whitewashed. There's a small lake at the bottom of the six-acre garden, breakfast is a feast (maybe scrambled duck eggs with smoked trout) and you can even arrive by horse — there are posts to tie up to. Locals do.

Rooms: 8: 4 doubles, 1 twin and 2 family; 1 twin with private bathroom.
Room price: £56-£85; singles £45.
Breakfast: Until 9.30am.
Meals: Dinner, 2 courses, £20; 3 courses, £25. Bar meals, lunch and dinner, £4-£15.
Closed: Never.

Directions: Approaching Falmouth on A39, follow Constantine signs. After about 7 miles, as you approach village, inn is clearly signed left, then right.

Entry no: 5   **Map no: 1**

The St. Mawes Hotel

The Sea Front
St. Mawes
Cornwall
TR2 5DW

Tel: 01326 270266
Fax: 01326 270170
E-mail: stmaweshotel@compuserve.com
Web: www.stmaweshotel.co.uk

Emma Burrows and Henry Hare

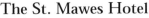

Emma's parents ran The St. Mawes for nigh on 30 years. She took over recently, gave the place a complete overhaul and, as the last drop of paint was drying, 3,500 gallons of water burst forth and flooded the entire place; they started all over again. The hotel is across the road from the sea and as the road goes nowhere, you won't be disturbed. Go for the balcony rooms and you can sit out there all day watching the boats float by — just wonderful. If you want, Henry will rent you something to whiz round in, take you water-skiing or simply deposit you on some distant, sandy beach with a hamper, then come back and pick you up later; more conventionally, there are small, local ferries. The hotel's hub is the lively ground-floor bar that, in summer, opens up onto the street like a French café. Inside, Mediterranean colours, wood floors, a couple of sofas in one corner and you can eat good bistro food here or more formally in the restaurant. Bedrooms are simple and stylish: wicker chairs, flowers, good beds and white walls to soak up the light so make sure you go for rooms with sea views or balconies.

Rooms: 8: 5 doubles and 3 twins.
Room price: £50-£134; singles £40-£100.
Dinner, B&B £46-£79 p.p.
Breakfast: 9-9.30am weekdays;
9-10.30am weekends.
Meals: Bar food from £3.95; dinner,
3 courses, from £17.50.
Closed: Never.

Directions: The hotel is on the seafront in the town. Parking available opposite in public carpark (£6 a day in high season, free in low season).

Polsue Manor

Ruanhighlanes
Nr. Truro
Cornwall
TR2 5LU

Tel: 01872 501270
Fax: 01872 501177
Web: www.chycor.co.uk/polsue-manor/

Annabelle and Graham Sylvester

The lost gardens of Heligan? What about the lost gardens of Polsue — they're *fabulous*. 'Lost' they may be, but the search is worth it with this wonderfully laid-back country house as your prize. Annabelle and Graham moved down for the lifestyle, to bring up their two small sons, to sail, to escape from London. They do everything themselves, so don't think the gardener is necessarily the gardener; it might be the cook, the barman, the waitress... who knows? This sense of fun echoes all around Polsue, softening its natural country house grandeur. Dinner at eight may come at quarter past, but you won't mind waiting while your wine warms on the Aga. Annabelle cooked professionally in London and her home-cooking is just right; my roast lamb was delicious. There's a big dining room with wooden floors, an elegant drawing room in yellow and blue and a snooker room is in the offing. Bedrooms have thick blankets, country eiderdowns, comfy beds. Cornwall-garden lovers will be in heaven — as will just about anyone. The swirly carpet is a national treasure and the Eden Project is nearby.

Rooms: 8: 4 doubles and 3 twin/doubles; 1 single with private shower.
Room price: £60-£78; singles from £35.
Breakfast: Until 9.30am.
Meals: Dinner at 8pm, 3 courses, £22.
Closed: Never.

Directions: A3078 south from Tregony. In Ruanhighlanes, take second right (signed Philleigh and King Harry Ferry). Polsue is a mile up on the left.

Entry no: 7   **Map no: 1**

Manor Cottage

Tresillian
Truro
Cornwall
TR2 4BN

Tel: 01872 520212
man.cott@cwcom.net
Web: www.manorcottage.com

Carlton Moyle and Gillian Jackson

Don't let the slightly shabby exterior of this engagingly unpretentious restaurant with rooms put you off — locals break out in nostalgic smiles at the mere mention of the place, their memory jogged about some sublime dish that Carlton once whisked up for them. This is a small, very relaxed operation and everything you come across is the work of either Carlton or Gillian: they painted the yellow walls, polished the wooden floors, hung the big mirror, arranged the pink lilies. They even planted the plumbago and passionflower that wander on the stone walls in the conservatory where you eat. Carlton cooks from Thursday to Saturday — the restaurant is closed for the rest of the week, presumably to let him get on with his other chores; he put in the bathrooms. They're excellent, some with hand-painted tiles. Bedrooms are small, but, for their price, superb and full of pretty things. You might have a Heal's of London bed, a hint of Art Deco or scented candles. Wonderful old farm quilts hang on the banister, so grab one and roast away till morning. A little noise from the road, but it's worth it.

Rooms: 5: 2 doubles; 1 double with private shower; 1 twin and 1 single sharing shower.
Room price: £44-£56; singles £22-£38.
Breakfast: 7.30-9.30am.
Meals: Dinner, 3 courses, £26. Restaurant open Thursday-Saturday only.
Closed: Occasionally.

Directions: East from Truro on A390 for about 3 miles. House on left when entering village and signed.

Number 6
6 Middle Street
Padstow
Cornwall
PL28 8AP

Tel: 01841 532093
Fax: 01841 532093

Karen Scott

If you dream of the Mediterranean, pack your bags and head to Padstow. Number 6 is the sort of place you hope to stumble upon in the back street of an unspoilt fishing village in the south of France. Karen came here to cook, to live by the sea, to fulfil the dream. Her place is perfect: small, informal and brilliantly decorated. It's not a place to come looking for spa baths and room service, but if you crave style without pretension, attentive but easy-going service and superb fish straight from the sea, then pick up the phone. Checkerboard floors, ferns in urns, wooden blinds and fired earth paints in the restaurant and a tiny courtyard garden full of pots and passionflower — book early if you want to eat here. Bedrooms are small, but perfectly formed: coir matting, the best cotton linen, piles of pillows on wooden beds and wonderful bathrooms that bring the beach to you. The house is bang next door to Rick Stein's deli. They can book you a table at his restaurant, but make sure you eat here first. Perfect. *Children over 12 welcome. Smoking in courtyard only.*

Rooms: 2 doubles.
Room price: £60-£65; singles £56.
Breakfast: 8.45-9.30am.
Meals: Dinner, 2 courses, £19.50; 3 courses, £23.50.
Closed: Occasionally in winter — please check.

Directions: Three miles south of Wadebridge, take the A389 west into Padstow. Parking is not available in village

centre, but you can drop off bags. You park a five-minute walk away. Ask when booking.

Entry no: 9   **Map no: 1**

Trebrea Lodge

Trenale
Tintagel
Cornwall
PL34 0HR

Tel: 01840 770410
Fax: 01840 770092

John Charlick and Sean Devlin

I'd wager a pound or two that people who 'discover' Trebrea either tell everyone or no-one about it and I'd guess mostly it's the latter. It has perfect combinations: formal but cosy, small but grand, warm and intimate, yet never oppressive or remotely pretentious. You start in the bright red-carpeted hall where wooden stairs flanked by fine large oils lead up to the drawing room. The view from here is uplifting, stretching across fields to cliff-topping Tintagel church, the Atlantic beyond. Up still further to the bedrooms that manage the clever trick of being crisp and elegant, yet cosy and homely as well. Beautiful furniture, bright colours, crisp linen and one has an enormous oak four-poster. Downstairs, there's a very snug smoking room and honesty bar piled high with magazines, where, in winter, lulled by a crackling fire, you fall asleep easily. Across the hall is a panelled dining room, candle-lit in the evenings, where Sean serves up great things. Outside, there are five acres of grounds and woodland and the North Cornish coast is only one mile away. *Children over 12 welcome.*

Rooms: 7: 3 twins and 4 doubles.
Room price: £74-£94; singles £60-£65.
Breakfast: 8.30-9.30am.
Meals: Dinner, 4 courses, £23. Packed lunches by arrangement.
Closed: January.

Directions: On B3263 leaving Tintagel to the north, turn right into Trenale Lane beside R.C. church. In Trenale, turn right towards Trewarmett. Hotel is 0.25 miles on left.

Map no: 1

Entry no: 10

Fowey Hall

Hanson Drive
Fowey
Cornwall
PL23 1ET

Tel: 01726 833866
Fax: 01726 834100
E-mail: info@foweyhall.com
Web: www.foweyhall.com

General Manager: Hazel Brocklebank

Fowey Hall claims to be the inspiration for Kenneth Graham's Toad Hall, so how fitting that it should now be a wonderful child-friendly hotel. And, if any adults fear 'child-friendly' is no more than a mere euphemism for 'grown-up-hell', then fear not: everyone has great fun here. For parents, a stunning 1899 mansion that sits at the top of the hill and looks down to the sea across Fowey's rooftops. There's a superb terrace for *al fresco* meals, glorious views, fabulous food in the panelled dining room and lots of time to enjoy it all — there's a crèche, a children's high tea party, nannies, baby sitters... you get the picture. It's just as good for children: there's an indoor pool, games' rooms galore, an escape-proof walled garden... simply masses and masses to do. Every detail has been thought of so that everyone can relax. The bedrooms (many interconnect) are excellent, with fine furniture, towelling bathrobes and good bathrooms; some even have balconies. Children sharing their parents' room stay free and there's a beach at the bottom of the hill.

Rooms: 25: 14 doubles, 10 suites and 1 twin.
Room price: £125-£160; suites £175-£295.
Breakfast: Until 10am. Children that stay free £3.50.
Meals: Dinner, 3 courses, £29.50. Childrens' tea at 5pm, £5. Lunch also available.
Closed: Never.

Directions: A390 south from Liskeard, then B3269 to Fowey. Straight over mini-roundabout and towards town. Half-way down steep hill, turn right into Hanson Drive. Hotel on right.

Entry no: 11

Map no: 1

The Cormorant Hotel
Golant
Nr. Fowey
Cornwall
PL23 1LL

Tel: 01726 833426
Fax: 01726 833426

Carrie and Colin King

Golant is well-hidden from Cornwall's tourist trail and The Cormorant is well-hidden from Golant. You drive along the quay (ignoring the 'no entry' signs), then climb a short, steep hill. The reward is a breathtaking view of the Fowey estuary flowing through a wooded landscape. Boats tug on their moorings and birds glide lazily over the water; it is a very English paradise. The view is so good that the architect made sure every room has it; ten of the eleven bedrooms have French windows, so they are fabulous to wake up in. They're not bad to sleep in either, with big comfy beds, pastel colours, good furniture and spotless bathrooms. There's a small bar with a good smattering of whiskies, a pretty dining room and a huge light-filled sitting room with log fire, colourful pictures and a big map of the estuary to help plan adventures — walks start from the door. The indoor pool is heated all year round and you can have tea under parasols on the terraced lawn in summer and watch the boats zip by. A marvellous spot. *Pets by arrangement.*

Rooms: 11 twin/doubles.
Room price: £76-£114; singles from £51.50.
Breakfast: Until 9.30am.
Meals: Dinner, 4 courses, from £19.
Closed: Never.

Directions: A390 west towards St. Austell, then B3269 to Fowey. After 6 miles, left to Golant. Continue into village, along quay and hotel signed right, up very steep hill.

Map no: 1

Entry no: 12

Talland Bay Hotel

Talland
Nr. Looe
Cornwall
PL13 2JB

Tel: 01503 272667
Fax: 01503 272940
E-mail: tallandbay@aol.com

Annie and Barrington Rosier

Decidedly old-fashioned, and with decidedly old-fashioned ideas about looking after people. If you want to be by yourself you may curl up with a book at the end of the garden, or just lie by the pool and listen to the seagulls. A peaceful place, with two acres of subtropical gardens and a beautifully mown lawn ending in a ha-ha and a 150-foot drop down to the bay, with long views out to sea. The house is surprisingly ancient, mentioned in the Domesday book and once owned by the famous Trelawney family. The air is fresh, the food is French — as is Annie — and very good. French windows open from sitting room, dining room (both panelled) and bar onto the paved terrace and pool. There's a little upstairs sitting area, too. The bedrooms are traditional-luxurious, Laura Ashley in parts, impeccable and bathed in light. The traditions go as far as croquet and a Cornish clotted cream tea, and other food looks good, too: lots of fresh fish and seafood from Looe, including lobster, crab and scallops.

Rooms: 21: 19 twin/doubles and 2 singles.
Room price: £84-£152; singles £42-£76.
Breakfast: Until 9.30am.
Meals: Dinner, 3 courses, £22. Light lunches £3.50-£8. Packed lunches from £2.50.
Closed: 10 January — mid-February.

Directions: From Looe, A387 towards Polperro. Ignore first sign to Talland. After 2 miles, left at crossroads and follow signs to hotel.

Entry no: 13

Map no: 1

Halfway House Inn
Fore Street
Kingsand, Cawsand Bay
Cornwall
PL10 1NA

Tel: 01752 822279
Fax: 01752 823146
E-mail: david.riggs@virgin.net
Web: www.connexions.co.uk/halfway/

Sarah and David Riggs

Kingsand is a dream, a shaded warren of narrow lanes and brightly-painted cottages, with the sea stretching out on one side and hills rising behind. At its heart is the Halfway House, a snug, traditional inn, where the local fishermen drop off their catch at the kitchen door before coming in for a pint. Inside, back-to-back woodburners warm both sides of the room, pictures of ships hang on stone walls and, somewhere, there's a barometer. Look carefully and you'll find a photo of the clock tower being drenched by a wave, then take 30 paces outside and you'll be standing 80ft below the clock! There's masses of fresh fish to tempt you — the fish soup is a meal in itself — but the philosophy here is 'eat whatever you want, wherever you want' so they'll do you ham, egg and chips if you fancy; Sunday lunches are huge and very popular. Bedrooms are simple and spotless with a dash of colour, a sprinkling of books and fresh flowers — nothing nasty, just excellent value. Sandy beaches, coastal walks, surfing, sailing, historic houses, gardens... something for everyone. Bring your bucket and spade.

Rooms: 6: 3 doubles, 1 twin, 1 single and 1 family.
Room price: £50; family £65; single £25.
Breakfast: 8.30-9.30am.
Meals: Lunch and dinner £5-£25.
Closed: Never.

Directions: 6 miles west of Saltash, leave A38 for Torpoint on A374. Follow signs, first, for Mount Edgcumbe Country Park (B3247), then, for Kingsand. Inn opposite Post Office. Public car park next door from £1 a day.

The Arundell Arms

Lifton
Devon
PL16 0AA

Tel: 01566 784666
Fax: 01566 784494
E-mail: arundellarms@btinternet.com

Anne Voss-Bark

Just a tiny pretence about liking fish, and fishing, would not be amiss — though Anne and her staff are so kind that they'd welcome anyone. She was once 'Woman Hotelier of the Year', an award richly deserved. Her husband was a contributor to *The Times* on fly-fishing, and most guests come with a strong sense of piscatorial purpose, perhaps for a fishing course. The hotel has 20 miles of its own water on the Tamar and five tributaries. You can be alone here all day, eyes peeled for an otter or kingfisher, fishing for wild trout, salmon, sea-trout at night. Then back to the country-house warmth and log fires of the hotel, and perhaps to an "exceptional" (*Daily Telegraph*) meal, where no doubt the piscivorous will be in raptures. But this is a haven for anyone, with a games room and skittle alley, for children and adults, and a good bar with a dartboard. We heard a guest whisper: "I'm in heaven".

Rooms: 27: 9 doubles, 11 twins and 7 singles.
Room price: £90-£113; singles £45-£74. Dinner, B&B £70-£80 p.p.
Breakfast: Until 10am.
Meals: Dinner, 3 courses, £29.50-£36.50; 5-course 'Menu of the Day' £29.50. Bar lunches and dinners from £5.
Closed: 24-26 & 31 December.

Directions: A30 south-west from Exeter, past Okehampton. The village of Lifton is 0.5 miles off the A30, 3 miles east of Launceston and signed. Hotel in centre of village.

Entry no: 15

Map no: 1

Lewtrenchard Manor

Lewdown
Nr. Okehampton
Devon
EX20 4PN

Tel: 01566 783256
Fax: 01566 783332
E-mail: s&j@lewtrenchard.co.uk
Web: www.lewtrenchard.co.uk

Sue and James Murray

A thrilling, historical mansion, outstanding in every way. I entered into the hall and almost expected to be set upon by hounds (probably quite rightly). Your senses explode with the magnificence: the roaring fire in the huge stone fireplace, the acres of panelling, the stained-glass crests, the mullioned windows... only the Victorian radiators belie the fact that you are not in 16th-century England. Sue and James arrive five minutes later (possibly by design to allow for the instinctive jaw dropping) and provide the perfect counterbalance to the formality of their home. Our tour takes in every corner — far too much to mention. Highlights include the hand-painted muses on panelling, Queen Henrietta Maria's four-poster bed and Anthony and Cleopatra, two African leopards, once the pets of James's father. But, this all fades to nothing on entering the 1602 gallery with its honeycombed, plaster-moulded ceiling, its grand piano, its 1725 bible... one of the most beautiful rooms I have ever seen. Bedrooms are exemplary — tremendous value for money, and the gardens, of course, are outstanding. Unmissable.

Rooms: 9: 2 four-posters, 1 suite, 4 twin/king doubles and 2 doubles.
Room price: £115-£160; suite £170; singles from £85.
Breakfast: 8-9.30am.
Meals: Lunch, £19.50 (booking essential). Dinner, 3 courses, £32.
Closed: Never.

Directions: From Exeter, leave A30 on slip road for A386. At T-junction, right, then 1st left, signed Lewdown. After 6 miles, left for Lewtrenchard and house signed left after 0.75 miles.

Map no: 1

Entry no: 16

Hazelwood House

Loddiswell
Nr. Kingsbridge
Devon
TQ7 4EB

Tel: 01548 821232
Fax: 01548 821318

Janie Bowman, Gillian Kean and Anabel Watson

Set amid 67 acres of woodland, meadows and orchards in an untamed river valley, Hazelwood House is no ordinary hotel. It is a place of exceptional peace and natural beauty, created more as a relaxed, unpretentious country house. It might not be for everyone, but those who like it will love it. Come through the front door, pass rows of Wellington boots and you enter a world to revive the spirit. Lectures and courses and evenings of music (classical or jazz) all play a part, all carried off with a relaxed and friendly approach. Anabel and Gillian came here 11 years ago and the place has evolved ever since. They have set up a charity, 'The Dandelion Trust', and are also involved with 'Through the Heart to Peace', a peace initiative started in 1993. The atmosphere outweighs any decorative shortfalls, the food is delicious and fully organic and they produce their own spring water. Outside, you can have cream teas on the veranda or roam past ancient rhododendrons and huge camellias to fields of wild flowers or grazing sheep.

Rooms: 15: 1 twin/double with child's bed and 1 twin; 8 twin/doubles, 3 family and 2 singles, all sharing 4 bathrooms. Self-catering cottages also available.
Room price: £50-£95; singles £35.25.
Breakfast: Until 10.30am.
Meals: Lunch from £8. Dinner, 2 courses, from £15; 3 courses, from £18. Packed lunches £5-£8.
Closed: Never.

Directions: A38 south from Exeter, then A3121 south. Left onto B3196 south. At California Cross, first left after petrol station. After 0.75 miles, left for Hazelwood. Gates on right.

Entry no: 17   **Map no: 2**

The Gunfield Hotel

Castle Road
Dartmouth
Devon
TQ6 0JN

Tel: 01803 834571
Fax: 01803 834772
E-mail: enquiry@gunfield.co.uk
Web: www.gunfield.co.uk

Mike and Lucy Swash

The Gunfield will soon be an institution in Dartmouth. At the heart of it are young, enthusiastic owners and staff, so it's lively and fun. Then there's the position right on the water's edge and the Devon coastal path, the waterside deck for breakfasts and BBQs in fine weather, the garden for sun-worshippers, the pontoon for boat taxis to the town quays and motor boat trips out to beaches. You can moor your own boat, too. The view follows you around wherever you go. The bistro, the restaurant and the lovely carved wooden bar all have river views, as do the great bedrooms. Colours are fun — terracotta, reds and oranges — the four-poster room has its own balcony and the octagonal turret rooms are exceptional. Back outside, there's also 'one-gun point', a grassy outcrop with a canon that hasn't moved since 1550, a good place to watch the traffic of the high seas: sailing dinghies, fishing boats, yachts and ocean cruisers all glide by. There are bicycles and water sports, you can go on wildlife cruises, even golf can be arranged. *Pets by arrangement.*

Rooms: 10: 1 four-poster, 4 twin/doubles and 2 doubles; 1 four-poster with private bath; 2 turret rooms (let to same party) sharing bath.
Room price: £60-£120; singles from £45.
Breakfast: Until 10am weekdays; 10.30am weekends.
Meals: Dinner, 3 courses, from £22.50. Lunches available, and BBQs in summer.
Closed: Never.

Directions: Into Dartmouth and follow signs to the Castle. Hotel 200 yards before Castle on left.

Fingals

Dittisham   **Tel:** 01803 722398
Dartmouth   **Fax:** 01803 722401
Devon   **E-mail:** richard@fingals.co.uk
TQ6 0JA   **Web:** www.fingals.co.uk

Richard Johnston

Where else can one find this magic? Richard miraculously combines a rare *laissez-faire* management style with a passionate commitment to doing things well. He is ever-present without intruding, fun without challenging, spontaneous without being demanding. This is his place, his style, his gesture of defiance to the rest of the hotel world. He does things his way, and most people love it. And he is backed by Sheila, whose kindness and perennial good nature are a constant source of wonder. The food is good, the meals around the big table memorable, the comfort indisputable. You may find children and dogs wandering freely, happy adults — certainly — and Sheila's ducks being marshalled home in the evening. The indoor pool beckons, sauna and jacuzzi too; there are ping-pong and croquet for all, perhaps tennis on the lawn, and cosy conversation in the bar. But don't be misled; there is peace and quiet, too. Perfect for the open-hearted.

Rooms: 12: 8 doubles, 1 twin and 1 family. Self-catering barn with 1 double and 1 twin sharing bathroom.
Room price: £70-£110. Variable single supp.
Breakfast: Flexible, any time after 9am.
Meals: Dinner £27.50.
Closed: 2 January — 26 March.

Directions: A381 south from Totnes, up hill, left towards Cornworthy/Ashprington. Turn right at ruined gatehouse near Cornworthy to Dittisham. Descend steep hill. Hotel signed on right after the bridge and up hill.

Entry no: 19

Map no: 2

Blackaller

North Bovey
Moretonhampstead
Devon
TQ13 8QY

Tel: 01647 440322
Fax: 01647 441131
E-mail: blackaller@dartmoor.co.uk
Web: www.dartmoor.co.uk/web/e142.asp

Hazel Phillips and Peter Hunt

Small and perfectly formed, this is the sort of place you dream of. Have absolutely *no* reservations about coming here unless you are after a city-slick hotel. Sparkling, polished pine floors, walking sticks for hikers, whitewashed walls to soak up Dartmoor's magical light, wood carvings, stone fireplaces and candles in the dining room. Peter and Hazel couldn't be nicer and keep themselves busy spinning wool, collecting honey, rearing sheep, making soups — the normal things in life. Don't think of eating elsewhere — the food here is gorgeous, much of it organic. Bedrooms are perfect — cosy and comfy with more of those white walls — but it's the relaxed mood of this superb little place that is priceless. Outside, stone walls and old water troughs full of flowers, then across the lawn the river tumbles past. In summer, sit out for a sundowner or come in November and watch the salmon run up. You are in the middle of nowhere here; walks from the front door are reason enough to come, but we would come for the laid-back simple humanity of the place.

Rooms: 5: 4 doubles; 1 single with private bathroom.
Room price: £64-£80; singles £31-£48.
Breakfast: 8.30-9am.
Meals: Dinner £23 (not Sundays or Mondays).
Closed: January & February.

Directions: From M5, A30 to Okehampton. Look for Marsh Barton sign onto B3212 to Moretonhampstead. There, take Princetown road, turn left at newsagent into Pound Street for North Bovey.

Kings Arms

Stockland
Nr. Honiton
Devon
EX14 9BS

Tel: 01404 881361
Fax: 01404 881732
E-mail: reserve@kingsarms.net
Web: www.kingsarms.net

Paul Diviani, John O'Leary and Heinz Kiefer

Stay for a week and you'll be a nearly-fledged local, a member of the skittles team, an expert in line dancing and probably tambourine-player for the folk club. You'll also be a stone or two heavier — this is the 'Devon Dining Pub of the Year' (1999), the menus seemingly endless: there's masses of fish, locally-reared game, even ostrich. Ramble at will and you'll find crackling fires, beams, gilt-framed mirrors, stone walls, cosy low ceilings and, eventually, the stone-flagged Farmer's Bar. It is here you meet the 'fair-minded, fun-loving locals who have the fortune to dwell in such a place' (one comes down from Birmingham) — they'll have you playing darts in minutes. Bedrooms are just what you'd hope for, not grand, but perfectly traditional with, maybe, a walnut bed or cushioned window seats: if you like inns, you'll be delighted. Outside, you can get lost in the Blackdown Hills or you can simply laze around inside with Princess Ida, the cat. As for Paul, "he's a tyrant to work for," said one of his staff with an enormous smile playing on his face.

Rooms: 3: 2 doubles and 1 twin.
Room price: £50; singles £30.
Breakfast: 9-10am.
Meals: Lunch from £4. Dinner, 3 courses, £14-£21.50.
Closed: Christmas Day.

Directions: From the centre of Honiton head for north-eastern junction of A303. Just before you join, Stockland is signed right. Straight ahead for 3.5 miles, then left and down to village.

Entry no: 21

Map no: 2

Combe House at Gittisham

Honiton
Nr. Exeter
Devon
EX14 3AD

Tel: 01404 540400
Fax: 01404 46004
E-mail: stay@thishotel.com
Web: www.thishotel.com

Ruth and Ken Hunt

Combe House claims a Saxon, Elizabethan and Caroline heritage and has stone-mullioned windows, oak panelling, huge high-ceilinged rooms, murals and a whiff of history at every turn. It is also set in 3,500 acres of beech woods and parkland that run down to the village of Gittisham (Prince Charles described it as "the ideal English village"), full of thatched cob cottages, a stunning Saxon church (some of Combe's previous owners are buried here in lavish tombs) and a village green. Amazingly, you'll find all of this only two miles from Honiton. Yet amid the splendour, it's Ruth and Ken who dazzle. The welcome is utterly genuine, the feel is more country house than hotel and they've managed to create an atmosphere that is both stately and informal. There are hot-water bottles to warm antique beds, luxurious bathrooms (some muralled), fine furniture everywhere and, as you'd expect, lush views down the valley. The food is superb — a feast of flavours — and you can walk your socks off without leaving the estate, or paddle around the walled flower garden. Wonderful.

Rooms: 15: 2 suites, 1 four-poster and 12 twin/doubles.
Room price: £108-£186; suites £225; singles from £80. Dinner, B&B from £83 p.p.
Breakfast: 7.30-10am.
Meals: Lunch, 2 courses, £10-£16. Dinner, 3 courses, £27.50.
Closed: Never.

Directions: A30 south from Honiton for 2 miles. Follow signs into Heathpark/Gittisham. House is signed in village.

Wigham

Morchard Bishop
Nr. Crediton
Devon
EX17 6RJ

Tel: 01363 877350
Fax: 01363 877350
E-mail: info@wigham.co.uk
Web: www.wigham.co.uk

Stephen and Dawn Chilcott

This ivy-clad house is a trimly-thatched Devon dream, hidden away on the side of a hill, half a mile from the lane. You get exactly what the picture suggests: roaring fires, baskets of logs, stone floors, low, beamed ceilings, tapestries on the walls, a curved settle here, an original 1590s oak screen wall there. Much of the wood furniture is locally made, the dining room table a great slab of polished elm around which you all sit for communal dinners. Upstairs, bedrooms are suitably cosy, with long views, timber-framed walls and generous bathrooms. But that is only half the story. Wigham is also a 30-acre, fully organic farm and — from the sausage at breakfast to the lamb at supper — the meat is all home-reared. Stephen, remarkably, farms it singlehandedly while Dawn stays in the kitchen making the breads, the soups, the ice creams. They even make their own butter and if you are lucky, you'll arrive as Stephen is washing the milk churns. If you want, help on the farm for a day; if not take home a box of organic meats, some organic wool or honey. There's a heated pool with a view, too. *No-smoking.*

Rooms: 5: 1 four-poster, 2 doubles and 2 twin/family.
Room price: Dinner, B&B £59-£75 p.p.
Breakfast: 8.30-10am.
Meals: Dinner, 3 courses, included in price.
Closed: Occasionally in winter.

Directions: A377 west from Crediton, then right, signed Morchard Bishop. There, leave village on Eastington road. Fork right by postbox in wall and house signed right at bottom of hill.

Halmpstone Manor

Bishop's Tawton
Barnstaple
Devon
EX32 0EA

Tel: 01271 830321
Fax: 01271 830826
E-mail: charles@halmpstonemanor.co.uk
Web: www.halmpstonemanor.co.uk

Jane and Charles Stanbury

'Halmpstone' means 'Holy Boundary Stone'. The house, a 1701 Queen Anne manor that had 22 bedrooms before the fire in 1633, faces south across to Dartmoor. The proportions remain delightful. Charles was born here and has run the farm for much of his life. The dining room is panelled, there are fresh flowers in every room (lilies perhaps), white linen tablecloths, pink walls, family photos in silver frames, china figures in the display cabinet, a bar in the hall... all very traditional. The bedrooms are immaculate, with a decanter of sherry (free), fresh fruit and flowers. Afternoon tea is included, as are the newspapers. The colours are pink and peach, with pink drapes on an Edwardian four-poster in one room; in no way designer-modern, but all very satisfying. The décor is formal, the food excellent (e.g. monkfish in a mustard sauce, fillet of beef...) and the service impeccable. Jane and Charles are very much 'hands-on' owners.

Rooms: 5: 2 four-posters and 3 twin/doubles.
Room price: £100-£140; singles £70.
Breakfast: Until 10am.
Meals: Dinner, 5 courses, £25.
Closed: Christmas & New Year.

Directions: From Barnstaple, south on A377. Turn left, opposite petrol station, after Bishop's Tawton, signed Cobbaton and Chittlehampton. After 2 miles, turn right. House on left after 200 yards.

Map no: 1

Entry no: 24

Broomhill Art Hotel and Sculpture Gardens

Muddiford
Barnstaple
Devon
EX31 4EX

Tel: 01271 850262
Fax: 01271 850575
E-mail: info@broomhillart.co.uk
Web: www.broomhillart.co.uk

Rinus and Aniet Van de Sande

Don't mistake this for a designer-trendy, London bijou hotel — this is the real thing: raw, relaxed, unpretentious. Rinus bought his first piece of art at the age of 17 and he hasn't been able to stop since (he's now a very young-looking 40-something). He and Aniet had a gallery in Holland, but after they fell in love with Devon, decided to ship the contents over here. Now you'll find 250 pieces of contemporary sculpture in their wild garden, 11 international exhibitions a year in the hotel, a ceramics shop and a programme that includes jazz, bebop, lectures and poetry... if it comes along, they put it on. Every piece you see is original (some in the bedrooms, too) and the range is wide: classical, abstract, conceptual... As you'd expect, there are no airs and graces (you can leave your pearls at home), the atmosphere is completely informal, the food is tasty, the wine flows. Bedrooms are simple, warm, comfy; you might find a wobbly shower head, but if you've come for the art, it won't worry you at all. Don't expect the lap of hotel luxury; do expect an experience unique in Britain.

Rooms: 5: 1 four-poster and 4 twin/doubles.
Room price: £55; four-poster £65; singles £35-£45.
Breakfast: 8-10am.
Meals: Lunch from £5. Dinner, 2 courses, £16.
Restaurant closed Sunday evenings.
Closed: 20 December — mid-January.

Directions: From Barnstable, north for Lynton on A39, then left onto B3230. From here, follow brown signs to the Sculpture Gardens and hotel.

Entry no: 25

Map no: 1

The Rising Sun Hotel

Harbourside
Lynmouth
Devon
EX35 6EQ

Tel: 01598 753223
Fax: 01598 753480
E-mail: risingsunlynmouth@easynet.co.uk
Web: www.risingsunlynmouth.co.uk

Hugo Jeune

A head-ducking, tide-rising, boat-bobbing place with a level of luxury entirely unexpected. As the tide rises so do the boats in the tiny harbour just across the road, creating an undeserved sensation of mobility as you idle in your four-poster under Jane Churchill fabric. The Rising Sun strides modestly through much of the village, absorbing a string of ancient houses and keeping their low beams and twisting spaces. Hugo has used reclaimed timber for beams and a local shipwright has tenderly carved those panels in the snug dining room, where the atmosphere is as delicious as the food. Design-and-fabric freaks can drop names to each other: Gaston y Daniela, Monkwell, Colefax and Fowler, Farrow and Ball, Telenzo... all applied with verve and superb effect. But don't be deceived; there is nothing pretentious here, just honest good taste in those small but perfect rooms, kind people and a most interesting little village. Walkers can head straight up the valley to the hills. *Children over eight welcome.*

Rooms: 16: 1 twin, 12 doubles, 2 singles and 1 cottage suite.
Room price: £94-£146; singles £63.
Dinner B&B £74.50-£97.50 p.p.
Breakfast: 8.30-9.30am.
Meals: Dinner, 3 courses, about £27.50.
Closed: Never.

Directions: From A39 turn into town centre and follow sign to harbour. Hotel overlooks harbour at the end on the left.

Huntsham Court

Huntsham
Nr. Bampton
Devon
EX16 7NA

Tel: 01398 361365
Fax: 01398 361456
E-mail: bolwigs@huntsham.freeserve.co.uk
Web: www.huntshamcourt.co.uk

Mogens and Andrea Bolwig

Two pianos in your bedroom and a fireplace primed for combustion — such may be your lot if you draw the short straw. The whole place has a rare aura of originality. As you enter you may wonder at the lack of staff to greet you, but they are there somewhere — solicitous, informal and competent. You are likely to find music filling the great hall, a fire roaring in the hearth, perhaps the clicking of billiard balls in the distance. Or if you are late the dinner party will be in full swing around the long table; later still and there may be games in the drawing room. But I don't want to give the impression of formality; far from it. This is one of the most easy-going and unpretentious hotels in the country, one that combines good taste, irony (viz. the '50s furniture and odds and ends), all in a surprisingly grandiose setting. It may be a touch faded in places, definitely not deluxe in others, but the mood is priceless. A great place for a private party.

Rooms: 14: 11 twin/doubles and 3 family.
Room price: £130-£150.
Breakfast: Flexible.
Meals: Dinner £35.
Closed: Never.

Directions: M5 junction 27, then follow signs to Sampford Peverell. On bridge here, turn sharp right. Continue 2 miles to Uplowman and then right for 4 miles to Huntsham.

Entry no: 27

Map no: 2

Bark House Hotel

Oakfordbridge
Nr. Bampton
Devon
EX16 9HZ

Tel: 01398 351236

Alastair Kameen and Justine Hill

Alastair left the family business to become a hotelier, trained at all the best places and then searched high and low for the right place to call his own. He found it a field away from the river Exe in a wooded valley, settled in and taught himself to cook, winning plaudits almost immediately. The day I visited, he was orchestrating a clean up in the garden; nothing, it seems, is beyond his grasp. The house is quietly stylish, not grand, but soothing — you look in vain for signs of bad taste; cosily low ceilings, a basket of logs by the fire, newspapers and magazines on tables, the rooms swimming in morning light. Fresh flowers, candles and fine linen napery in the restaurant suit Alastair's excellent cooking. Upstairs, bedrooms are simple, spotless and perfectly cosy, with flowers from the garden and a bit of oak furniture. One has a beautiful, curved, bay window. The service is superb for a place this size; morning tea is brought to your room and breakfast is a feast — flaked almonds with your yoghurt, fresh juice, fruit and porridge. There's Mike, too, handy man, porter and waiter — it's that sort of place.

Rooms: 5: 2 doubles, 2 twin/doubles; 1 double with private bath.
Room price: £65-£90; singles from £34.50. Dinner, B&B £51-£61 p.p.
Breakfast: 8.30-9.30am.
Meals: Light lunches by arrangement. Dinner, 3 courses, £21.50.
Closed: 2 weeks in November & 2 weeks in January.

Directions: A396 north from Tiverton towards Minehead. Hotel on right, 1 mile north of junction with B3227.

Porlock Vale House

Porlock Weir
Somerset
TA24 8NY

Tel: 01643 862338
Fax: 01643 863338
E-mail: info@porlockvale.co.uk
Web: www.porlockvale.co.uk

Kim and Helen Youd

Exmoor National Park runs into the sea here, tiny lanes ramble down into lush valleys while headlands rise to meet the waves. At the hotel, you can spurn two feet and wheels, saddle up a horse and ride off into the sunset. Well, not quite, but this is also an exceptional riding school, so come to jump, to brush up your dressage, or to hack across the moors. All levels from beginner to Olympic medalist, so don't be shy. You don't have to come to ride. Come instead to sit out on the terrace and watch the deer eat the garden (they do), or walk down across fields and paddle in Porlock Bay. Whatever you do, come back to the simple splendour of this relaxed country house. Good, hearty food in the dining room, crackling log fires and leather sofas in the hall, books and games scattered about the place. Bedrooms are big, bright and comfortable with sofas if there's room; most have sea views and the bigger rooms are huge. Make sure you see the beautiful Edwardian stables; you may find the blacksmith at work in the yard, and the smell of polished leather in the tack room is just fantastic. Great people, too.

Rooms: 15: 9 doubles, 5 twins and 1 single.
Room price: £64-£104; singles £32-£84. Dinner, B&B £50-£72 p.p.
Breakfast: 8.30-9.45am weekdays; 9-10.15am weekends.
Meals: Lunch from £5. Dinner, 3 courses, £19.50.
Closed: 2 weeks in January.

Directions: West past Minehead on A39, then right in Porlock, signed Porlock Weir. Through West Porlock and hotel signed right.

Entry no: 29

Map no: 2

Langley House Hotel and Restaurant

Langley Marsh
Wiveliscombe, Taunton
Somerset
TA4 2UF

Tel: 01984 623318
Fax: 01984 624573
E-mail: user@langley.in2home.co.uk

Anne and Peter Wilson

The entrance hall was once an alleyway between two 15th-century farm cottages. In 1720 two became one and it turned into a gentleman's residence, the gentleman being good enough to have it panelled. It's now very much Anne and Peter's place, warm and elegant and full of comfort. The drawing room is the highlight downstairs. With wooden floors, thick rugs and scarlet walls, it feels more like home, all visible signs of a hotel having been banished. Likewise the bedrooms. Some are casually grand, others cosy, but all have that old country house feel. Back downstairs, the serious stuff begins. Peter and Anne came here to cook (though they didn't decide who would until they got here). Now, in characteristically informal style, they run a fabulous eating den. There's a garden, too, with a half-acre, walled, kitchen garden where they grow as much as they can. Behind it sheep graze on the hillside and buzzards fly off to Exmoor five miles away.

Rooms: 8: 1 four-poster, 1 family suite, 2 twin/doubles and 4 doubles.
Room price: £93-£127.50; singles from £77.50.
Breakfast: Until 9.30am.
Meals: Dinner, 3 courses, £27.50; 4 courses, £32.50.
Closed: Never.

Directions: From Taunton, B3227 to Wiveliscombe town centre, then right signed Langley Marsh. Hotel on right after 0.5 miles.

Bindon Country House Hotel

Langford Budville
Wellington
Somerset
TA21 0RU

Tel: 01823 400070
Fax: 01823 400071
E-mail: BindonHouse@msn.com

Lynn and Mark Jaffa

An extraordinary, beautiful building that hides on the edge of woodland where wild flowers flourish. Four years ago this was a derelict mansion, now it is merely a mansion, thanks to Mark and Lynn who laboured long and hard to get things just right. Enter through the large glass front door and wonder at the crispness of the tiled entrance hall, the stained glass, the huge wall tapestries, the plaster-moulded ceilings, the oak, galleried-staircase, the glass-domed roof. Keep going into the snug panelled bar, past the wrought-iron candlesticks, for coffee served with piping-hot milk and delicious home-made biscuits. In summer, the hall doors open up and you can move outside to sit by the magnificent stone balustrading and gaze out over the rose garden and down to the uninhabited dovecote. Bright bedrooms come in different sizes, the two oval rooms at the front of the house being *huge*, with, maybe, window seats, tremendous wallpaper, a high brass bed or a Victorian cast-iron bath. The food, too, is gorgeous and the pool heated to 90°!

Rooms: 12: 1 four-poster, 1 single and 10 twin/doubles.
Room Price: £95-£185; singles £85.
Breakfast: 7.30-9.30am weekdays; 8-10am weekends.
Meals: Lunch, 2 courses, £12.95. Dinner, 5 courses, £29.50.
Closed: Never.

Directions: North out of Wellington on B3187. After 1.5 miles, left at very sharp S-bend, signed Langford Budville. In village, right towards Wiveliscombe, then 1st right again. House signed on right after 1.5 miles.

Entry no: 31

Map no: 1

Little Barwick House

Barwick Village
Yeovil
Somerset
BA22 9TD

Tel: 01935 423902
Fax: 01935 420908

Emma and Tim Ford

This restaurant with rooms may have changed hands, but the emphasis on producing superb food in a relaxed atmosphere remains. Emma and Tim represent the new vanguard of hoteliers who are bringing a depth of experience mixed with a new-found freedom to do their own thing: flair, bravery and masses of ability are all in evidence, all set off by a sense of vocation and commitment rare in Britain these days. Step out of your car and immediately the smell of something irresistible will waft your way. Whatever can be is home-made: marmalades, chutneys, sorbets and ice creams, breads, shortbreads, jams — even pasta; the food here is superb. As for the house, that's not bad either. Emma has brought the graceful Georgian interior back to life, creating a fresh and airy contemporary feel: natural colours on the walls, stripped floorboards, polished stone floors, with anything stuffy or frilly banished to the tip. In winter, prices start from as little as £42 a night each for Dinner, B&B — simply incredible value. House champagne is available by the glass, so spoil yourself at breakfast.

Rooms: 6: 2 twins and 4 doubles.
Room price: £84-£93. Dinner, B&B from £55 p.p.
Breakfast: Flexible.
Meals: Lunch from £10.50. Dinner, 3 courses, £25.95.
Closed: 2 weeks in January.

Directions: A37 south from Yeovil. Left at first roundabout (by Red House pub). Down hill, past church and house signed left after 200 yards.

Map no: 2

Entry no: 32

Glencot House
Glencot Lane
Wookey Hole, Nr. Wells
Somerset
BA5 1BH

Tel: 01749 677160
Fax: 01749 670210
E-mail: glencot@ukonline.co.uk

Jenny Attia

Jacobean elegance spills over from this beautiful late-Victorian mansion into its 18-acre parkland setting. Inside, it's just as you would expect: four-poster beds, carved ceilings, walnut panelling, magical hallways filled with ancient furniture and bric-a-brac, plants and flowers everywhere. The drawing room is the magnet of the house; you'll meet the other guests here, all staring at the ceiling. The room is panelled top-to-toe with a mix of four woods and there's an inglenook fireplace the size of a room; in winter the flames leap six feet high. Hard to believe it's all en suite — and mod-cons too. Glencot was rescued from a state of dilapidation by Jenny and her husband; long hours of toil have brought it back to life. Don't miss the garden. The house has a magnificent terrace with stunning stone balustrade and wide, gracious steps that sweep you down to the river Axe. There are fountains too, a waterfall and an old stone bridge to take you over to the cricket pitch where the village team plays in summer. *Pets by arrangement.*

Rooms: 13: 3 four-posters, 4 doubles, 3 twins and 3 singles.
Room price: £86-£104; singles from £62
Breakfast: 7.30-9.30am weekdays; 8-9.45am weekends.
Meals: Dinner, 3 courses, from £25.50. Packed lunches by arrangement.
Closed: Never.

Directions: From Wells follow signs to Wookey Hole. Before village, look for pink cottage on left. 100 yards on, sharp left at finger post. House on right in Glencot Lane.

Entry no: 33   **Map no: 2**

The George
Norton St. Philip
Bath
Somerset
BA3 6LH

Tel: 01373 834224
Fax: 01373 834861

David and Tania Satchell

I dream of such places, where once an ostler would calm your snorting steed after its urgent canter across the Downs and direct you under the massive stone arch, across the cobbled courtyard and into the snug bar where logs crackled and wenches served ale under the darkened oak beams. Oh well... but The George must have been like that, even though it has been brilliantly converted into a luxury hotel. The building is one of Somerset's finest, a 12th-century inn in continuous use — an English record. There are 16th-century wall paintings, timber and stone everywhere, an ancient balconied corridor above the courtyard, and rear views across the cricket pitch to the church. The village street passes in front, but quietly at night, and the village, too, is handsome. The bedrooms are magnificently re-done with timber reproduction beds and furniture, bare floorboards in some, plain woollen carpet in corridors, luxury in all... impeccable.

Rooms: 8: 3 four-posters, 4 doubles and 1 twin.
Room price: £80-£90; singles £60.
Breakfast: Until 10am.
Meals: Dinner, 3 courses, about £18. Bar meals £3.95-£7.95.
Closed: Never.

Directions: A36 south from Bath, then A366 west for 1 mile. The George is in the middle of the village.

Hunstrete House

Pensford
Nr. Bristol
Somerset
BS39 4NS

Tel: 01761 490490
Fax: 01761 490732
E-mail: user@hunstretehouse.co.uk
Web: www.hunstretehouse.co.uk

House manager: David Hennigan

At last a grand country house hotel where you're encouraged to leave your
Wellington boots at the back door and curl up, shoeless, in front of the fire for tea.
There's been a house here for over 1,000 years (the Lewin of Bristol once paid a rent
of 10 salmon a year for it), but what stands today goes back to the 1650s when it
was built as a hunting lodge. It's impossible to pick out just one feature for praise:
elegant long curtains, oils everywhere, gilt-framed mirrors, chandeliers, columns,
high ceilings, striking fabrics... just room after room full of exquisite antiques, all
with large windows giving long views out past plinths and urns to deer park beyond.
Weeping pear trees and terracotta pots in the courtyard where you can eat in
summer; croquet, a tennis court and bedrooms full of antiques with all the
trimmings (bathrobes, bowls of fruit, old radios). Stroll through the magnificent six-
acre Victorian walled garden on your way to the outdoor pool and see the gardeners
picking carrots for the pot — they ask the chef what he wants everyday. All this
within easy striking distance of Bath and Bristol.

Rooms: 23: 2 suites, 2 four-posters,
1 single and 18 twin/doubles.
Room price: £125-£195; singles from
£85; suites from £280. Dinner,
B&B £100-£170 p.p.
Breakfast: 7.30-10am.
Meals: Lunch from £14.95. Dinner,
3 courses, from £35.
Closed: Never.

Directions: South from Bristol on A37,
then left at Chelwood roundabout onto
A388. After 4.2 miles, left and hotel first
left again.

Entry no: 35

Map no: 2

Winford Manor Retreat

Winford
Nr. Bristol
Somerset
BS40 8DW

Tel: 01275 472262
Fax: 01275 472065
E-mail: omegatrust@aol.com
Web: www.winfordmanorretreat.com

James Fahey

A retreat centre where you set your own agenda. Join in if you want, or follow your nose and walk in the fields. Nothing here is imposed upon you — you are simply given the space and time to explore whatever side of yourself you want to in a calm and understanding environment. Not whacky — don't come in search of answers, but perhaps to forget the questions. The aim here is to remove prejudice and to value the individual. Organised retreats range in content from 'Healing for Life' to 'The God Within' or you may find health retreats where you can try out alternative therapies like cranial osteopathy, yoga or reflexology. All you need bring is a toothbrush and an open mind. "We're not here to change you, but if you want to change, this is a good place to do it." There's a great respect for privacy — it's a place to find real peace — and non-believers are as welcome as anyone. Books everywhere, simple bedrooms (warm and spotless), communal dining, silent suppers, good food, open country all around. A very special place.

Rooms: 35: 27 twins and 8 singles.
Room price: Full board £32.50-£37.50 p.p.
Breakfast: 8.30am.
Meals: All meals included in price.
Closed: Never.

Directions: A38 south from Bristol. Left onto B3130, signed Winford. There, 2nd right, signed Winford Manor. House at top of hill.

The Queensberry Hotel and Olive Tree Restaurant

Russel Street, Bath
Bath and N.E. Somerset
BA1 2QF
Tel: 01225 447928
Fax: 01225 446065
E-mail: enquiries@bathqueensberry.com
Web: www.bathqueensberry.com

Stephen and Penny Ross

The Queensberry is an old favourite, grand but totally unpretentious and immensely enjoyable. It is rare to find a hotel of this size and elegance still in private hands, rarer still to find the owners so actively deployed. Stephen is 'everywhere' and even though he no longer cooks in the famed basement restaurant, his Dauphinoise potatoes remain, rightly, legendary. Penny keeps her eye on the walls. The bedrooms are magnificent — contemporary and dramatic, with bold inspirational colours and fabrics. If you feel like spoiling yourself, have breakfast brought up to you: croissants, orange juice, fresh coffee, warm milk and a newspaper. Then, pad around in wonderful white bathrobes feeling a million dollars. The bath runs in seconds, the shower imitates a monsoon. At night, pop down to supper and when you get back your bed will have been turned down, your towels refreshed. As for the home-made fudge after supper... just wonderful! All this in a John Wood house in the centre of Bath, a minute's walk from the Assembly Rooms.

Rooms: 29: 28 doubles and twins and 1 four-poster.
Room price: £120-£210; singles from £90.
Breakfast: 7.30-9.30am; 8-10am on Sundays. Continental included; Full English £9.50.
Meals: Lunch from £12.50. Dinner from £21.
Closed: Christmas & New Year.

Directions: Take London Road (A4) towards Bath centre until it becomes Paragon. First right into Lansdown, second left into Bennett St, then first right into Russel St.

Entry no: 37   **Map no: 2**

Paradise House

Holloway
Bath
Bath and N.E. Somerset
BA2 4PX

Tel: 01225 317723
Fax: 01225 482005
E-mail: info@paradise-house.co.uk
Web: www.paradise-house.co.uk

David and Annie Lanz

It must be well nigh impossible to stay at Paradise House and not enter the garden. The view — a 180-degree spectacle of the city — is magical. You see it at the end of the corridor when you enter and immediately it draws you out. The Royal Crescent and the Abbey, floodlit at night, are dazzling advertisements for Bath. In summer, hot air balloons float across low enough for you to hear the roar of the flame. Wonderful — as are the rooms, a mix of yellows and blues, some with huge bay windows for those views, another with a four-poster. All have a soft country feel with drapes, wicker chairs and good bathrooms. Downstairs, the sitting room has lovely stone arched French windows (wherever possible, the house seems to be made of glass). In summer, it moves outside. Two doors up on Holloway (the old Roman Road), the old Monastery is now owned by a music teacher. He sometimes leaves his door open when he plays, so tea in the garden really can be something very special. Bells may peal too. Only seven minutes walk from the centre.

Rooms: 9: 1 four-poster, 1 family, 4 twins and 3 doubles.
Room price: £65-£130; singles £55-£75.
Breakfast: Until 9.30am.
Meals: An easy walk to all Bath's restaurants.
Closed: Christmas week.

Directions: From Bath train station follow one-way system to Churchill Bridge. Take A367 exit from roundabout up hill. After 0.75 miles turn left at 'Day and Pierce'. Left down hill into cul-de-sac. On left.

Map no: 2

Entry no: 38

Apsley House
141 Newbridge Hill
Bath
Bath and N.E. Somerset
BA1 3PT

Tel: 01225 336966
Fax: 01225 425462
E-mail: info@apsley-house.co.uk
Web: www.apsley-house.co.uk

David and Annie Lanz

Apsley House takes its name from the Duke of Wellington's main London residence
which had the mighty address 'No.1 London'. The Iron Duke is thought to have
lived here, though if he did the tempo was probably a little stiffer than it is now with
David and Annie at the helm. Take a drink from the bar, then collapse into one of
the sofas in the drawing room. It's full of great furniture and fabrics, tallboy porter
chairs, gilt mirrors and rich Colefax and Fowler curtains. There's also a huge arched
window overlooking the garden. The dining room is separated by an arch and
antique screens and shares the same warm elegance, with fresh flowers on all the
tables and nice little touches like jugs of iced water at breakfast. Upstairs most of the
pretty bedrooms are huge and have good bathrooms with power showers. Morning
papers are dropped off at your door, your clothes can be laundered, and there's a car
park too, which in this city is precious indeed. *Children over five welcome.*

Rooms: 9: 1 four-poster, 5 twin/doubles
and 3 doubles.
Room price: £70-£110; singles £45-£65.
Breakfast: Until 9am weekdays;
9.30am weekends.
Meals: Available locally.
Closed: Christmas.

Directions: A4 west into Bath. Keep right
at first mini-roundabout. Continue for
about 2 miles, then follow 'Bristol A4'
signs. Pass Total garage on right. At next lights, branch right. Hotel on left after 1
mile.

Entry no: 39   **Map no: 2**

Hotel du Vin and Bistro
The Sugar House
Narrow Lewins Mead
Bristol
BS1 2NH

Tel: 0117 925 5577
Fax: 0117 925 1199
E-mail: admin@bristol.hotelduvin.co.uk
Web: www.hotelduvin.com

Manager: Charles Morgan

Robin Hutson and his team get better and better as they cover the country with their re-invention of the grand townhouse hotel, the 'grand' turning 'casual' to the joy of all. This, their latest venture, will win awards (as have the other two), but most notable is the challenge inherent in their prices: if they can offer such luxury for £125, others must look to their laurels. Lots of space, stone walls, boarded floors, rugs, squishy sofas and sandblasted beams. The courtyard entrance has parasols, tables and chairs sprinkled around a fountain while in the glass-fronted lobby, a fire flies up a 100-foot chimney — a remnant of the building's days as a warehouse. Up the steel staircase, spectacular bedrooms have a minimalist Manhattan-loft feel: low-slung furniture, handmade beds, off-white walls and hessian; big bathrooms — the best I've ever seen — have walk-through, power showers, baths, too. But always, at the heart of a Hotel du Vin, there's the bistro, French to the core, full of life and a great place to be. You can also play billiards or walk into the *humidor* and buy a Havana.

Rooms: 40: 30 doubles, 5 twins and 5 suites.
Room price: £99-£125; suites £150-£185.
Breakfast: 7-9.30am weekdays; 8-10am weekends. Continental £7.50; Full English £10.50.
Meals: Lunch and dinner, 3 courses with bottle of house wine, about £35 in bistro.
Closed: Never.

Directions: M4, junction 19, then M32 into Bristol. Follow signs to city centre and past big Bentalls store on your left. After about 500 yards double back on yourself at traffic lights. Hotel is visible from main road down a small side road after 100 yards on left.

Map no: 2   **Entry no: 40**

Summer Lodge

Summer Lane
Evershot
Dorset
DT2 0JR

Tel: 01935 83424
Fax: 01935 83005
E-mail: reservations@summerlodgehotel.com
Web: www.summerlodgehotel.com

Nigel and Margaret Corbett   Manager: Daniel Hostettler

Nine logs on the fire couldn't tempt the cat, who preferred to bathe proprietorially in sunlight on the carpet, and when the smart French waiter brought morning coffee, he stepped over her nonchalantly while his tray spiralled effortlessly down to the table. Summer Lodge is a nostalgic trip back to 'old-school' England, to old-fashioned comforts and marvellous service. "We try to do the little things well," says Nigel. Thus you get the turndown service, the fresh milk and ice buckets in bedrooms, the morning newspaper waiting at your breakfast table, the freshly-baked breads and sumptuous biscuits — the sheer generosity of spirit. There's humour, too (it wouldn't be properly 'old-school' if there wasn't), so search for the alternative brochure in the sitting room. In the courtyard Margaret's multitude of tubs blaze brightly and if you stray further afield, you'll find the pool, the tennis court, croquet on the lawn. Don't forget to eat — the food here is perfection: afternoon tea is legendary, there are freshly-baked croissants for breakfasts in bed and a cheeseboard to thrill a Frenchman.

Rooms: 19 twin/doubles.
Room price: £120-£285; singles from £85. Dinner, B&B from £100 p.p.
Breakfast: 7.30-10am.
Meals: Lunch, 2 courses, £12.50.
Dinner, 3 courses, £42.50.
Closed: Never.

Directions: South from Yeovil on A37. After about 5 miles, right, signed Evershot. 1st left in village into Summer Lane. Hotel signed right.

Entry no: 41

Map no:

The Acorn Inn

Evershot
Dorchester
Dorset
DT2 0JW

Tel: 01935 83228
Fax: 01935 83707
E-mail: lee@acorn-inn.co.uk
Web: www.acorn-inn.co.uk

Susie and Martyn Lee

An inn for nearly 400 years, The Acorn has a tale or two to tell; Thomas Hardy called it the Sow and Acorn and let Tess rest a night here. Martyn and Susie are locals who took over recently, their mission being to preserve all the traditions of an old inn while giving the creature comforts a 21st-century zap. The effect is bedrooms that creak with age *and* style; canopied four-posters rest on uneven floors. In Tess (all the rooms have a Hardy connection) the pub sign hangs outside the window and there's an Edwardian seven-foot mahogany bed. Downstairs, panelled and beamed bars echo to the merry chink of glass and cutlery. Much local laughter too for this is above all a locals' pub, the heart of village life. There are also open fires, a skittle alley, a small beer garden and, if you keep going, deer parks and ancient woods for revitalising Sunday strolls.

Rooms: 9: 4 doubles, 3 twins,
2 four-posters.
Room price: £80-£120; singles £55.
Breakfast: Flexible.
Meals: British menu in restaurant and bar
from £3.25-£12.95.
Closed: Never.

Directions: One mile off A37 Yeovil-
Dorchester road, in centre of Evershot
village.

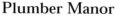

Plumber Manor

Sturminster Newton
Dorset
DT10 2AF

Tel: 01258 472507
Fax: 01258 473370
E-mail: book@plumbermanor.com

Richard, Alison and Brian Prideaux-Brune

The *enormous* old sofa on the landing is surely the most uncomfortable thing I have ever sat on, but it is irresistibly vast and the only discomfort Plumber has to offer. While the sofa might be old, the family is positively ancient. They go back to William the Conqueror and have lived "in the area" ever since, the last 300 years right here at Plumber. Outside, there's a large, sloping lawn, a white bridge over the river and deck chairs scattered about the well-manicured garden. Inside, the house remains more home than hotel with huge family portraits crammed on the walls (everything in this house seems to be *big*); the atmosphere is relaxed and informal without a trace of pomposity. Bedrooms in the main house are more homely; those in the converted stables are bigger with fresher colours and fabrics. Best of all at Plumber is the family triumvirate of Brian (in the kitchen), Richard (behind the bar and guaranteed to provide laughter) and Alison (simply everywhere). They know exactly how to make you feel at home. *Pets by arrangement.*

Rooms: 16: In house: 2 doubles and 3 twin/doubles; 1 twin/double with private bath. In Courtyard: 10 twin/doubles.
Room price: £95-£145; singles from £80.
Breakfast: Until 9.30am.
Meals: Dinner, 2 courses, from £19; 3 courses, from £22.50.
Closed: February.

Directions: In Sturminster Newton take the road south to Hazlebury Bryan for 2 miles. The house is on the left.

The Compasses Inn

Lower Chicksgrove
Tisbury
Wiltshire
SP3 6NB

Tel: 01722 714318
Fax: 01722 714318

Jon and Caren Bold

One's first impression is of having arrived at the perfect English pub. So is the second impression. The setting is almost over-the-top: crinkly-roaded village of thatched cottages and beamed walls. The pub seems to have settled into the ground, the bedroom windows just above the level of the lawn. You instinctively duck into the sudden darkness of the bar, to have your nostalgia nourished by a long wooden room, flagstones, cubicles, piano, fireplace — the works. Jon and Caren are fresher and more modern than their pub, and are a charming counterpoint to the suitably dark and cosy interior. The bedrooms are as perfect as the pub, each leading off an attractive little carpeted lobby and furnished simply, properly, cosily. Pine beds, coloured duvets, plain carpets, nothing grand and nothing ugly. Beyond the windows is the serenity of Wiltshire at its sweetest. And the food: far better than you'd expect of a pub. Modest, ineffably pretty, and great value.

Rooms: 4: 3 doubles and 1 twin.
Room price: £55; singles £40.
Breakfast: Flexible.
Meals: Lunch and dinner £3-£25.
Closed: Restaurant closed Sundays. Bar and restaurant both closed on Mondays.

Directions: West from Salisbury on A30. Pass through Fovant, take third right, signed Lower Chicksgrove, then first left down single track road to the village.

Map no: 2

Entry no: 44

Howard's House

Teffont Evias
Nr. Salisbury
Wiltshire
SP3 5RJ

Tel: 01722 716392 or 716821
Fax: 01722 716820
E-mail: paul.firmin@virgin.net
Web: www.howardshousehotel.co.uk

Paul Firmin

Howard's House has all the ingredients of an English idyll: a quiet village, gently rising hills, a soaring church spire and the occasional rattle of a tractor; it's the last house in the village too, with one toe in deep country. It's no less English inside with a stone-flagged hall, stone-mullioned windows, open fires in winter, the scent of flowers from the garden in summer. There's masses of space — *no* cluttering in this house — and every room seems to be swimming in light. The style is of elegant simplicity: warm pastel colours in all the rooms with a sprinkling of good floral fabrics and lots of fresh flowers. The bedrooms are faultless, bright and crisp, with fresh fruit and home-made biscuits, bathrobes and big, white towels. Some have views of the garden — more English perfection — which stretches out past terrace, fountain and croquet pitch to fields and hills beyond. It's all utterly immaculate as is Paul's lauded modern British cooking. It's the sort of place where the sun shines, even in January.

Rooms: 9: 1 four-poster, 1 twin/double, 1 family and 6 doubles.
Room price: £125-£145; singles from £75
Breakfast: Until 10am.
Meals: Dinner, 3 courses, £19.95.
A la carte from £24.95.
Closed: Occasionally.

Directions: A350, then B3089 east to Teffont. At sharp left-hand bend in village, turn right, following brown hotel sign. Hotel on right after 0.5 miles.

Entry no: 45   **Map no: 2**

The Red Lion

High Street
Lacock
Wiltshire
SN15 2LQ

Tel: 01249 730456

Chris and Sarah Chappell

Lacock, built around the 13th-century abbey, is a beautifully preserved National Trust village and when the BBC filmed part of *Pride and Prejudice* here, the dashing Mr D'Arcy was sensible enough to stop at The Red Lion for refreshments. The inn dates from the early 1700s and is beamed and airy, with big open fires and tankards that hang from the bar. There are rugs on stone flagging in one bar, bare wood floors in the other, so take you pick, order a drink and sit down to some fine home-cooked food, amid timber frames, old settles and hanging Victorian bird cages. In summer you can eat outside in the garden, with country views towards the abbey. Climb the shallow tread of the stairs to excellent bedrooms that retain a Georgian style: old oak dressers, half-testers, crowns above beds, antique furniture, a beam or two. Breakfast — the full Wiltshire works — is eaten in a pretty, first-floor room that looks out onto the High Street.

Rooms: 4: 3 doubles and 1 twin.
Room price: £65-£75; singles from £45.
Breakfast: 8-8.30am weekdays; 9-9.30am weekends.
Meals: Lunch from £6. Dinner, 3 courses, about £15.
Closed: Never.

Directions: Lacock is signed just off A350 between Chippenham and Melksham. The inn is on the High Street.

The Royal Oak Hotel

The Square
Yattendon
Berkshire
RG18 0UG

Tel: 01635 201325
Fax: 01635 201926

Corinne and Robbie Macrae

Corinne, who is French, would never forgive me if I didn't mention her garden; she loves it, and rightly so. It is English through and through, walled by ancient red bricks, bordered on one side by gently-sloping tiled roofs, with lots of colour and shade. There's also a French twist — vines under which you can eat (or fall asleep). Yattendon has a deep country feel: unspoiled, quiet and pretty, with a village store, old red-brick cottages and the handsome Royal Oak — a 300-year-old inn. Inside, Robbie, who cooks, and Corrine have mixed the traditional and the contemporary to great effect: cool yellows and greens in the stunning restaurant (you'll eat well here); a warm and elegant sitting room with rugs and open fire; a smart, but traditional bar, with a terracotta-tiled floor, old red-brick walls and timber frames. The bedrooms, too, are excellent. They are fresh, uncluttered with a hint of French chic: lace and good linen, antiques and big white towels in spotless bathrooms — nothing nasty in sight. A good place to escape to at weekends and only an hour from London.

Rooms: 5: 4 doubles and 1 twin/double.
Room price: £115-£125; singles £95.
Breakfast: 7-9.30am. Full English £9.50; Continental £6.50.
Meals: Brasserie lunch and dinner £9.50-£25. Restaurant dinner, 3 courses, £27.
Closed: Never.

Directions: M4, junction 13, then A34 south for under 1 mile. Take first left past petrol station, then first left again onto B4009. Continue through Hermitage, then branch right to Yattendon.

Entry no: 47

Map no: 3

The Wykeham Arms

75 Kingsgate Street
Winchester
Hampshire
SO23 9PE

Tel: 01962 853834
Fax: 01962 854411

Tim Manktelow-Gray

The Wykeham is too good to be true, the sort of place that you could never recreate. It is English to the core and full of its own traditions. In the bars, ceilings drip with 'collectables', the walls are packed with pictures (I defy you to find space to hang a postage stamp) and fiercely loyal locals chat, pint in hand. It's grand too, a throwback to the past and brimming with warm colours and atmosphere. There are small red-shaded lamps on old school desks, a roaring fire and a nicely cluttered dining room. At heart it remains a pub, but it's easy to mistake it for something smarter; the bedrooms in the main house are more like those of a stately home. Across the narrow Cathedral-shaded street — another throwback — the St. George has a log-fired snug, more good rooms and your own post office. There is much to discover, not least the food. When they tried to take the rack of lamb off the menu once, a small scale rebellion erupted. It went straight back on. *Children over 14 welcome.*

Rooms: 13: 1 suite, 3 twins, 8 doubles and 1 single.
Room price: £79.50-£117.50; singles from £45.
Breakfast: 7.30-9am weekdays; 8-10am weekends.
Meals: Lunch from £5. Dinner, 2 courses, from £13. Restaurant closed Sundays.
Closed: Christmas Day.

Directions: Immediately south of Cathedral between Winchester College and Cathedral. Access via south gate, Canon Street.

Map no: 3

Entry no: 48

Hotel du Vin and Bistro

Southgate Street
Winchester
Hampshire
SO23 9EF

Tel: 01962 841414
Fax: 01962 842458
E-mail: admin@winchester.hotelduvin.co
Web: www.hotelduvin.com

Manager: Nigel Buchanan

Flair and high standards in an easy atmosphere... a rare find. Every tiny, exquisite detail has been thought of. It's all very French too: old wooden floors and tables in the bistro, big, wooden windows onto the garden (*al fresco* dining in summer) and a mirrored champagne bar in gold and blue with bergère sofas, prized by locals, on which to loll like kings for the night. Elsewhere are sweeping expanses of cream walls hung with prints and oils and some very handsome furniture. The bedrooms have power showers and deep baths, strikingly simple colours and fine fabrics. Rooms are split between the bustling main house and the quieter Garden rooms; light sleepers should go for the latter. The food and wine are the *raison d'être* of this hotel and the staff, too, are excellent — artisans who speak with passion about their work. You can play *boules* in the garden.

Rooms: 23: 22 doubles & 1 suite.
Room price: £85-£125; suite £185.
Breakfast: 7-9.30am weekdays; 8-10am weekends. Continental £7.50; Full English £10.50.
Meals: Lunch and dinner, 3 courses with bottle of house wine, about £35.
Closed: Never.

Directions: M3, junction 11, signed Winchester South. At first roundabout follow signs to St. Cross & Winchester. After 2 miles, hotel is on left.

Entry no: 49   **Map no: 3**

Master Builder's House Hotel

Bucklers Hard
Beaulieu
Hampshire
SO42 7XB

Tel: 01590 616253
Fax: 01590 616297
E-mail: res@themasterbuilders.co.uk

Christine Bayley

The first thing you need to know is that the Master Builder's House is utterly comfortable. In the bedrooms there are good fabrics, king-size beds and power showers; downstairs, there's fine, comfortable furniture in rooms with great views down to the river Beaulieu. But this is an end-of-the-road idyll — you can only go further by boat — and if, during its recent renovation, they had made it grander, the house would have lost some of the warmth that makes it so special. There's a traditional terracotta-floored pub, full of sailors in summer, a hall that seems to tumble down to the water, a riverview restaurant (turn left by the flying buttress), and a terrace for *al fresco* meals. Yachts and sailing boats glide down to the Solent (you can take river trips), the marshland is full of birdlife. It's a one-hour walk up stream to Beaulieu and the New Forest stretches out to the west. There's a rich history, too. Henry Adams built much of Nelson's fleet on the grass above the water and the ancient slipways that launched warships still survive. A wonderful spot.

Rooms: 25 twin/doubles.
Room price: £145-£195; singles £110.
Breakfast: 7.30-10am weekdays;
8-10am weekends.
Meals: Lunch, 3 courses, from £18.50.
Dinner, 3 courses, £24.50. Bar food also
available.
Closed: Never.
Directions: From Lyndhurst take B3056
south past Beaulieu turn-off, then take first
left, signed Bucklers Hard. The hotel is signed left after one mile.

Westover Hall

Park Lane
Milford-on-Sea, Lymington
Hampshire
SO41 0PT

Tel: 01590 643044
Fax: 01590 644490
E-mail: westoverhallhotel@barclays.net
Web: www.westoverhallhotel.com

Nicola and Stewart Mechem

A hotel, but family-run and without the slightest hint of stuffiness. It was built for Siemans in 1897 to be the most luxurious house on the south coast; a fortune was lavished on wood alone. It is still vibrant with gleaming oak and exquisite stained glass and it's hard to stifle a gasp when you enter the hall — it's a controlled explosion of wood. The Mechems are generous and open-minded, keen that people should come to unwind and treat the place as home. Private parties can take over completely and throw the rule book towards the window. The bedrooms are exemplary. Some have sea views, all are furnished with a mix of the old and the contemporary and have spotless bathrooms. The whole place indulges you in massive luxury. Romantics can take to the bar or restaurant and gaze out to sea. The more active can dive outside and walk up the beach to Hurst Castle. Alternatively, sink into steamer chairs on the sun-deck at the back for great views of the Needles. A Mediterranean beach hut is in the offing, too.

Rooms: 13: 3 twins, 8 doubles, 1 single and 1 family.
Room price: £110-£140. Dinner, B&B £77.50-£92.50 p.p.
Breakfast: Flexible.
Meals: Dinner, 3 courses, £27.50. Light lunches £5-£10.
Closed: Never.

Directions: From Lymington take signs for Milford-on-Sea (B3058). Continue through village. House on left up hill.

Entry no: 51

Map no: 3

The George Hotel at Yarmouth

Quay Street
Yarmouth
Isle of Wight
PO41 0PE

Tel: 01983 760331
Fax: 01983 760425
E-mail: jacki@thegeorge.co.uk

Jacki Everest

The position here is just fabulous with the old castle on one side, the sea at the end of a sun-trapping garden; yet walk out through the front door and you're in the heart of Yarmouth, the oldest town on the island. Handy too, if you're a corrupt Governor, intent on sacking ships that pass. Admiral Sir Robert Holmes moved here for that very reason in 1668, demolishing a bit of the castle to improve his view. Inside, the grand feel still lingers, though the house has probably been rebuilt since Sir Robert left. The entrance is large, light and stone-flagged; the next-door drawing room is panelled and echoes to the sound of the dice from the backgammon board. Upstairs, all the big bedrooms are also panelled, one with a huge four-poster and two with timber balconies and views out to sea. Meals can be taken outside in the garden bar. You can also eat in the buzzy, cheerful, yellow and wood brasserie or the sumptuous, Michelin-starred, burgundy dining room. A very welcoming hotel and an attractive island base.

Rooms: 16: 15 twin/doubles and 1 single.
Room price: £145-£192.50; singles from £90. Dinner, B&B rates available.
Breakfast: 8-10am weekdays; 8.30-10.30am weekends.
Meals: Lunch and dinner in brasserie from £13.95. Dinner in restaurant £39.75.
Closed: Never.

Directions: Take Lymington ferry to Yarmouth, then follow signs to town centre.

Biskra Beach Hotel and Restaurant

17 St. Thomas's Street
Ryde
Isle of Wight
PO33 2DL

Tel: 01983 567913
Fax: 01983 616976
E-mail: info@biskra-hotel.com
Web: www.biskra-hotel.com

Barbara Newman and Hamish Kinghorn

On the terrace there are wooden chairs and tables, canvas umbrellas, a palm tree and views across a ripple of sea back to the mainland. The beach starts on the other side of the wall while the hot tub is a full 10 paces away. Barbara, who is as easy-going as the hotel, lived in the Middle East and she has infused every inch of Biskra with a casual, colonial elegance. The house, with its high ceilings and big windows, is alive with ideas: sisal matting everywhere, driftwood furniture, painted tongue-and-groove panelling, sofas to curl up on, art floating on walls, Mediterranean colours, and candles in the restaurant at night. Bedrooms are just as stylish with crisp white linen, director's chairs, swathes of curtain, bathrobes and most have sea views. Two have large deck balconies with steamer chairs. In the breakfast room, exquisite murals of Afghan rugs tease the senses. The food is excellent (you can eat on the terrace in summer) and there are 15 deep-water moorings, so arrive under sail. In winter, leave your alarm clock at home and let the fog horn wake you. Wonderful.

Rooms: 14: 9 doubles and 5 twins.
Room price: £57-£120.
Breakfast: Until 10am.
Meals: Lunch from £7.50. Dinner, 3 courses, £22-£30.
Closed: Never.

Directions: Entering Ryde from the west, follow signs to town centre. Take 1st left before Nat West bank. Hotel at bottom of hill, on left, signed.

Entry no: 53

Map no: 3

Seaview Hotel
High Street
Seaview
Isle of Wight
PO34 5EX

Tel: 01983 612711
Fax: 01983 613729
E-mail: reception@seaviewhotel.co.uk
Web: www.seaviewhotel.co.uk

Nicholas and Nicola Hayward

If you know the Isle of Wight, you know the Seaview. It is one of the island's institutions — smart, buzzing, and down by the sea, full of thirsty sailors. Nicky and Nick bought it back in 1980 and, sea lovers that they are, they have made this their ship on land. The terrace, with its railings, mast and flag, is like the prow of a boat — a great place to sit in summer. In the back bar, you can learn your knots, in the front bar you can brush up your semaphore. Wander the stripped wood floors and pass port holes, ship's wheels, lanterns, even sails in the smart back restaurant, where you can eat superb seafood. Bedrooms upstairs have everything you need, but it's the tiptop service that sets the place apart: beds are turned down, a full-cooked breakfast can be brought to your room and the staff couldn't be nicer — nothing here is too much trouble. Bigger rooms at the front have sea views from bay windows; smaller rooms at the back are very good value, some have little balconies and all are quiet. The sea is half a minute's walk away (if that) and you can learn to sail close by.

Rooms: 18: 3 doubles and 13 twin/doubles. (Also, 2 twins in self-catering cottage next door.)
Room price: £70-£125; singles from £55.
Breakfast: Until 10am.
Meals: Lunch and dinner £5-£25.
Closed: Christmas.

Directions: Leave Ryde to the south on B3330. Seaview is signed left after 1.5 miles.

Priory Bay Hotel

Seaview
Isle of Wight
PO34 5BU

Tel: 01983 613146
Fax: 01983 616539
E-mail: reception@priorybay.com
Web: www.priorybay.co.uk

Andrew Palmer

Medieval monks thought Priory Bay special. So did Tudor farmers and Georgian gentry who all helped sculpt this tranquil landscape into a rural haven. From the main house and tithe barns, the parkland rolls down to a ridge of trees. The land drops down to long clean sands and a shallow sea. It's all hotel-owned and as Mediterranean as Britain gets. You can hire boats, there's a summer beach café in the trees, and fishermen land their catch here, so walk down for the freshest mackerel breakfasts. The house has huge rooms that fuse classical French and contemporary English styles. The sun-filled drawing room has wonderful windows (chairs obligingly face out to sea), the dining room is muralled and everywhere there is exquisite furniture. The bedrooms are luxurious; some have fresh colours and a modern feel, others oak panelling, maybe a crow's nest balcony and telescope. They grow as much as they can, there are nature tours in the grounds (peregrine falcons, red squirrel and badgers) and there's a nine-hole golf course, too.

Rooms: 26: 16 twin/doubles and 10 family.
Room price: £90-£190; singles from £50. Dinner, B&B £55-£100 p.p.
Breakfast: Until 9.30am weekdays; 10am weekends.
Meals: Table d'hôte, 3 courses, £25. Picnic hampers available.
Closed: Never.

Directions: B3330 south from Seaview.
Through Nettlestone, then left up road signed to Nodes Holiday Camp. The hotel drive is signed left.

Entry no: 55

Map no: 3

The Millstream Hotel and Restaurant

Bosham Lane
Bosham
Sussex
PO18 8HL

Tel: 01243 573234
Fax: 01243 573459
E-mail: info@millstream-hotel.co.uk
Web: www.millstream-hotel.co.uk

Antony Wallace

Bosham (pronounced bozzum) has a busy past: a fishing port in Roman times, the launching pad for Harold's Norman expedition and, legend has it, the place where King Canute got his feet wet. These days the tide really has turned and Bosham is now a very gentle, very English, summer paradise for sailors, its tidal waters their playground. Half a mile from the water (if that) The Millstream has become a sanctuary for landlubbers and the occasional old sea dog who prefers the comforts of land at night. You can't blame him; The Millstream has the feel of 'the place to be'. In summer, the front garden fills with parasolled tables for cream teas. Inside, a tapestry acts as a bar shutter. There is a long, light, yellow sitting room with good comfortable furniture and a big, equally light, dining room for good, well-priced food; everywhere, there's the sound of chatter. Bedrooms are kept fairly simple: pretty fabrics, pastel colours, comfy beds, good lighting and spotless bathrooms. Chichester Festival Theatre is close, and worth a trip. Or come and learn to sail.

Rooms: 35: 3 suites, 5 singles, 10 twins and 17 doubles.
Room price: £115; suite £150; singles from £72. Dinner, B&B from £60 p.p.
Breakfast: Until 9.30am.
Meals: Lunch, 2 courses, £11.50. Dinner, 3 courses, £21.50.
Closed: Never.

Directions: From Chichester, A259 west through Fishbourne. At Swan roundabout, follow brown hotel signs left, then right at T-junction. Hotel on right in village.

Map no: 3

Entry no: 56

The Old Railway Station

Station Road
Petworth
Sussex
GU28 OJF

Tel: 01798 342346
Fax: 01798 342346
E-mail: mlr@old-station.co.uk
Web: www.old-station.co.uk

Lou Rapley

Without doubt the most beautiful railway station in Britain... and the fact that trains no longer stop here should not deter you — this is one platform where you'd be happy to wait a year! It was built in 1894 and the king used to come here on his way to Goodwood. Lou has renovated immaculately, bringing back the soft Edwardian grandeur: stripped wooden floors, tasselled lamps, busts, writing desks, a gramophone, old black and white pictures, shuttered windows, rising ferns and a 20-foot vaulted ceiling. Breakfast in winter is accompanied by an open fire while in summer you can have your bacon and eggs out on the platform. The biggest problem here is deciding where to sleep: the Pullman carriages are exceptional (you almost expect to bump into Poirot) and were last used to transport the Admiralty to the Queen's coronation. So, too, are the rooms in the station with tongue-and-groove walls, marble bathrooms and maybe a brass bed, all with a colonial freshness to them. Great food at the pub at the top of the drive. For stressed commuters and lovers of luxury. *Children over 10 welcome.*

Rooms: 6: 5 doubles and 1 twin.
Room price: £84-£94; singles £62-£65.
Breakfast: 8-10am.
Meals: Available locally.
Closed: Never.

Directions: A285 1.5 miles south of Petworth. Turn into Badgers pub forecourt, then follow drive on right down to Old Railway Station.

Entry no: 57   Map no: 3

Bailiffscourt Hotel

Climping
Sussex
BN17 5RW

Tel: 01903 723511
Fax: 01903 723107
E-mail: bailiffscourt@hshotels.co.uk
Web: www.hshotels.co.uk

Sandy and Anne Goodman   **Manager: Martin Harris**

Everything about Bailiffscourt is exhilarating. It is beautiful to the eye, the architect having searched high and low for soft, golden Somerset sandstone, the gardens and grounds are a simple paradise and as you stroll in peace from barn to coach house, you feel as if you are walking around an ancient monastery. Inside, the rooms are big and have a perfect medieval atmosphere, set off brilliantly by bold colours, rich fabrics and large tapestries on the walls. There are (of course) mullioned windows, heavy, ancient beams, even an entire ceiling of wood in the restaurant. The bedrooms, too, are perfect with carved four-posters, oak chests and waterfalls of cushions, 600-year-old doors, fabulous bathrooms and decanters of sherry. But, best of all is the truth! Bailiffscourt, incredibly, is a 'genuine fake', built in the 1930s from innumerable medieval bits and bobs; one of the buildings was moved here brick by brick, and only the 13th-century chapel is authentic. It is quite magnificent and there's even a beach at the end of the garden.

Rooms: 31 doubles.
Room price: £140-£310; singles from £135.
Breakfast: 7.30-9.30am weekdays; 8-10am weekends.
Meals: Lunch from £14.50. Dinner £35.
Closed: Never.

Directions: From Littlehampton, A259 west. At the brown sign for Bailiffscourt, turn left into Climping St and continue up lane to hotel.

Map no: 3   Entry no: 58

Sussex Arts Club
7 Ship Street
Brighton
Sussex
BN1 1AD

Tel: 01273 727371
Web: www.sussexarts.com

Mary Sassi

"Shabbily chic, not *The Ritz*, but we loved it," said one review. A place to move at your own pace: come down for breakfast at ten, then grab the papers and stretch out on the *chaise longue*. A Singaporean Raffles-style bar where members stand six deep at weekends (come early for the leather sofas) and a domed ballroom for salsa, poetry, talks or blues — and the Friday night disco. Upstairs, past the photos of luminaries who have stayed (and returned), a small theatre for the occasional production, then, ever upwards, great bedrooms. Your climb will be rewarded with a pick from: a brass four-poster, maybe a low-slung French bed, marble-topped side tables, Art Deco furniture, summery colours, and thick rugs. One room has a pet seagull (on the outside) and there's the tiny Tinker single, too. Don't come with any pre-set notions of it being grand, but it's hard to think of a place that offers such dynamic, laid-back, effortless fun. Turn right out of the front door and you land on the beach, or left and you're strolling past antique shops in Brighton's famous Lanes.

Rooms: 7: 1 four-poster, 5 doubles and 1 single.
Room price: £80-£100; single £50.
Breakfast: Flexible; Continental only.
Meals: Dinner £12-£25.
Closed: Never.

Directions: From Palace Pier, west along seafront. Ship Street is 200 yards on right, just after The Old Ship Hotel. Nearby carparks from £8 a day.

Ockenden Manor

Ockenden Lane
Cuckfield
Sussex
RH17 5LD

Tel: 01444 416111
Fax: 01444 415549
E-mail: ockenden@hshotels.co.uk
Web: www.hshotels.co.uk

Sandy and Anne Goodman   **Manager: Mr Kerry Turner**

The first thing you notice about Ockenden is how handsome it is, with a soft
sandstone grandeur, tall brick chimneys, magnolia trees and runaway lawns. Inside,
the aesthetic treat continues, much of it the indirect legacy of fire as the house burnt
down in 1608 and was re-built soon after. The oak panelling is all original,
stretching from floor to ceiling in the dining room. The detail is more recent, added
by Anne and Sandy: decanters of port, cut-glass crystal glasses, green leather
armchairs and good prints in the bar. There's a crisp, elegant drawing room full of
stunning furniture, much of it under vases of fresh flowers. The bedrooms are split
between the original house and the 1990 addition, but all have a smart 'country
house' look helped along by lots more antiques and, predominantly, Colefax and
Fowler and Zoffany materials. You'll find oils on the walls, bathrobes in spotless
bathrooms, starched linen sheets to sleep on. Some of the bedrooms are also
panelled. Close to Gatwick, but much more than an airport stopover.

Rooms: 22: 6 four-posters, 11 doubles,
4 twins and 1 single.
Room price: £127-£265; singles from
£99.
Breakfast: Until 10am. Continental
included; Full English £5.
Meals: Lunch, 2 courses, from £10.
Dinner, 3 courses, from £31.
Closed: Never.

Directions: A23 south from M23, then
B2115 south-east to Cuckfield. In village, turn right, opposite Talbot Inn, into
Ockenden Lane. Hotel signed.

Map no: 3   **Entry no: 60**

The Griffin Inn

Fletching
Nr. Uckfield
Sussex
TN22 3SS

Tel: 01825 722890
Fax: 01825 722810
Web: www.thegriffininn.co.uk

Bridget, Nigel and James Pullan

On a chilly Tuesday morning in January the locals were queuing up outside before opening time. This is not that surprising — The Griffin, voted best dining pub in Sussex, is the sort of local you'd move to the village for. Warmed by six smouldering fires and with the obligatory 500-year-old beams, settles, red carpets and panelling, its sense of perfection comes from the occasional touch of scruffiness — this inn has been allowed to age. Black and white photos on the walls, a small club room for racing on Saturdays and, in summer, two cricket teams. Bedrooms are perfect — tremendous value for money. The style is of crisp, uncluttered country-inn elegance. You might have a free-standing Victorian bath, the shower heads are huge, there are bathrobes, rag-rolled walls, lots of old wood furniture, beams and uneven floors; rooms in the coach house are quieter. In summer jazz bands play in the garden, the backdrop being a 10-mile view across the Ashdown Forest to Sheffield Park; there are spit roast barbecues, too. Run with gentle passion by the Pullan family as a true 'local.' Perfect.

Rooms: 8: 7 four-posters and 1 twin.
Room price: £60-£85; singles £50-£75.
Breakfast: Flexible.
Meals: Lunch from £5. Dinner, 3 courses, £15-£25.
Closed: Christmas Day.

Directions: A22 south from East Grinstead. Turn right at Nutley, signed Fletching, and straight on for 2 miles into village.

Stone House

Rushlake Green
Heathfield
Sussex
TN21 9QJ

Tel: 01435 830553
Fax: 01435 830726
Web: www.stonehousesussex.co.uk

Peter and Jane Dunn

One of the bedrooms has a huge en suite bathroom with enough room for a sofa and two chairs around the marble bath, but does that make it a suite? Jane thought not. The bedroom is big, has a beautiful four-poster, floods with light and, like all the rooms, has sumptuous furniture and seemingly ancient fabrics, all typical of the generosity of both house and owners. Stone House has been in the Dunn family for a mere 500 years and Peter and Jane have kept the feel of home. Downstairs, amid the splendour of the drawing room, there's still room for lots of old family photos; across the hall in the library, logs piled high wait to be tossed on the fire. Weave down a corridor to ancient oak-panelling in the dining room for Jane's cooking (Master Chef award!) and, having eaten it, walk out to the superb, half-acre, walled kitchen garden and see where it's all grown — they're 99% self-sufficient in summer. There are 1,000 acres to explore and you can fish for carp. Indulgent picnic hampers for Glyndebourne (chairs and tables, too) are an added treat.

Rooms: 7: 1 suite, 3 twin/doubles, 2 four-posters, 1 double/single.
Room price: £100-£215; singles from £55-£80.
Breakfast: 8.30-9.45am.
Meals: Dinner £24.95. Lunch £24.95 by arrangement.
Closed: 24 December — 2 January.

Directions: Take B2096 from Heathfield, fourth turning on right, signed Rushlake Green. Continue to village, then first left by the green. House signed to left.

Little Hemingfold Hotel

Telham   **Tel:** 01424 774338
Battle   **Fax:** 01424 775351
Sussex
TN33 0TT

Allison and Paul Slater

The south east of England is much underrated in terms of rural beauty, but drive up the bumpy track that leads to Little Hemingfold and you could be miles from the middle of nowhere. People who want to get away to the simplicity of deep country will love it here. It's comfortably rustic (a little like renting a remote country cottage, though here you don't have to cook or clean) with open fires, bergère sofas and armchairs, books and games, lots of flowers and floods of light. Breakfast in the yellow dining room is under beams; at night the candles come out for delicious home-cooked dinners. The bedrooms are all over the place, some in the main house, others across the small, pretty courtyard. They are fairly earthy, four having woodburning stoves — again that feel of deep country — with a four-poster perhaps, maybe a sofa, glazed-brick walls and simple bathrooms. Outside, a two-acre lake to row and fish or swim in, a grass tennis court (the moles have got the better of the croquet lawn), woodland to walk in and lots of peace and quiet. *Pets are very welcome.*

Rooms: 12: 10 twin/doubles; 2 family with private bathroom.
Room price: £80-£90; singles £40-£70. Dinner, B&B £52-£62 p.p.
Breakfast: 8.30-9.30am.
Meals: Dinner, 4 courses, £22.50.
Closed: 3 January — 11 February.

Directions: A2100 from Battle towards Hastings. House signed left about 1.5 miles past Battle, by 'sharp left' road sign. Farm track is 0.5 miles.

Entry no: 63   Map no: 4

Jeake's House

Mermaid Street
Rye
Sussex
TN31 7ET

Tel: 01797 222828
Fax: 01797 222623
E-mail: jeakeshouse@btinternet.com
Web: www.s-h-systems.co.uk/hotels/jeakes.html

Jenny Hadfield

Rye — one of the Cinque Ports — is a perfect town for whiling away an afternoon; wander aimlessly and you'll come across the tidal river, old fishing boats, arts and crafts shops and galleries. Jeake's House is hidden away at the top of the hill — the heart of old Rye — on an ancient cobbled street. The house has a colourful past as, variously, wool store, school and home of American poet Conrad Potter Aitken. The dining room is an old Baptist chapel, now painted deep red and full of plants, busts, books, clocks and mirrors. It is galleried and you can make a grand entrance, walking down for breakfast. Jenny is engagingly easy-going and has created a lovely atmosphere. The rooms are pretty, not fussy, with good furniture and all are excellent value. There are old four-posters and a big attic room up a mind-your-head stairway, beams and timber frames and views over roof tops and chimneys to open country. Downstairs, there's a small library for rainy days and, in winter, a fire in the hearth. A super little hotel. *Children over 12 welcome.*

Rooms: 13: 10 doubles and 1 honeymoon suite;
1 double and 1 single sharing bathroom.
Room price: £51-£92; singles £26.50-£60.
Breakfast: 8-9.30am; 8.30-10am on Sundays.
Meals: Available locally.
Closed: Never.

Directions: Entering Rye, pick up and follow 'Town Centre' signs under the arch into High St. Third left at Lloyds Bank and first right into Mermaid St. House on left and signed. Private parking nearby £3 a day.

Map no: 4

Entry no: 64

Romney Bay House

Coast Road
Littlestone, New Romney
Kent
TN28 8QY

Tel: 01797 364747
Fax: 01797 367156

Helmut and Jennifer Gorlich

Designed by Clough Williams-Ellis — creator of Portmeirion — for American star Hedda Hopper, this is an atmospheric dreamscape. The whole house has a lingering 1920s house-party feel. There's an honesty bar full of colour, a drawing room with deep sofas to sink into and a pretty dining room and conservatory for wonderful Jennifer-cooked delights — don't miss tea. Everything has been thought out and is just right, a perfect home from home. You can unwind with a book in front of the fire, go for long beachside walks, or simply fall in love with the sheer romance of the place: nothing disappoints. Upstairs, there's a library lookout with a telescope (on a clear day you can see France), books and games. The bedrooms are elegant, full of everything you'll need, and with great bathrooms. There's lots of pretty furniture, half-testers and sleigh beds, and most of the rooms look out to sea. Add to this Jennifer and her undying enthusiasm and Helmut and his great sense of humour and you have a very special place indeed.

Rooms: 10: 8 doubles and 2 twins.
Room price: £75-£130; singles £55-£90.
Breakfast: Flexible.
Meals: Dinner, 4 courses, £29.50. Light lunches at the weekend from £5.50. Cream teas £4.50.
Closed: Christmas & mid-June.

Directions: M20, junction 10, A2070 south, then A259 east through New Romney. Turn right to Littlestone. At sea, turn left and continue for 1 mile.

Entry no: 65

Map no: 4

The Sandgate Hotel and La Terrasse Restaurant

The Esplanade
Sandgate, Folkestone
Kent
CT20 3DY

Tel: 01303 220444
Fax: 01303 220496

Zara and Samy Gicqueau

A hotel for Francophiles who miss the ferry. Samy is from the Loire, met Zara in the kitchen of a Paris restaurant, worked with Raymond Blanc at *Le Manoir* and now has a Michelin star all of his own. The food here is heavenly, the atmosphere entirely French. Smart Gallic waiters dressed in waistcoats speak impeccable English (in rich French accents, of course) and trays swivel down from shoulders with theatrical flair. The hotel has a comfortable formality; it's relaxing, yet things are done 'just right'. In the morning, door handles and hinges are polished to perfection and each speck of dust is busted. It stands across the road (some noise) from the sea and first-floor rooms have balconies, so breakfasts can be special. Home-made *croissant, pain au chocolate, brioche* and freshly-squeezed orange juice are brought up to you; bring your telescope and peer across to France. Bedrooms are very good value for money, fairly simple with good basics (pretty fabrics, new furniture, comfy beds). If you don't get a balcony room, champagne on the terrace will compensate. More than a channel stopover.

Rooms: 14: 10 doubles, 2 twins and 2 singles.
Room price: £58-£76; singles £45.
Breakfast: 7.30-9.30am.
Meals: Lunch and dinner: weekdays, 3 courses, £22.50; weekends, 5 courses, £31. A la carte, 3 courses, £35-£40.
Closed: January & 10 days in October.

Directions: M20, junction 12, then follow signs for Folkestone. Right at lights, signed Sandgate. After a mile, right at bottom of hill and hotel on right when you reach the sea.

Map no: 4

Entry no: 66

Wallett's Court Country House Hotel

Westcliffe, St. Margaret's at Cliffe   **Tel:** 01304 852424
Dover   **Fax:** 01304 853430
Kent   **E-mail:** wc@wallettscourt.com
CT15 6EW   **Web:** www.wallettscourt.com

Chris, Lea and Gavin Oakley

Wallett's Court is *old*. Odo, half-brother of William the Conqueror, held this land in Norman times, and Jacobeans restored the house in 1627. When the Oakleys renovated in 1975, the house gave up long-held secrets. From a ceiling fell 17th-century tobacco pipes; in a hidden passageway hung 17th-century paintings. The Oakley's passion, commitment and care have all paid off and the house feels warm and genuine. Old features catch the eye: ancient red-brick walls in the drawing room, an oak staircase with worn, shallow steps in the hall. Bedrooms in the main house are big and have heaps of character and there's also an impeccably behaved ghost. There are good, quiet rooms in the barn and cottages and, above the spa complex (indoor pool, sauna, steam room and spa), four excellent, contemporary rooms have recently been added. There's tennis, a terrace with views towards a distant sea and, within a mile, white cliffs for breezy walks, towering views, rolling mists and wheeling gulls. Great food, too, with puddings to diet for!

Rooms: 15: 13 doubles and 2 family rooms split between the main house, stables, barn and cottage.
Room price: £80-£150; singles £70-£110.
Breakfast: Until 9.30am weekdays; 10am weekends.
Meals: Dinner, 3 courses, £27.50. Lunch, 3 courses, £17.50.
Closed: 24 December — 2 January.

Directions: From A2/A20 follow signs to Deal on A258. Turn right to St. Margaret's at Cliffe. House 1 mile on right and signed.

Entry no: 67

Map no: 4

The Ringlestone Inn

Ringlestone Hamlet
Nr. Harrietsham
Kent
ME17 1NX

Tel: 01622 859900
Fax: 01622 859966
E-mail: bookings@ringlestone.com
Web: www.ringlestone.com

Michael Millington-Buck   **Manager: Michelle Stanley**

Two old sisters once ran The Ringlestone. If, when you arrived, they liked the look of you, they'd lock you in. If they didn't, they'd shoot at you! Michael and his daughter Michelle have let the tradition slip and run their 1635 ale house with a breezy conviviality. Glass beer tankards dangle above the bar, a woodburner throws out heat from the inglenook and old *Punch* cartoons hang on the original brick and flint walls between oak beams and stripped wooden floors. They stock 30 fruit wines and liqueurs as well as excellent local ales and you can sit in settles or on Ringlestone's quirky, tiny, yet very comfy chairs. Across the lane in the farmhouse, bedrooms are perfect: oak furniture, sublime beds, crisp linen and big, luxurious bathrooms. The food is delicious — try a Ringlestone pie — and in the garden, you can play *Pétanque* (they hold competitions here). The inn has a children's licence, they sometimes host vintage car rallies and Leeds Castle is close by. As for Michael's breakfasts — they'll keep you going for a week. Good walking, too.

Rooms: 3: 1 four-poster and
2 twin/doubles.
Room price: £85; singles £79.
Breakfast: 8-9.45am. Full English £11.50;
Continental £8.50.
Meals: Lunch from £5. Dinner £8-£25.
Closed: Christmas Day.

Directions: M20, junction 8. After 0.25
miles, left at 2nd roundabout, signed
Hollingbourne. Through Hollingbourne,
up hill, then right at brown 'Knife and Fork' sign. Pub on right after 1.5 miles.

Kennel Holt Hotel

Goudhurst Road
Cranbrook
Kent
TN17 2PT

Tel: 01580 712032
Fax: 01580 715495
E-mail: hotel@kennelholt.demon.co.uk
Web: www.kennelholt.co.uk

Sally and Neil Chalmers

Kennel Holt is definitely Elizabethan — the scrolled beams date it to 1520 — and probably a huntsman's lodge, with the soaring Jacobean-style chimneys added by the Victorians. The house ticks along to the easy beat of a small, relaxed country house with lots of original touches: cut-glass decanters on the honesty bar, tinsel prints on the walls and Neil's rustic mix of Mediterranean flavours in the restaurant. Best of all is the panelled library, a big warm room with comfy old sofas, open fire, rugs, a collection of Edwardian books and a large collection of old records which you can throw on the record player. The bedrooms also have the country house feel: good beds, beams, great furniture, a couple of four-posters, proper eiderdowns and lots of good books. Outside, the five-acre garden has topiary, a rain-fed pond, a weeping willow, croquet and a putting green. The hotel even has its own shoot that runs from November to February. Sissinghurst is five minutes away and 40 historic houses and gardens are within a half-hour drive.

Rooms: 10: 2 four-posters, 2 singles, 1 twin and 5 twin/doubles.
Room price: £145-£175; singles £90.
Breakfast: Until 10am.
Meals: Dinner, 3 courses, £27.50. Lunch for 6 people or more by arrangement. Restaurant closed Monday evenings.
Closed: End of January/beginning of February for 3 weeks.
Directions: The hotel is 3 miles west of Goudhurst on the A262 and signed.

Hotel du Vin and Bistro

Crescent Road
Royal Tunbridge Wells
Kent
TN1 2LY

Tel: 01892 526455
Fax: 01892 512044
E-mail: admin@tunbridgewells.hotelduvin.co.uk
Web: www.hotelduvin.com

Manager: Matt Callard

You enter immediately and literally into the spirit of the place — an ocean of wooden floor and high ceiling with animated chatter spilling out from the bars and bistro. This enormous hall is the hub of the house, leading to bars and bedroom stairs and, even though the bedrooms are magnificent, you'll want to get back down and join the fun. The Burgundy bar buzzes with local life; open fires and facing sofas lead inevitably to 'later' dinners. The yellow-walled, picture-crammed bistro is distinctly French with more wooden floors and, in tribute to Kent, hop strings tumble from the windows. Afterwards, wander into the Havana Room (the bullet holes are fake) for a game of billiards and a cigar or take coffee in the Dom Perignon room where huge hand-painted copies of the Impressionists hang boldly on the walls. Bedrooms come in different sizes (the biggest is *huge*) and all have fantastic bathrooms. You sleep on Egyptian linen; one would expect no less.

Rooms: 32 doubles.
Room price: £75-£139.
Breakfast: 7-9.30am weekdays; 8-10am weekends. Continental £7.50; Full English £10.50.
Meals: Lunch and dinner, 3 courses with bottle of house wine, about £35.
Closed: Never.

Directions: M25, then A21 south. After 13 miles, exit signed Tunbridge Wells. A264 into town, right at lights into Calverley Rd. At mini-roundabout, left into Crescent Road.

Map no: 4   **Entry no: 70**

The Beaufort

33 Beaufort Gardens
London
SW3 1PP

Tel: 020 7584 5252
Fax: 020 7589 2834
E-mail: thebeaufort@nol.co.uk
Web: www.thebeaufort.co.uk

Sir Michael and Lady Wilmot   **Manager:** Jackie Kennedy

This was the first private house-hotel to open; privacy, attention to detail and individual treatment are the keynotes still. A lovely 1880s terrace house in a quiet cul-de-sac off Knightsbridge, it is home to the world's largest collection of original English floral watercolours (Sir Michael used to work for James Goldsmith and is used to aiming high) and offers all drinks, including *grand cru* champagne, on the house, 24 hours a day. Supremely elegant pastel-coloured bedrooms come with all the trimmings: CD player, video recorder and fax, bowls of fruit, Swiss chocolates, fresh flowers and sparkling bathrooms. Continental breakfast comes to your room on Wedgwood china, cream tea is served downstairs every afternoon. Tiptop service and a gentle atmosphere make it exceptional in central London, a five-minute walk from Harrods. Hyde Park is close, too.

Rooms: 28: 18 twin/doubles, 7 suites and 3 singles.
Room price: £211.50-£305.50; suites £350; singles £182.50-£194.
Breakfast: Flexible; Continental only.
Meals: Room service offers light snacks. Good restaurants locally.
Closed: Never.

Directions: Leave Knightsbridge tube by the Brompton Road exit. Pass Harrods and Beaufort Gardens is the first road on the left (after Hans Road).

Entry no: 71   **Map no: 3**

Two Hyde Park Square

London
W2 2JY

Tel: 020 7262 8271
Fax: 020 7262 7628
E-mail: reservation@apartments-hps-london-paris.co.uk
Web: www.apartments-hps-london-paris.co.uk

Martyn Lawson

Two Hyde Park Square may not be a hotel, but you'll be hard pressed to find better value than this so close to the centre of town. What you get is a serviced apartment (you live in it, they clean it!), made up of bedroom, a sitting area, a bathroom and a small kitchenette (but with hundreds of restaurants on your doorstep you don't have to self-cater). The rooms are perfect, furnished with absolutely everything you need to be comfortable: good fabrics and beds, demure carpets, TV and phone, and furniture that may not be antique, but you won't worry for a moment that it isn't. Every room is as clean as a whistle, the kitchens have all the equipment you could possibly need, there are tiny balconies, and though some rooms are quite compact, the open-plan design works well. Downstairs, you get a 24-hour reception in the big lobby, there's an underground car park (£10 a day) and you are a three-minute walk from Oxford Street. For long-term stays in London, it's unbeatable value, and if Martyn can't find you a place here, don't worry; he has similar places all over town.

Rooms: 75 twin/doubles.
Room price: £88-£129.50 (minimum 5 night stay).
Breakfast: Available locally.
Meals: Availably locally.
Closed: Never.

Directions: In Hyde Park Square, London W2.

Entry no: 72

Number Ten

10 Manchester Street
London
W1M 5PG

Tel: 020 7486 6669
Fax: 020 7224 0348
E-mail: stay@10manchesterstreet.fsnet.co.uk
Web: www.10manchesterstreet.com

Manager: Neville Isaac

In a city where a good night's sleep can often cost a fortune, Number Ten has good rooms without frills at reasonable prices. The smaller doubles here cost £120 a night, which, given that you're only a five-minute walk from Oxford Street, is good value indeed. Rooms are simple and spotless, with good use of space and natural colours, comfortable beds and crisp linen. Bathrooms are fine, too, and you get all the little bits: TVs, mini hi-fis, a box of chocolates and fans in case we ever get a summer. Bay trees stand guard outside this 1919 red-brick building, while inside staff wait to usher you into the lift and to carry your bags up to your room. There's a bright and breezy sitting room with sea-grass matting and a basement breakfast room. No restaurant, but you are given an excellent London-wide restaurant guide and the best advice on the hottest night spots. Theatre tickets can be booked, taxis called. The Wallace Collection, which has just re-opened after years of magnificent restoration, is at the end of the road; don't miss it.

Rooms: 46: 9 suites, 13 doubles, 5 small doubles and 19 twins
Room price: £120-£150; suites £195.
Breakfast: 7-11am. Continental included; Full English £5.
Meals: Available locally.
Closed: Never.

Directions: Bond Street tube. Left onto Oxford Street. 3rd left into Duke Street. Straight over Manchester Square into Manchester Street and on right.

Portobello Gold
95-97 Portobello Road
Notting Hill
London
W11 2QB

Tel: 020 7460 4910
Fax: 020 7460 4911
E-mail: mike@portobellogold.com
Web: www.portobellogold.com

Michael Bell and
Linda Johnson-Bell

Portobello Gold is a cool little place on one of London's trendy roads. It's a bar, a restaurant, an internet café and it also has five bedrooms. The latter are basic and have very small en suite showers, but they're clean and have good beds. Clearly, if you are after luxury, then this is not for you, but if the hippy in you is still active and you're after a cheap place to stay in London, this reliable and very friendly place will do the trick. Downstairs, you can sit out on the pavement in wicker chairs and watch Portobello life amble by, or hole up inside on stools at the bar for a beer with the locals. Wooden floors, an open fire and modern art on the walls. Wander through to the restaurant and you come across a conservatory that's more like a jungle. Here, while four canaries sing, you eat good food, much of it — maybe Irish rock oysters — fresh from the sea. Linda writes about wine, so expect to drink well. Michael is a cyber-visionary, hence the first-floor internet café. For a fiver, he'll put a PC in your room and you can surf away all night; stay down in the lounge and it's free. Portobello market starts outside the front door.

Rooms: 5: 4 doubles and 1 single.
(2 doubles share separate wc.)
Room price: £52-£75; singles £45-£65.
Breakfast: Continental, from 7.30am, included; Full English, 11am-2pm, £4.
Meals: Bar meals all day from £6. Dinner, 3 courses, £20-£25.
Closed: 2 weeks over Christmas maybe.

Directions: Notting Hill tube, then north onto Pembridge road. Keep right at mini-roundabout, then first left into Portobello road. On left after 1/2 a mile.

The Centre of England

Norfolk
Suffolk
Essex
Oxfordshire
Gloucestershire
Worcestershire
Herefordshire
Shropshire
Derbyshire
Lincolnshire

"To travel is to discover that everyone is wrong about other countries."
– Aldous Huxley

The White Hart Inn

High Street
Nayland, Nr. Colchester
Suffolk
CO6 4JF

Tel: 01206 263382
Fax: 01206 263638
E-mail: nayhart@aol.com
www: www.whitehart-nayland.co.uk

Michel Roux

Manager: Franck Deletang

Michel Roux's 'other place' is exquisite on all counts, but the way things are done here is second to none. The service is remarkable, the staff fired by a sense of proud vocation — a rarity in Britain these days. The inn dates back to the 15th century and has kept its timber-framed walls and beams. The inside has been opened up a bit — not so much as to remove the 'ramble', but just enough to give it a light, airy feel — and its here that you feast on "scrumptious food" (to quote an enraptured guest) and sup from a vast collection of New World wines: "people like to travel when they drink," says Michel. Exemplary bedrooms have a striking, yet simple country elegance: yellow walls and checked fabrics, crisp linen and thick blankets, beams (two have almost vaulted ceilings), piles of cushions, sofas or armchairs. The single has wonderful art, some have wildly-sloping floors and one has original murals that may be the work of Constable's brother. All have excellent bathrooms. Superb.

Rooms: 6: 4 doubles, 1 twin/double and 1 single.
Room price: £71.50; singles £66.
Breakfast: 8-10am.
Meals: Lunch, 2 courses from £11. Dinner, 3 courses, about £26.50. Restaurant closed Mondays.
Closed: Never.

Directions: Nayland is signed right 6 miles north of Colchester on the A134 (No access from A12). The hotel is in the village centre.

Map no: 4

Entry no: 75

The Great House

Market Place
Lavenham
Suffolk
CO10 9QZ

Tel: 01787 247431
Fax: 01787 248007
E-mail: info@greathouse.co.uk
Web: www.greathouse.co.uk

Régis and Martine Crépy

A little pocket of France run by a charming couple with French staff. They have pulled off a trick rare in the UK, creating a superb hotel that feels like a home. The 18th-century front hides a 15th-century house, full of surprises and utterly lovely. Each of the bedrooms has antique desks and chests of drawers to offset the superb marble of the perfect bathrooms. Some have views over the bustling, historic market place, one has a big Jacobean oak four-poster — an island surrounded by a sea of rugs — another is a huge beamed double up in the roof with sofas and armchairs. Most rooms have their own private sitting room as well. You can't escape the beams, the fresh flowers, the sheer generosity and good taste of it all. Nowhere is this more true than in the restaurant — the very essence of France in the middle of Suffolk. The cheese board alone is a work of art, but the sheer splendour of the food brings guests back again and again. Catch the early sun in the courtyard for breakfast or wait awhile and eat *al fresco* on warm and lazy summer nights. A fabulous little place.

Rooms: 5 doubles.
Room price: £80-£130; singles from £55. Dinner, B&B from £61 p.p.
Breakfast: 7.30-9.30am.
Meals: Lunch from £11. Dinner from £21.95 (restaurant closed Mondays).
Closed: First three weeks in January.

Directions: Lavenham is on A1141. The Great House is in the market place. Take Market Lane, at the corner of Newsagents', signed Guildhall.

Entry no: 76

Map no: 4

Ounce House

Northgate Street
Bury St. Edmunds
Suffolk
IP33 1HP

Tel: 01284 761779
Fax: 01284 768315
E-mail: pott@globalnet.co.uk

Simon and Jenny Pott

An extremely handsome 1870 red-brick townhouse that is but a stroll from the heart of this ancient town, one of England's loveliest. Bury has a rich history. The Romans were here, its Norman abbey attracted pilgrims by the cartload and the wool trade made it rich in the 1700s. A gentle, one-hour stroll takes you past 650 years of architectural wonder — special indeed. The house, more home than hotel, is pristine, furnished with fine antiques. Double doors between drawing room and dining room let light flood in all day long. You'll find a huge mahogany dining table for sumptuous breakfasts, a wildly-ornate, carved fireplace in a grand drawing room and leather armchairs and an honesty bar in the snug library. Fine, homely bedrooms are packed with books, mahogany furniture, local art and piles of magazines; the room at the back of the house has a pretty view of the garden. Tickets to the theatre can be arranged. They'll pick you up from the railway station and there are 35 restaurants within five minutes of the house, so take your pick.

Rooms: 3: 2 doubles and 1 twin.
Room price: £85-£90; singles £60.
Breakfast: Flexible.
Meals: Available locally.
Closed: Never.

Directions: Leave A14 at northern junction for Bury and follow signs to centre. At first roundabout, left into Northgate Street. House on right after 1 mile.

Map no:

Entry no: 77

The Cornwallis Country Hotel and Restaurant

Brome
Eye
Suffolk
IP23 8AJ

Tel: 01379 870326
Fax: 01379 870051

Jeffrey and Beth Ward

The good old English aristocracy! Sir Thomas Cornwallis made his fortune as treasurer of Calais, his grandson's grandson, Charles, was a 'spendthrift and gambler' who escaped the 'silken cord of Tyburn' and the 2nd Earl surrendered to George Washington at Yorktown, Virginia in 1781. The Cornwallis, grand as it is, was no more than a dower house to such illustrious men. The original 1561, timber-framed house is now squashed between rather grand additions and the inside is part tavern, part country house. Bedrooms have mahogany dressers, writing desks, sofas, and big, old beds, while up in the eaves you can bathe under 14th-century beams. Downstairs, order a pint of organic beer in the fine, timber-framed bar, then walk over the 100ft-deep well (now covered by glass) on your way to a settle in front of the woodburner. They have their own cricket pitch, hot air balloons land here in summer and the yew topiary in the garden is among the oldest and grandest in Britain. An avenue of mature lime trees leads up the driveway — aristocratic indeed. *Pets by arrangement.*

Rooms: 16: 4 four-posters, 2 twins, 1 family and 9 doubles.
Room price: £90-£125; singles from £72.50. Dinner, B&B from £70 p.p.
Breakfast: 7-9am weekdays; 7.30-9.30am weekends.
Meals: Lunch and dinner £9-£25.
Closed: Never.

Directions: From A140 1 mile south of Diss, take B1077 south towards Eye. Hotel down private drive on left after 20 metres and signed.

Entry no: 78

Map no: 1

The Old Rectory

Campsea Ashe
Nr. Woodbridge
Suffolk
IP13 0PU

Tel: 01728 746524
Fax: 01728 746524

Stewart Bassett

Stewart encourages a house-party atmosphere in this listed Georgian rectory right next to the church: an honesty bar under the stairs; an east-facing morning room for breakfast; a wooden-floored, terracotta-walled winter dining room and a brightly-coloured conservatory with rugs and flagstoned floor for lazy summer dinners. It's all fired by Stewart's twin passions — entertaining and cooking. He used to run a restaurant and still can't keep out of the kitchen. There are home-made jams, extra strong marmalade and fruit compots at breakfast, coffee, tea and home-baked cakes 'on the house' all day long and dinners conjured up with fresh local produce in the evenings. The drawing room is big, bright and full of comfortable sofas and armchairs (the TV banished to a distant corner) with low sash windows that look out to the garden and fields beyond. Upstairs, bedrooms hit the right note: cotton sheets and duvets, soft fabrics and good furniture. It's all deeply relaxing, not least because of Stewart. Riverboat trips can be arranged.

Rooms: 7: 1 four-poster, 3 doubles,
2 twins and 1 single.
Room price: £60-£75; singles £37.50-
£47.50.
Breakfast: Until 9.30am.
Meals: Dinner, 3 courses, £18. Restaurant
closed Sunday evenings.
Closed: Over Christmas.

Directions: North from Ipswich on A12
for 15 miles, then right onto B1078. In
village, over railway line and house on right
just before church.

Map no: 4   **Entry no: 79**

The Dolphin

Peace Place
Thorpeness, Nr. Aldeburgh
Suffolk
IP16 4NA

Tel: 01728 454994
Fax: 01728 454300
E-mail: info@thorpeness.co.uk
Web: www.thorpeness.co.uk

Tim Rowan-Robinson

Thorpeness is a one-off, the perfect antidote to 21st-century holidays. The village was the turn-of-century brainchild of G.S. Ogilvie, who set out to create a holiday resort for children, free of piers and promenades, with safety assured. His master stroke is the Meare — a 64-acre lake, never more than three feet deep, that was inspired by Ogilvie's friend, J.M. Barrie, creator of *Peter Pan*. Children can row, sail and canoe their way up creaks and discover islands that may have a lurking (wooden!) crocodile round the corner. The Dolphin — in the middle of the village — is a great little inn. It has three very good bedrooms in cottage style with old pine furniture, soft colours and spotless bathrooms. Downstairs, there are two lively bars, open fires, wooden-floors in the dining room and outside, a terrace and lawn for BBQs and *al fresco* dinners. You can play tennis at the Country Club, there's a great golf course, an unspoilt sand and pebble beach, a summer theatre company and even a 'house in the clouds'. A paradise for families and excellent value for money.

Rooms: 3 twin/doubles.
Room price: £60-£65; singles £45.
Breakfast: Until 9.30am weekdays;
10am weekends.
Meals: Lunch and dinner, 2 courses, from
£10. Packed lunches by arrangement.
Closed: Christmas Day.

Directions: From A12 at Farnham, take
A1094 to Aldeburgh seafront. Turn left
and follow coast road for 2 miles into
Thorpeness. The Dolphin is on the right
and signed.

Entry no: 80   **Map no: 4**

The Crown

High Street
Southwold
Suffolk
IP18 6DP

Tel: 01502 722275
Fax: 01502 727263

Michael Bartholomew

"Rooted in our place, we have always been proud to do different and to do it well".
Thus spake Adnams, the brewery, local owners of The Crown. Southwold is almost
an island, bounded on all sides by creeks, marshes, the River Blyth and the sea.
Almost unchanged for a century, it has a strong Dutch element in the brickwork of
the older houses, a gleaming white lighthouse, numerous pubs (mostly Adnams)
and a small museum. Scores of notable figures have come here to retreat from the
frenzy of the outside world. Above all there is the Sailors' Reading Room, tiny, snug,
heart-warming, nostalgic. As for The Crown, well you'll just have to come and see.
It is pub, wine bar, restaurant and small hotel, with a terrific wine list, imaginative
food and a bustling atmosphere of cheerful informality. You look in vain for signs of
traditional hotel poor taste. The bedrooms are small, comfortable and 'decent' —
nothing spectacular, but that is the hotel's mood. Perfect... as is the beer.

Rooms: 12: 4 doubles, 3 twins and 2
singles; 1 twin, 1 double and 1 family
(double interconnecting with twin), all
with private bathrooms.
Room price: £75; family room £100;
singles from £50.
Breakfast: Until 9.30am. Continental
included; Full English £4.
Meals: Lunch £15.50-£18.50.
Dinner £20.50-£25.50.
Closed: Never.

Directions: From A12 take A1095 to Southwold. The Crown is on the High
Street.

Map no: 7   Entry no: 81

The Norfolk Mead Hotel

Coltishall
Norwich
Norfolk
NR12 7DN

Tel: 01603 737531
Fax: 01603 737521

Jill and Don Fleming

You *can* paddle your canoe from the bottom of the garden all the way along the river Bure to the Broads, but they *are* a few miles away! A better idea is to potter about in one of the hotel's rowing boats and stay closer to home. It's a great position, and it is more than that, for there are 12 acres of lawns, mature-trees, a walled garden and swimming pool, even a one-acre fishing lake. Come for the owners, the food and the easy-going luxury of a lovely old Georgian country house — the sort you can usually only dream of. The bedrooms, all different, are super-comfortable, with the best-quality linen and every tiny, most frivolous need anticipated. The food is just as good, all fresh and local, maybe samphire from Blakeney or home-made ice cream. A fine entrance hall with high-backed sofas and open fire unwind you immediately. Big, gracious, beautifully proportioned yet perfectly relaxing. And if that's not enough, you can have a massage or a manicure, so expect to be pampered in every way.

Rooms: 10: 3 twins, 6 doubles and
1 family suite.
Room price: £75-£110; singles £65-£90.
Breakfast: 8-9am weekdays; 8.30-9.30am
weekends.
Meals: Lunch £8.50-£12.95.
Dinner £15.50-£25.
Closed: Never.

Directions: B1150 north to Coltishall.
Over humpback bridge and first right. Turn
down drive before church. House signed.

Entry no: 82

Map no: 7

Elderton Lodge and Langtry Restaurant

Gunton Park
Thorpe Market
Norfolk
NR11 8TZ

Tel: 01263 833547
Fax: 01263 834673
E-mail: enquiries@eldertonlodge.co.uk
Web: www.eldertonlodge.co.uk

Martin and Christine Worby

Shades of Scotland in this peaceful north Norfolk shooting lodge set a in deer park with Gunton Tower graceful in the distance. Gunton Hall, just over the brow, was a favourite with Edward VII and Lilly Langtry and the local railway station was put in especially to bring down their champagne — 1000 cases at a time! Pictures of Lillie Langtry hang on the walls, as does a framed letter she wrote. The house echoes to her time. Tasselled lamps, old rugs, leather sofas, trophies and oils — all the deep country trimmings and comforts. A very comfortable place, run with ease by Christine and Martin. It's worth splashing out and going for the more expensive rooms. They are bigger and are furnished with Edwardian antiques. There are rich fabrics, plush headboards and, in most rooms, you can lie in bed and look out across parkland to the tower. Candlelit dinners in the warm and elegant restaurant, breakfasts amid hanging ferns in the Victorian, tiled conservatory. Deer graze all around and there's a varied programme of 'special interest' weekends, too. *Children over 10 welcome.*

Rooms: 11: 2 twins and 9 doubles.
Room price: £90-£105; singles from £57.50. Dinner, B&B from £52.50 p.p.
Breakfast: 8-9am weekdays; 8.30-10am weekends.
Meals: Lunch, 2 courses, £9.50. Dinner, 3 courses, £25.
Closed: 2 weeks in January.

Directions: 3 miles north of North Walsham on A149 and signed left.

Map no: 7   **Entry no: 83**

The Hoste Arms

The Green
Burnham Market
Norfolk
PE31 8HD

Tel: 01328 738777
Fax: 01328 730103
E-mail: thehostearms@compuserve.com
Web: www.hostearms.co.uk

Paul and Jeanne Whittome   **Manager: Emma Tagg**

At the risk of being excoriated for plagiarism I will quote at large from Hoste brochures. "Paul's partial deafness is often mistaken for rudeness. Local fishermen frequent the bar. The fine old bedrooms are occupied by anyone from film-stars to captains of industry, though thankfully most guests are none of these. In its 300-year history The Hoste has been courthouse, livestock market, art gallery, brothel. Paul, once a bouncer in a shanty pub in Australia, has not shrunk since then but has converted brilliantly from ejector to welcomer." The Hoste seems to have won every prize going, deservedly (in February 1999, *The Times* voted it their second favourite hotel in England, their 27th in the world, and gave it a 'Golden Pillow' award). The place has a genius of its own: brave and successful mixtures of colour, deep-sinking chairs, panelled walls, bold reds, beamed fireplaces, food to be eaten with rapture, anywhere and anytime, and a jazz pianist on Friday nights in winter. Brilliant.

Rooms: 28: 6 junior suites, 4 four-posters, 4 twins, 8 doubles, 1 family and 5 singles.
Room price: £86-£120; four-posters and suites £102-£140; singles £64-£95.
Breakfast: 8-10.30am.
Meals: Lunch and dinner £3.50-£25.
Closed: Never.

Directions: From King's Lynn, north on A149, then A148 and, after about 2 miles, left onto B1153. At Great Bircham, branch right onto B1155 and continue through Stanhoe to Burnham Market. In village.

Entry no: 84   **Map no: 7**

Strattons

4 Ash Close
Swaffham
Norfolk
PE37 7NH

Tel: 01760 723845
Fax: 01760 720458

Vanessa and Les Scott

A classical, 1700s villa, hidden away in its own peaceful courtyard, a minute's walk from the market square. A real find, with a distinctly rural French feel (you expect to come across a clucking free-range hen or two), the gardens reassuringly unmanicured, with urns and terracotta pots in abundance. The interior is spectacular. Les and Vanessa (they met at art school) have managed to cover every square inch with something wonderful. Bold colours, busts and sculptures, chests piled with books, bunches of dried roses, rugs on stripped floors — this is a succulent dreamscape, as if you've walked into a small, French château. Bedrooms are exquisite. Take your pick from: a tented bathroom, murals and stained glass, two sofas in front of a smouldering fire, *tromp d'oeil* panelling, a raised four-poster bed, stripped wooden floors, rich fabrics... you get the picture. Glimpse the church spire from the room in the eaves or sit by murals in the lower-ground floor bistro for Vanessa's gorgeous food. A real treat — the four-poster room is sheer heaven. Don't miss it.

Rooms: 6: 1 four-poster, 2 twins and 3 doubles.
Room price: £90-£115; four-poster £150; singles from £70.
Breakfast: 7.30-9am weekdays; 8-10.30am weekends.
Meals: Dinner, 4 courses, £33.
Closed: Christmas & New Year.

Directions: Ash Close runs off the north end of the market place between W H Brown estate agents and Express cleaners.

Map no: 7

Entry no: 85

Langar Hall

Langar
Nottinghamshire
NG13 9HG

Tel: 01949 860559
Fax: 01949 861045
E-mail: langarhall-hotel@ndirect.co.uk
Web: www.langarhall.com

Imogen Skirving

Langar Hall is one of the most engaging and delightful places in this book — reason enough to come to Nottinghamshire — and Imogen's exquisite style and natural *joie de vivre* make this a mecca for those in search of a warm, country house atmosphere and a place to connect with other people. The house sits at the top of a hardly noticeable hill in glorious parkland, bang next door to the church. Imo's family came here 150 years ago. Much of what fills the house came here then and once inside you feel intoxicated by beautiful things: statues and busts, the odd Doric column, ancient tomes in overflowing bookshelves, huge oils on the walls. Bedrooms are spectacular, some resplendent with antiques, others more contemporary with fabrics draped from beams or *tromp d'oeil* wallpaper. When you ring to book, you are talked through each room, much as a sommelier talks you through each wine. Magnificent food, too (as if you needed to ask!), my fruit brulée the best pudding I ate all year. There's Shakespeare on the front lawn in summer, too. A cultural paradise.

Rooms: 12: 1 four-poster, 1 suite, 2 twins and 8 doubles.
Room price: £100-£150; suite £175; singles £75-£95.
Breakfast: 7-10am weekdays; 8.30-10am weekends.
Meals: Lunch, 2 courses, £10. Dinner, 3 courses, £17.50; à la carte £30.
Closed: Never.

Directions: A52 from Nottingham towards Grantham. Right, signed Cropwell Bishop, then straight on for 5 miles. House next to church on edge of village and signed.

Entry no: 86

Map no: 6

Hambleton Hall

Hambleton
Oakham
Rutland
LE15 8TH

Tel: 01572 756991
Fax: 01572 724721
E-mail: hotel@hambletonhall.com
Web: www.hambletonhall.com

Stefa and Tim Hart

Manager: Rupert Elliot

One of the finest hotels in Britain — simple as that. This 1881 shooting box stands half a mile up from its tree-lined shore with an imperious view across Rutland Water. Sink into steamer chairs by the heated swimming pool, then lie mesmerised. Inside, a scarlet bar with rich acres of curtain, opulent sofas, columns by the fireplace and oils on the walls — a place for cocktails. Fine plaster-moulded ceilings in the big, gracious drawing room, a Michelin star in the high-ceilinged restaurant and upstairs, glorious bedrooms. Expect silk print wallpaper, Egyptian cotton linen, antique sofas at the end of king-size beds, marble bathrooms and lake views. Meticulous attention to detail, too, inspired by Tim and Stefa and executed by an impeccable staff; they are kind and natural and nothing is too much trouble. After tea on the balustraded terrace, walk through the rose garden to the paddock and the lake shore. Hambleton is on a small peninsular — you can follow the water round; in summer, hot air balloons pass over.

Rooms: 17: 2 four-posters, 12 twin/doubles and 3 doubles.
Room price: £165-£320; singles from £140.
Breakfast: Flexible. Continental included; Full English £12.
Meals: Lunch from £16.50. Dinner £35-£60.
Closed: Never.

Directions: From A1, A606 west towards Oakham for about 8 miles, then left, signed Hambleton. In village, bear left and hotel signed right.

Map no: 6

Entry no: 87

The Old Bridge Hotel

1 High Street
Huntingdon
Cambridgeshire
PE18 6QT

Tel: 01480 424300
Fax: 01480 411017
E-mail: oldbridge@huntsbridge.co.uk

John Hoskins and Martin Lee

The rather busy traffic system that circles Huntingdon may put some people off which is a shame as this is a lovely hotel and the double (if not triple) glazing ensures peace and quiet. If you want, you can spurn the roads altogether and arrive by boat as the hotel is flanked on one side by the river Ouse and has its own jetty. Walk up from car park or river, past flower-filled urns to hanging baskets and the ivy-clad, 18th-century walls of what started life as a bank and became a hotel in 1910. Inside, the breezy feel of a grandish hotel greets you: back-to-back sofas in the bar (the locals flock here at the weekends), Mediterranean murals in the conservatory restaurant and panelled elegance in the formal dining room, where a buddha sits in the fireplace. John is a 'Master of Wine' so expect *vins extraordinaires*, many of them available by the glass, to go with Martin's superb food. Bedrooms are excellent, with regal fabrics, bold colours, antique furniture, super bathrooms and CD players. Cambridge and Ely are both close by.

Rooms: 23: 2 four-posters, 3 twins, 6 singles and 12 doubles.
Room price: £95-£125; four-posters £129-£139; singles £79.50.
Breakfast: 7-10am.
Meals: Lunch, 2 courses, £14.95. Dinner, 3 courses, about £25.
Closed: Never.

Directions: Leave A14 for Godmanchester and Huntingdon. Follow signs into town and hotel on left just over bridge.

Entry no: 88

Map no: 3

The Falcon Hotel

Castle Ashby
Nr. Northampton
Northamptonshire
NN7 1LF

Tel: 01604 696200
Fax: 01604 696673
E-mail: falcon@castleashby.co.uk

Michael and Jennifer Eastick

A stone-built inn, originally a farm, which dates from 1594 and sits just across the road from the castle after which this dreamy village is named. The castle grounds are spectacular and they are open to the public; there are craft shops in the village, too. The Easticks came here recently after Michael decided he needed another change of job — he has been a farmer and a racing driver, among other things. These days he is quite content being a hotelier, making sure his cellar bar is full of beer, that the oils hang symmetrically on the smart Regency-stripped walls, that the fire crackles with bounteous logs and that guests get well fed and watered in the pretty stone-walled restaurant. In summer, you can eat out in the garden and watch the cows saunter up to the dairy while flower beds burst with colour and sheep graze beyond. Some bedrooms are in the house, others are next door but one in the cottage (the 83 year-old ex-postmistress lives in-between). All are pretty, with country-cottage fabrics, bright yellows and blues, bath robes, fresh flowers and gentle village views.

Rooms: 16: 13 twin/doubles and 3 singles.
Room price: £85-£99.50 (excluding special event weekends); singles from £69.50. Dinner, B&B from £69.50.
Breakfast: 7-9.30am weekdays; 8-9.30am weekends.
Meals: Lunch, 2 courses, £14.95. Dinner, 3 courses, £23.50
Closed: Never.

Directions: Castle Ashby is signed north from the A428, 1.5 miles west of Yardley Hastings.

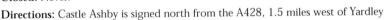

The Stonor Arms

Stonor
Oxfordshire
RG9 6HE

Tel: 01491 638866
Fax: 01491 638863
E-mail: stonorarms.hotel@virgin.net
Web: www.stonor-arms.co.uk

Sophia Williams

It is hard to believe you are so close to London — The Stonor, wrapped in the end of the Chiltern Hills, has the feel of deep country. Footpaths lead out to hills and forest, red kites circle above the deer park at Stonor House (open to the public), and lanes lead up to pretty villages. Key notes at the hotel are the tiptop service, a high degree of elegance and the relaxed informality of the place. Close to Henley-on-Thames, the hotel has strong links with the regatta and the grand, stone-flagged bar has oars on the ceiling, old rowing photos on the walls and leather sofas and armchairs in which to sit and enjoy it all. In summer, life spills out into the very pretty walled garden, both candle- and flood-lit at night. Antique-furnished bedrooms tend to be huge and come with all the extras: bathrobes, turndown service, morning papers delivered to your room and peace and quiet. Conservatory breakfasts can be eaten in the garden in good weather or you can have them in bed instead. A place to come and spoil yourself.

Rooms: 10: 3 doubles and
7 twin/doubles.
Room price: £125-£155; singles £99.
Dinner, B&B from £62.50 p.p.
Breakfast: 7-10am weekdays; 8-10am weekends.
Meals: Bar meals from £7. Dinner,
3 courses, £25-£30.
Closed: Never.

Directions: M40, junction 6, then B4009 to Watlington. There, B480 towards Nettlebed for 2 miles, then left, signed Stonor. House in village.

Entry no: 90

Map no: 3

The Old Trout Hotel

29-30 Lower High Street
Thame
Oxfordshire
OX9 2AA

Tel: 01844 212146
Fax: 01844 212614
E-mail: mj4trout@aol.com
Web: www.theoldtrouthotel.co.uk

Mark and Ruth Jones

Once a merchant's house and now a trimly-thatched restaurant with rooms where Mark and Ruth serve up great food and good humour in equal measure. Come in off the street and you find a cosy, clutter-free interior of low ceilings, red brick walls, a big rustic fireplace, beams and a gleaming stone floor. The whole of the downstairs has been given over to the restaurant and Mark's unrushed hospitality has made this a lively local haunt. Go for bedrooms in the main house. One is entered through the smallest hotel door in Britain (leading to the tallest four-poster, perhaps?). All have bags of character, most notably their sloping floors; one end of each room is about two feet higher than the other. In the converted stables, rooms are small, though each has a four-poster and all rooms have good fabrics. There's also Mark's sense of humour — The Old Trout is named after a recent Prime Minister! The piscatorial pleasures of your plate — maybe grilled Barracuda with mussels and green beans — are all market-fresh.

Rooms: 8: 4 four-posters, 1 double and 3 singles.
Room price: £75-£85; singles £60.
Breakfast: Until 9.30am.
Meals: Lunch, 2 courses, £10.50. Dinner, 3 courses, about £25.
Closed: 24 December — 8 January.

Directions: M40, junction 8, then A418 into Thame. Hotel on right on entering town.

Bath Place

4-5 Bath Place, Holywell Street
Oxford
Oxfordshire
OX1 3SU

Tel: 01865 791812
Fax: 01865 791834
E-mail: bathplace@compuserve.com
Web: www.bathplace.co.uk

Yolanda Fawsitt

Bath Place is unlike anything else you are ever likely to come across. Close to the Bodleian Library and surrounded by four colleges, this courtyard is a throwback to Dickensian England, a warren of four cottages that seem to have been squashed together and pushed up into the sky. Alleyways burrow through, connecting the world to the ancient Turf pub next door. Predictably, it is dripping with history. The last remnant of city wall stands right behind, the model for the pre-Raphaelites was born in room 11, and Dorothy Sayers lived in room 5. It just goes on. Before the war, well-heeled undergrads roomed here and sometimes turn up, aged 85, on nostalgic whims! It's a mad, wonderful, rambling place. One of the staircases is for mountaineers only and the sheer romance of the rooms is staggering; they may not be grand, but you wouldn't want them to be. It's all overseen by delightful staff, the irrepressible Kathleen and her daughter Yolanda, a wonderful, down-to-earth person. *Pets by arrangement.*

Rooms: 13: 2 suites, 2 twins and
9 doubles.
Room price: £95-£140; singles from £90.
Breakfast: Continental buffet until
9.30am weekdays; 10am weekends.
Meals: Available in Oxford.
Closed: Christmas & New Year.

Directions: In the centre of Oxford head
south from St. Giles. Keep left and turn left
at T-junction into Broad St. Straight across
lights and into Hollywell St. Hotel signed
on right.

Entry no: 92

Map no: 3

Old Parsonage Hotel

No. 1 Banbury Road
Oxford
Oxfordshire
OX2 6NN

Tel: 01865 310210
Fax: 01865 311262
E-mail: info@oldparsonage-hotel.co.uk
Web: www.oxford-hotels-restaurants.co.uk

Ian Hamilton

1660 must have been a good year for cooks. Edward Selwood, the wealthy chef of nearby St. John's College, completed his house that year and the original oak door still hangs. Inside, clever use of design details and materials have kept the old-house feel and the intimacy of a private club (Oscar Wilde is reputed to have stayed here). The hall has marble floors, the original fireplace and huge pots of dried flowers. Splendid bedrooms have smart florals and checks, some in the old house have fireplaces and panelling; all have glorious bathrooms. There's a first-floor roof garden, lush with plants, for tea or sundowner and a snug sitting room downstairs for those seeking quiet. But all roads seem to lead to the Parsonage bar/restaurant, a slight misnomer as it is the hub of the hotel. Newspapers hang on poles, walls are heavy with pictures and people float in all day long for coffee, drinks and good food. First-class service from real people too, and they'll do just about anything they can to help.

Rooms: 30 twin/doubles.
Room price: £150-£175; singles £125; suites £195.
Breakfast: Until 11am.
Meals: Lunch and dinner, 2 courses, from £15.
Closed: 24-27 December.

Directions: From A40 ring road, south at Banbury Road roundabout to Summertown and towards city centre. Hotel is on right next to St. Giles' church.

The Old Bank

92-94 High Street
Oxford
Oxfordshire
OX1 4BN

Tel: 01865 799599
Fax: 01865 799598
E-mail: info@oldbank-hotel.co.uk
Web: www.oxford-hotels-restaurants.co.uk

Manager: Ian Hamilton

The original safe, too heavy to remove, now guards the wine cellar! Built of mellow golden stone, the hotel is in the heart of old Oxford, flanked by colleges and cobbled streets. Rooms at the top have views across the fabled skyline of spires, towers and domes — a sublime panorama of architectural splendour — but no-one misses out; there's a viewing platform at the very top. Downstairs, the big old tillers' hall has turned into a bar and grill — the 'hip' hub of the hotel — with stone floors, a zinc-topped bar, huge modern oils on the walls and big arched windows that look out onto the High Street. In summer, you can eat on the deck at the back, beneath umbrellas or the shade of lime trees. The bedrooms are superb and just as contemporary — stylishly clean-cut with natural pastel colours, the best linen, velvet and silk. Some have big bay windows or views to the back and they're full of all the 21st-century gadgetry you'd ever want. A five-minute stroll will take you through Merton College, The Meadows and down to the river. Perfect.

Rooms: 44: 1 suite and 43 twin/doubles.
Room price: £155-£300; singles from £135.
Breakfast: 7-10am. Full English from £7.95; Continental from £5.
Meals: Lunch and dinner £8-£25.
Closed: 25-26 December.

Directions: Cross Magdalen Bridge towards city centre. Keep left through first set of lights, then first left into Merton St. Follow road right, then first right into Magpie Lane. Car park second on right.

The Feathers Hotel

Market Street
Woodstock
Oxfordshire
OX20 1SX

Tel: 01993 812291
Fax: 01993 813158
E-mail: enquiries@feathers.co.uk
Web: www.feathers.co.uk

Martin Godward

Once a draper's, then a butcher's, this serenely English townhouse hotel has stayed true to its roots and now has a Michelin-starred restaurant and rooms lavished with fine fabrics. The four 17th-century houses have labyrinthine corridors that lead to the four original staircases, which have the odd mind-your-head-beam. Elsewhere, smouldering fires, stone floors, oils and antiques, an elegant upstairs sitting room, a pretty terraced bar and garden, and Johann the parrot. Window boxes to fit the season help frame glimpsed views of Woodstock outside. The restaurant is part library, half-panelled with soft yellow walls and low ceilings. Bedrooms are beautiful: some are smaller than others, but most have marble bathrooms and all have period furniture, towelling bathrobes, purified water and home-made shortbread; one suite has a steam bath. Play backgammon in the study while devouring sinful teas. Hot-air ballooning and chauffeured-punting can both be arranged and you can stroll to Blenheim Palace along Woodstock's pretty streets.

Rooms: 22: 4 suites, 10 doubles, 7 twins and 1 single.
Room price: £130-£185; suites £235-£290; singles from £109.
Breakfast: 7.30-9.45am.
Meals: Lunch, 2 courses, from £17.50. Dinner, 3 courses, about £38. Tasting menu, 6 courses, £48.
Closed: Never.

Directions: From Oxford, A44 north to Woodstock. In town, left after traffic lights. Hotel on left.

Map no:

Entry no: 95

Falkland Arms

Great Tew
Chipping Norton
Oxfordshire
OX7 4DB

Tel: 01608 683653
Fax: 01608 683656

Paul Barlow-Heal and S-J Courage

In a perfect Cotswold village, the perfect English pub. Five hundred years on and the fire roars in the stone-flagged bar under a low-slung timbered ceiling that drips with jugs, mugs and tankards. Here, the Hop is treated with reverence; ales are changed weekly and old pump clips hang from the bar. Tradition runs deep; they stock endless tins of snuff with great names like Irish High Toast and Dr. Kalmans. In summer, Morris Men stumble on the lane outside and life spills out onto the terrace at the front, and into the big garden behind. This lively pub is utterly down-to-earth and in very good hands. The dining room is tiny and intimate with beams and stone walls; every traditional dish is home-cooked. The bedrooms are snug and cosy, not grand, but fun. Brass beds and four-posters, maybe a heavy bit of oak and an uneven floor — you'll sleep well. The house remains blissfully free of modern trappings, nowhere more so than in the bar, where mobile phones meet with swift and decisive action! *Children over 14 welcome.*

Rooms: 6: 5 doubles and 1 single.
Room price: £65-£85; singles £40.
Breakfast: At 9am.
Meals: Lunch from £4. Dinner from £8.
Closed: 24-27 December, 31 December & 1 January.

Directions: A361 from Chipping Norton, then right onto B4022. Pub is signed.

The Tollgate Inn and Restaurant

Church Street
Kingham
Oxfordshire
OX7 6YA

Tel: 01608 658389
Fax: 01608 659467

Penny Simpson

Kingham is a well-kept secret — one of the few Cotswold villages to have escaped the tourist trail. Among the soft sandstone cottages you'll find the obligatory church, pub, and green and a surprise, The Tollgate — a Georgian farmhouse turned restaurant with rooms. Penny has drawn on her deep experience in hotels to bring a fresh country feel to the inside. Old beams have been stripped and stone floors polished back to life. A wall has been knocked down to open the place up, smart red check sofas have been brought in and pastel colours put on the walls. The bedrooms have had the same treatment — simple, yet striking: coir matting, sanded wood furniture, rag-rolled walls (lilacs, blues, even electric green in one room), good lighting, cotton duvets and fresh flowers. The family room is huge and airy with a vaulted, beamed ceiling. But you've come to eat, and Matthew Laughton's cooking — much of it organic — doesn't disappoint; my poached pear infused with mulled wine was exceptional. In summer you can eat in the front garden with the house floodlit behind you.

Rooms: 10: 8 doubles, 1 twin and 1 family.
Room price: £50-£105; singles from £45.
Breakfast: 8.30-10am.
Meals: Lunch from £4. Dinner, 3 courses, from £18.50.
Closed: 2 weeks in January. Restaurant closed Mondays.

Directions: A44 to Chipping Norton, then B4450 to Churchill. In Churchill, right, signed Kingham. There, left at green. Hotel on right, signed.

Map no: 3

Entry no: 97

Burford House

99 High Street
Burford
Oxfordshire
OX18 4QA

Tel: 01993 823151
Fax: 01993 823240
E-mail: stay@burfordhouse.co.uk
Web: www.burford-house.co.uk

Jane and Simon Henty

It's good to see the owner of a hotel wiping the sauce off his fingers before shaking your hand. Burford House is small enough for Simon and Jane to influence every corner; this is also their home. It's a delight, small and intensely personal, redecorated with elegant good taste without any loss of character: oak beams, good fabrics, antiques, simple colours, log fires, immaculate bedrooms and a little garden for afternoon teas, all in this exquisite Cotswold town — with a sense of fun that avoids any hint of stuffiness. There's an honesty bar, with home-made sloe gin and cranberry vodka to be sipped from cut-glass tumblers, no less. Handwritten menus promise ravishing breakfasts too; Simon cooks, Jane bakes. Classical music wafts about the place, there are fresh flowers everywhere and Jumble the cat. It's a serenely comfortable place where you can unwind, and unwind a little more. Guests return time after time to do so.

Rooms: 7: 2 four-posters, 2 twins and 3 doubles.
Room price: £90-£120; singles from £75.
Breakfast: Until 9am weekdays; 9.30am weekends.
Meals: Light lunches and afternoon teas available. Restaurant closed Mondays. Dinner available in Burford.
Closed: 2 weeks in January/February.
Directions: In the centre of Burford.

Entry no: 98   **Map no: 3**

The Lamb Inn

Sheep Street
Burford
Oxfordshire
OX18 4LR

Tel: 01993 823155
Fax: 01993 822228

Caroline and Richard De Wolf

Surely the best hotel address ever — especially with the owners' name! This honourable inn must be one of the finest in the country. It dates in part from 1420 (it used to be a dormy house) and, in the old bar, the footsteps of monks and thirsty locals have worn a gentle groove into the original stone floor. Make a grand tour and you'll come across four fires, two sitting rooms, rambling corridors, rugs to warm stone floors, mullioned windows, old parchments framed on the walls and a porter's chair with a high enough back "to keep the draught off a giant's neck." In the restaurant, ferns hang above the wooden floor, beneath the conservatory roof, with a couple of Doric columns thrown in for good measure; inevitably, the food is sheer perfection. Bedrooms are just as good: plump-cushioned armchairs, heavy oak beams, antiques of every hue and colour, brass beds, half-testers, four-posters. The whole place has a mellow magic, rather like its owners. Richard and Caroline have been here 18 years; the locals, sensibly, won't let them leave until they match the 40 years the previous owners managed!

Rooms: 15: 1 four-poster, 10 doubles and 4 twins.
Room price: £100-£120; singles from £65.
Breakfast: 8-9.30am.
Meals: Dinner, 3 courses, £25.
Closed: Christmas Day & Boxing Day.

Directions: North from A40 into Burford. Sheep Street is the first left going down the High Street.

Map no: 3

Entry no: 99

The New Inn at Coln

Coln St-Aldwyns
Nr. Cirencester
Gloucestershire
GL7 5AN

Tel: 01285 750651
Fax: 01285 750657
E-mail: stay@new-inn.co.uk
Web: www.new-inn.co.uk

Brian and Sandra-Anne Evans

Built by decree of Elizabeth I, this is a lovely coaching inn in a sleepy Cotswold village. There is old-fashioned hospitality at its best, with roaring fires and low beamed ceilings, a place for locals too. The New Inn is Brian's and Sandra-Anne's life — you sense this in their relaxed, personal welcome. They, and their staff, take the time to talk you through a local walk, the ales on tap, the wonderful menu; chef Stephen Morey's food is "divine". Sandra-Anne's sumptuously designed bedrooms have everything — a four-poster here, a half-tester there, a romantic floral theme brilliantly developed. Those in the converted dovecote have views out to open country where the river meanders serenely. In summer, you can sip drinks lazily outside under the generous shade of parasols. Golf, biking and horse riding can all be arranged; or you can walk out into the countryside from the front door, past Highland cattle (we think!) in the fields and swans on the river.

Rooms: 14: 10 doubles, 3 twin/doubles
and 1 single.
Room price: £96-£115; singles £80.
Breakfast: 8-9.30am.
Meals: Dinner, 2 courses, £22.50;
3 courses, £26.50.
Closed: Never.

Directions: Leave A40 soon after Burford,
taking B4425 towards Bibury. After
Aldsworth, turn left to Coln St-Aldwyns.

The Swan Hotel at Bibury

Bibury
Gloucestershire
GL7 5NW

Tel: 01285 740695
Fax: 01285 740473

Elizabeth Rose **Manager: John Stevens**

The Swan must be the most photographed hotel in Britain and for good reason — the setting here is pure Cotswold bliss. The inside is no less enchanting, the sky-blue panelling in the entrance hall so impressive it's been listed. Everywhere there is something wonderful: Macintosh chairs sprinkled about, a baby grand piano in the lobby. The dining room is spectacular — a monument to 1920s opulence with high ceilings, claret wallpaper, oils and chandeliers — and a great place to eat. Bedrooms are equally indulgent, with a mix of old and contemporary furniture, maybe an Art Deco mirror or a ceramic bedside light the size of a barrel; every room I saw had something delightfully extravagant. There are Italian-tiled bathrooms, bathrobes and old Roberts radios; the hotel even has its own spring water. Retire at night and you'll find the bed turned down; wake in the morning and your newspaper is waiting outside your room. Go for rooms with a view to the front — the trout farm across the road is an artistic triumph. You can fish, too; the hotel has a beat nearby.

Rooms: 18: 3 four-posters, 1 family,
5 twins and 9 doubles.
Room price: £165-£235; singles
from £99.
Breakfast: 7.30-10am.
Meals: Lunch from £5. Dinner, 3 courses,
£28.50.
Closed: Never.

Directions: A429 north out of Cirencester,
then B4425 to Bibury. Hotel by bridge in
village.

Map no: 2 **Entry no: 101**

Lords of the Manor

Upper Slaughter
Nr. Bourton-on-the-Water
Gloucestershire
GL54 2JD

Tel: 01451 820243
Fax: 01451 820696
E-mail: lordsofthemanor@btinternet.com
Web: www.lordsofthemanor.com

General Manager: Iain Shelton

What a name — a form of linguistic time travel. The bar, more gentleman's club than anything else, is deeply rich with old wooden floors, low lighting and the smell of smouldering logs. It has a large bay window with facing leather sofas. This is the place to sit. Here you can stare out on rolling parkland, a perfect English landscape. A sense of tradition swirls around you, but it hasn't stopped progress; the restaurant is nicely contemporary. It looks out onto the walled orchard, where pears grow in bottles; when ready, they're made into *Poire William*, then imbibed. Bedrooms are split between the main house and the converted granary; they're what you'd expect, some beamed in the eaves, others with stately four-posters. There are fruit and sherry and a feeling of high calm. You can sleep easy too — the name 'Slaughter' has no sinister history. It comes from *scolostre* meaning 'muddy place'; the walk over to Lower Slaughter is a good way to find out.

Rooms: 27: 3 suites, 3 four-posters, 2 singles and 19 twin/doubles.
Room price: £145-£295; singles from £99.
Breakfast: 8-10am.
Meals: Lunch, 2 courses, £16.50. Dinner, 3 courses, £32.50. Picnic hampers available.
Closed: Never.

Directions: From Cirencester, A429 north about 16 miles, then left signed The Slaughters. In Lower Slaughter, left over bridge. Continue to Upper Slaughter and hotel signed right in vilage.

Entry no: 102   **Map no: 3**

Lower Brook House

Lower Street
Blockley, Moreton-in-Marsh
Gloucestershire
GL56 9DS

Tel: 01386 700286
Fax: 01386 700286
E-mail: lowerbrookhouse@cs.com

Marie Mosedale-Cooper

Marie is full of life — not the sort of person to stand in the way of progress. Lower Brook House started life as a B&B and evolved into a restaurant with rooms, but it's more than that still. Ancient stone floors, timber-framed walls, fresh flowers everywhere... and stacks of beautiful things. Settle into coral sofas next to the huge inglenook fire, toss on a log and start *War and Peace*. Next door in the restaurant, a gallery of family rogues hang on crimson walls while on tables you'll find cut-glass crystal, hand-painted crockery, the best starched linen. In summer you can have breakfast and dinner in the garden, the latter surrounded by scented candles. Bedrooms are compact but with all the paraphernalia to pamper you — bathrobes, bowls of fruit, garden flowers as well as fresh colours, stone mullioned windows, the odd exposed timber roof. The food is delicious — maybe steamed fillet of sea bass or roast loin of venison. There's a working kitchen garden and you can even watch brown trout commuting up the brook.

Rooms: 7: 2 four-posters, 3 doubles and 2 twin/doubles.
Room price: £80-£96; singles from £60.
Breakfast: 8-10am.
Meals: Lunch by arrangement. Dinner, 3 courses, £21.
Closed: Never.

Directions: West from Moreton-in-Marsh on A44, then right (B4479) into Blockley. House on right at bottom of hill and signed.

Map no: 3   **Entry no: 103**

The Churchill Inn

Paxford
Chipping Campden
Gloucestershire
GL55 6XH

Tel: 01386 594000
Fax: 01386 594005
E-mail: the_churchill_arms@hotmail.com

Leo Brooke-Little and Sonia Kidney   **Manager: Richard Barnes**

Above all, The Churchill is fun. The bar is vital, full of life and warm, too, with stone floors and wooden tables. The feel is fresh, an engaging mixture of old and new, the atmosphere relaxed and informal and bubbling over with happy chatter. The staff are friendly and natural and no one seems to stand too much on ceremony; it is, you might say, very 'user friendly'. The locals seem to like it that way. I arrived at two o'clock on a Tuesday afternoon and they were grudgingly starting to leave after lunch. The bedrooms, right above the bar, are equally fun and stylish. "Frills and drapes are not us" says Sonia. Beams, old radiators and uneven floors obviously are. There are good fabrics and pastel colours with country views from the heart of the village. Although two rooms are small, good use of space keeps you from feeling closed in. And the food here is good, the sticky toffee pudding perfect, according to one usually cantankerous Sunday critic. Such perfection might explain the prayer stool in one corner!

Rooms: 4 doubles.
Room price: £60; singles £40.
Breakfast: Until 10am.
Meals: Dinner £20. Lunch £15.
Closed: Never.

Directions: From Moreton-in-Marsh, take A44 towards Worcester/Evesham. Through Bourton-on-the-Hill, take right at end to Paxford. Straight through Blockley, over railway track and tiny bridge into Paxford. Inn is in village on right.

The Wilderness

Worldsend
Farfromhere
Gloucestershire

Tel: 01234 567890
E-mail: dontstay@thisplace.co.uk

Freda Rome and Wanda Lust

Do you long to leave the city far behind and return to nature? Have you dreamt of nights wrapped up in the peace and quite of ancient woodland? Are you a hunter-gatherer? This delightful country hideaway is far beyond the reach even of cars (you walk in) and has had its walls removed to increase your sense of freedom. It works a treat. The seasons come to you: leaves fly by in autumn, snow drifts through in winter (bring a shovel). In spring there's no need to buy flowers — you'll find them growing in your bed; you may get to sleep on cherry blossom, too. Summers are particularly special. The bedroom, which is the bathroom, is also the sitting room, which is the dining room. Delicious meals are freshly prepared by trees, bushes, hills, rivers — all in season. A bit cold in winter and those who wish to take to the hills should probably do so. *Al fresco* dining all year round, so bring your thermals and an umbrella. The wildlife is spectacular; some will find it far too close for comfort.

Rooms: 1 open-plan double.
Room price: Free.
Breakfast: Nuts in May.
Meals: Fully organic.
Closed: Not in the slightest.

Directions: If you go down to the woods today...

Map Ref. No: 3

Entry no: 105

The Malt House

Broad Campden   **Tel:** 01386 840295
Nr. Chipping Campden   **Fax:** 01386 841334
Gloucestershire
GL55 6UU

Nick, Jean and Julian Brown

The very epitome of Englishness, a substantial house in the heart of an untouched village, with climbing roses, magnolia trees and deck chairs in the garden. A place that echoes to the past: you almost expect the vicar to call for tea or for a post boy to bring a telegram explaining that the London train is running late! The mellow Cotswold walls of this 1530 house hold a soft and unexpected grandeur: bright wood floors, ancient panelling, a Renaissance oil painting hanging on a wall of shimmering gold and an original fireplace throwing out the crackle of smouldering logs beneath a 17th-century mantelpiece that rises to within a foot of the ceiling. Nick is easy-going and never tires of seeing faces light up as guests walk in. They stay lit up — there's no dropping of standards in the bedrooms where mullioned windows, sloping floors, gilt mirrors, a beam or two, and muralled bathrooms all wait. Also, contemporary splashes of colour in the fine garden suite, pretty views of the orchard paddock and food to keep you smiling for days.

Rooms: 8: 1 four-poster, 1 garden suite and 6 twin/doubles.
Room price: £89.50-£108; garden suite £117; singles from £59.50. Dinner, B&B from £74 p.p.
Breakfast: 8-9.30am weekdays; 8.30-10am weekends.
Meals: Dinner, 3 courses, £29.50.
Closed: Christmas.

Directions: A44, then B4081 north into Chipping Campden. First right, signed Broad Campden. House on left after 1 mile.

Entry no: 106   **Map no: 3**

Wesley House
High Street
Winchcombe
Gloucestershire
GL54 5LJ

Tel: 01242 602366
Fax: 01242 609046
E-mail: reservations@wesleyhouse.co.uk
Web: www.wesleyhouse.co.uk

Matthew Brown

Winchcombe was the 6th-century capital of Mercia. Wesley House, a 14th-century half-timbered townhouse, entices you straight off the High Street and seduces you once you're inside. Old timber-framed white walls, a terracotta-tiled floor and a large crackling fire — all are perfect for lazy afternoons spent flicking through the papers. The downstairs is open-plan, the dining area stretching back in search of countryside — and finding it; French windows lead out to a small terrace where breakfast and lunch or evening drinks can all be enjoyed with the gentle Cotswold hills as a backdrop. The bedrooms have more of those ancient whitewashed, timber-framed walls that need little further decoration. They're warm, smart, well-lit and compact with good wooden beds, crisp sheets and the occasional head-cracking bathroom door. Fresh milk and coffee in every room and you can breakfast in bed with home-baked bread, croissant and *pain au chocolat*, even kumquat, orange and whisky marmalade. One room has a lovely balcony. *Children over seven and babies welcome.*

Rooms: 5 doubles.
Room price: £75-£85; singles £48.
Breakfast: Until 10am.
Meals: Dinner, 3 courses, £28.50. Lunch from £6.95.
Closed: 16 January — 10 February.

Directions: From Cheltenham take B4632 to Winchcombe. Wesley House is on the High Street.

Map no: 2   **Entry no: 107**

Hotel on the Park

Evesham Road
Cheltenham
Gloucestershire
GL52 2AH

Tel: 01242 518898
Fax: 01242 511526
E-mail: stay@hotelonthepark.co.uk
Web: www.hotelonthepark.co.uk

Darryl Gregory

Symmetry and style to please the eye in the heart of the spa town of Cheltenham. The attention to detail is staggering — everything has a place and is just where it should be. The style is crisp and dramatic, a homage to the Regency period in which the house was built, but there's plenty of good humour floating around, not least in Darryl himself, who's brilliant at making you feel at home. He's the first to encourage people to dive in and enjoy it all. There are lovely touches too: piles of fresh hand towels in the gents' cloakroom, where there's a sink with no plug hole — you'll work it out; newspapers hang on poles, so grab one and head into the drawing room where drapes swirl across big windows. In the restaurant you'll come across Doric columns, Greek and Roman busts, lots and lots of fun too. Upstairs all the bedrooms are fabulous, crisp and artistic, all furnished to fit the period. The whole house is a treat, classically dramatic, and it's great fun to be a part of it all.

Rooms: 12: 4 twins, 6 doubles and
2 suites.
Room price: £121-£171; singles £78.50.
Breakfast: Until 9.30am weekdays; 10am
weekends.
Meals: Dinner, 3 courses, from £21.50.
Closed: Never.

Directions: From town centre, join one-way system and exit at signpost to Evesham. Continue down Evesham Road. Hotel signed on left opposite park.

Painswick Hotel

Kemps Lane
Painswick
Gloucestershire
GL6 6YB

Tel: 01452 812160
Fax: 01452 814059
E-mail: reservations@painswickhotel.com
Web: www.painswickhotel.com

Helen and Gareth Pugh

The Painswick is an absolute gem, immaculate inside and out. It once was home to a wealthy rector. He married a Catholic, unwise at the time, so he built her a small private chapel. It is now a cocktail bar with a black and white tiled floor and a gold-leaf, plaster-moulded ceiling — just wonderful. But to single out one room for praise is unfair — they are all superb, all treated with stunning simplicity. There's a semicircular pine-panelled dining room (the tables are set to perfection), a pale yellow, clutter-free country house morning room and a big, bright and elegant sitting room that opens onto a small porticoed balcony with valley views. The bedrooms are no less magnificent: sparkling antiques, Balinese thrones, a mahogany four-poster, maybe a porter chair; even the simpler rooms feel luxurious. Yet amid all this grandeur, Helen and Gareth have kept the mood splendidly relaxed. Outside, there's the Slad Valley — home of writer Laurie Lee — to discover. It was here that he drank his cider with Rosie.

Rooms: 19: 2 four-posters, 11 doubles, 2 twins, 2 family and 2 singles.
Room price: £110-£185; singles from £75.
Breakfast: Until 10am.
Meals: Dinner, 3 courses, £26.50; 6 course (*dégustation*) menu, £60.
Closed: Never.

Directions: From Stroud, A46 north to Painswick. Turn right at St. Mary's church.
Follow road left, then first right. Hotel signed on right.

Map no: 2   **Entry no: 109**

Heavens Above at The Mad Hatters Restaurant

3 Cossack Square
Nailsworth
Gloucestershire, GL6 0DB

Tel: 01453 832615

Carolyn and Mike Findlay

Mike and Carolyn are inspiring. They were smallholders once, lived at the top of the hill, worked the land, kept livestock, made bellows — and earned £2,500 a year. Seven years ago they rolled down hill into town and opened a fully-organic restaurant. The locals flocked in and still do — the food here is quite delicious, some still grown back up the hill. You might get fabulous fish soup, lamb with garlic and rosemary and a mouth-puckering lemon tart. It's a place with real heart, not designed to impress, which is probably why it does. Cookery books are squashed into a pretty pine dresser and there are mellow stone walls, big bay windows, stripped wooden floors, simple pine tables. Exceptional art hangs on the walls and the place is airy with a warm rustic feel to it. Please don't worry that the bedrooms are not en suite and that you have to walk round the back to get to them. They are delightful — huge, like an artist's studio, with shiny wood floors, whitewashed walls and rag-rolled beams. A fabulous little place run with great passion and humanity. It may not be the Dorchester, but I'd stay here any day instead. *No-smoking.*

Rooms: 3: 1 double, 1 twin and 1 family.
Room price: £50-£60; singles £28-£35.
Breakfast: Flexible.
Meals: Lunch from £6.50. Dinner,
3 courses, £20-£25 (restaurant closed
Sunday evenings and Mondays).
Closed: Never.

Directions: M5, junction 13, A419 east to
Stroud, then A46 south into Nailsworth.
Right at roundabout, immediately left and
restaurant on right, opposite the Britannia pub.

Entry no: 110   Map no: 2

Glewstone Court Hotel

Glewstone
Ross-on-Wye
Herefordshire
HR9 6AW

Tel: 01989 770367
Fax: 01989 770282
E-mail: glewstone@aol.com

Christine and Bill Reeve-Tucker

A relaxed country house — grand, yet nicely lived-in, with an authentic 'house party' feel. Not a place to stand on too much ceremony. Kick off your shoes in the sitting room bar, sink into an elegant sofa in front of the fire and let Bill pour you a large gin and tonic. At lunchtime, you can eat on your lap here or at the table by the window, but there's a smartish restaurant, too, if you prefer. The centre of the house is early Georgian with a wooden staircase that spirals up to country house bedrooms. The honeymoon suite is enormous, while elsewhere, big bedrooms have pretty Christine-stencilled cupboards and walls, maybe a brass bed or quilted bedspreads. The electric pink room is wonderful and, like all the others, looks out onto plum, cherry, apple and pear orchards; the blossom goes on and on in spring. In the garden, an ancient cedar of Lebanon towers and there's a fountain out there, too. Christine cooks brilliantly, much of it organic, and Bill looks after you with great style. People in search of a small and friendly, informal country house will be in heaven.

Rooms: 8: 7 doubles and 1 single.
Room price: £75-£105; singles £45-£75.
Breakfast: Until 9.45am.
Meals: Dinner, 3 courses, about £26.
Bar/bistro main courses from £7.50.
Closed: 25-27 December.

Directions: From the A40 Ross-Monmouth road, turn right one mile south of Wilton roundabout, signed Glewstone. Hotel on left after half a mile.

Penrhos Court Hotel

Kington
Herefordshire
HR5 3LH

Tel: 01544 230720
Fax: 01544 230754
E-mail: reservations@penrhos.co.uk
Web: www.penrhos.co.uk

Martin Griffiths and Daphne Lambert

Penrhos is magnificent by any standards, but when you enter the cruck hall — a stone-flagged medieval masterpiece — bear in mind that 20 years ago it was a pile of medieval rubble. Daphne and Martin did most of the renovation themselves, keeping even the tiny details historically accurate, and the effect is jaw-dropping: tapestries on the walls, a 14th-century snug sitting room with a wooden ceiling, a huge fireplace where they burn great knotted lengths of wood (walk in, lift up your head and see the sky) and, outside, a stone barn, cow byre and puddleduck pond. But without a doubt, the highlight is the hall where you eat at night sitting at rough-hewn slabs of oak, illuminated by candlelight. Daphne cooks (she also runs a school of food and health) and the restaurant is fully organic (no red meat) reflecting their eco-friendly philosophy; they host a yearly 'green cuisine' festival here. The bedrooms have immense character and are big and bright; upstairs views to the hills, downstairs French doors onto a pretty garden. Bring your boots and walk. A heavenly experience.

Rooms: 15: 2 four-posters, 3 twins and 10 doubles.
Room price: £80-£120; singles from £55.
Breakfast: 8-9am weekdays; until 9.30am weekends.
Meals: Dinner, 4 courses, £31.50.
Closed: January.

Directions: Off A44 Leominster to Kington road, 1 mile east of Kington on the right. Hotel signed 200 yds down a smooth track.

Entry no: 112

Map no: 2

The Mill at Harvington

Anchor Lane
Harvington, Evesham
Worcestershire
WR11 5NR

Tel: 01386 870688
Fax: 01386 870688

Simon and Jane Greenhalgh

Not a bad house for a miller! He baked Birmingham's bread until 1898 when the river froze over, breaking the mill's waterwheels, a fate from which it never recovered. But he left a legacy: Russian Pine beams (imported for the great weight they could support) with shipping marks branded in Cyrillic. The house dates from the 1700s though you enter through the 'Chestnut Tree', a bright 1990s addition with glass walls and a trim wooden roof. Like the rest of the house, it looks out onto the huge lawned garden that runs down to the river Avon. In summer, parasolled tables are liberally sprinkled around, so pick one up and plonk it wherever you like, then sit back and watch canal boats chug by. Alternatively, sink into deep sofas in the sitting room or hang your head out of one of the bedroom windows — they, too, all look 'the right way'. The rooms are all good, "comfortable, not luxurious", says Simon, who always wears a bow-tie. Good fabrics, drapes and lots of king-size beds all prove his point. *Children over 10 welcome.*

Rooms: 21: 5 twins and 16 doubles.
Room price: £86-£121
Breakfast: Until 9.30am.
Meals: Dinner, 3 courses, £23. Light lunches also available.
Closed: 24-29 December.

Directions: A46 north of Evesham, then B4088 to Norton. In village, right, signed Bidford. After 1.5 miles, hotel signed right over bridge. Drive on left after about half a mile.

The Howard Arms

Lower Green
Ilmington
Warwickshire
CV36 4LT

Tel: 01608 682226
Fax: 01608 682226
E-mail: howard.arms@virgin.net
Web: www.howardarms.com

Robert and Gill Greenstock

Once upon a time Robert and Gill ran the Cotswold House hotel in Chipping Campden with a rare mix of flair, quirkiness and professionalism. It was a great place. Now, after a deserved sabbatical, they have cast their fairy dust over The Howard and the results are magical. The place buzzes with good-humoured babble, good beer gushes from a most genial bar and, at the far end of the attractive flagstoned bar-room, there is a dining area that is irresistible. It has an unexpected elegance for a pub, great swathes of bold colour and some noble paintings. People come from far away for the food. The bedrooms are taking shape, of average size, solidly comfortable and attractive, with perhaps, creamy white bedcovers and good wooden furniture. The village is a surprise, literally tucked under a lone hill and with a most unusual church, surrounded by a sort of extended village green and orchards. It is a place to spend a few days walking, listening to the buzzing of bees, and then to retire to The Howard to treat yourself — before the theatre at Stratford, perhaps.

Rooms: 3: 1 twin and 2 doubles.
Room price: £60-£70; singles from £37.50.
Breakfast: 8.30-11am.
Meals: Lunch and supper £7-£19 (kitchen closed Sunday evenings).
Closed: Never.

Directions: North from Moreton-in-Marsh on A429. After about 5 miles, left for Darlingscott and Ilmington. Pub in village centre.

Entry no: 114

Map no: 3

The Fox and Goose

Armscote
Nr. Stratford-upon-Avon
Warwickshire
CV37 8DD

Tel: 01608 682293
Fax: 01608 682293
Web: www.foxandgoose.co.uk

Sue Gray

Sue is one of those irrepressible innkeepers with an instinctive feel for what works. She took on a pub that had seen better days, stripped it back to its walls, pulled up the carpets, put in earthy wooden floors, then coated the walls with Farrow and Ball paints. The whole place is fresh, informal, vibrant — a 'happening' place. Purple, crushed velvet stools in the stone-flagged bar, shutters on all the windows, an open fire and woodburner, and heavy oak beams — fixtures and fittings from the 17th century, style from the 21st. She also added an excellent dining room for food that's "not too fancy, but very well cooked" — maybe Thai chicken, rib-eye steaks or home-made pasta; on Sundays take your pick from goose, beef and lamb, all roasted to perfection. Bedrooms above the restaurant are spectacular, though fairly compact. Big, comfy beds have 'jester hat' padded headboards, there are bold colours — blues, reds and yellows — on the walls, stripped wooden floors and CD players. Grab a disc from reception, light the candles in the bathroom, fill the tub, take in your glass of wine... There's a garden, too.

Rooms: 4 doubles (6 people maximum).
Room price: £90; singles £50.
Breakfast: 8.30am-midday.
Meals: Lunch and dinner £4.50-£20.
Closed: Christmas Day & New Year's Day.

Directions: A3400 south from Stratford-upon-Avon for 8 miles, then right for Armscote just after Newbold-on-Stour. In village.

Map no: 3   **Entry no: 115**

Mr Underhill's at Dinham Weir

Dinham Bridge   **Tel:** 01584 874431
Ludlow
Shropshire
SY8 1EH

Chris and Judy Bradley

With Chris and Judy at the helm, Mr Underhill's started life in Suffolk, travelled 18,000 frustrating miles around England looking for a new home and finally found one at the foot of Ludlow castle. It brought its Michelin star with it (a movable feast?) and was worth all that bother — the position right on the river Teme is dreamy. In summer, you can eat outside in the garden and watch the river flow by. The restaurant is long, light and airy, modern, warm and fun, and there's lots of glass to help you enjoy the view. The bright bedrooms are upstairs at the other end of the house — the only noise you'll hear is the river — and though some are small-ish, good design by Judy has made them feel bigger. They're almost Shaker in style: simple fabrics, crisp linen, king-size beds (one a canopied four-poster without the posts) and river views. All are good and restful. Back downstairs, you're bound to meet a roaming 20-year-old cat by the name of Frodo, king of all he surveys, and after whose alias, as Tolkien-lovers will confirm, the restaurant is named. Good people with huge commitment.

Rooms: 6 doubles (refurbishing winter 2000).
Room price: £75-£105; singles £65-£85.
Breakfast: Until 9.30am.
Meals: Dinner £27.50-£30.
Closed: Never.

Directions: Drive into centre of Ludlow, heading for castle. Take road called 'Dinham' to left of castle and follow down short hill, turning right at bottom before crossing river. On left and signed.

Entry no: 116   Map no: 5

The Hundred House Hotel

Norton
Nr. Shifnal
Shropshire
TF11 9EE

Tel: 01952 730353
Fax: 01952 730355
E-mail: hphundredhouse@compuserve.com

Henry, Sylvia, David and Stuart Phillips

A watering hole in the true sense, where the traditions of a good inn live on. Henry and Sylvia came here 14 years ago (Henry once kept chickens, but they didn't keep him) and they have infused the entire place, both inside and out, with deep charm. You enter to a world of blazing log fires, old brick walls, panelling and terracotta-tiled floors. Dried flowers hang from the beams, blackboard menus trumpet roast rib of beef, Moroccan lamb or Italian pork, and in the restaurant, Sylvia's wild and wonderful collage art hangs on wild and wonderful walls (one is gold). Quirky bedrooms come in different shapes and sizes. Patchwork quilts on brass beds, a half-tester in the purple and gold room, carafes of shampoo and bubble bath in the bathrooms. Some of the rooms even have swings while pillows are sprinkled with lavender water, presumably home-made as outside you will find the outstanding herb and flower gardens (they're open to the public). Wander out with your pint and find a quiet spot to share with a few stone lions. Henry, an innkeeper of the 'old school', has a great sense of humour, too.

Rooms: 10: 5 doubles, 2 twins, 2 family and 1 single.
Room price: £95-£120; singles £69.
Dinner, B&B from £65 p.p.
Breakfast: 7-9am weekdays;
8.30-10.30am weekends.
Meals: Dinner and lunch in brasserie from £3.50. Dinner, 3 courses, £28.
Closed: Christmas Day.

Directions: On A422 in village of Norton between Shifnal and Bridgnorth.

Pen-y-Dyffryn Country Hotel

Rhydycroesau
Nr. Oswestry
Shropshire
SY10 7JD

Tel: 01691 653700
Fax: 01691 650066
E-mail: stay@peny.co.uk
Web: www.peny.co.uk

Miles and Audrey Hunter

On a road that goes nowhere, this old rectory was commissioned in 1845 by its first rector, Robert Williams, who compiled the first Cornish dictionary. He was a bit stuffy apparently, the very opposite of Miles and Audrey, who are low-key and easy-going and have given the house much unpretentious charm. The entrance hall doubles as a bar, the bar itself an old *chiffonier* — "a posh sideboard," says Miles — with menus tucked away in the drawers. The bedrooms are 'comfy old house', with good fabrics and some with hand-painted furniture. One little double has its own flight of stairs and is sweet and romantic; the two 'old stable' rooms are big, more contemporary and have private terraces; nearly all the rooms have spectacular views. There's a sitting room to curl up in, a restaurant for all tastes, organic beers and wines and a terrace at the front for drinks and that view. The five acres of Pen-y-Dyffryn start at the top of the hill and roll down to Wales; the river at the foot of the beautiful valley marks the natural border.

Rooms: 10: 4 twins, 4 doubles, 1 single and 1 family room.
Room price: £74-£96; singles £60.
Breakfast: 8-9.30am.
Meals: Dinner, 3 courses, £21.
Closed: Christmas & 1-14 January.

Directions: From A5 head to Oswestry. Leave town on B4580 signed Llansilin. Hotel on left just before Rhydycroesau.

Entry no: 118

Map no: 5

Frogg Manor

Fullers Moor
Broxton, Chester
Cheshire
CH3 9JH

Tel: 01829 782629
Fax: 01829 782459

John Sykes

To quote from Frogg literature: "Classic bourgeois country house hotel? Not exactly, but an immensely enjoyable Englishman's home offering an unlikely combination of plush surroundings, 1930s music and frogs." The frogs are ceramic and stem from an old girlfriend called Froggy, who hopped off some time ago. The name has stayed though, as has John, your engagingly eccentric host. If you prefer your hotels to be a little more matter-of-fact, then perhaps this is not for you, but don't think it is a screamingly crazy place. Far from it. Strikingly individual at every turn, John has decorated with great panache. There are bergère sofas, ornate fireplaces, bold colours and a flamboyant Victorian elegance. Bedrooms are excellent, have everything you could ever possibly need (or forget) and are super value for money, but it's worth splashing out and going for Wellington, an extraordinary room. Entered via a secret bookcase door, it reveals an Aladdin's Cave of wonderful things. The food is exceptional — you've never seen a menu like it.

Rooms: 6: 1 suite and 5 doubles.
Room price: £70-£90; suite £135; singles £50-£100. Dinner, B&B from £75 p.p.
Breakfast: A la carte (£2-£17) served 24 hours, Monday-Saturday; 9-10.30am on Sundays.
Meals: Lunch from £16.80. Dinner, 3 courses, from £31.50.
Closed: Never.

Directions: South from Chester on A41, then left onto A534 at roundabout. Pass hotel on right, take first right and drive on right.

Map no: 5

Entry no: 119

Belle Epoque Brasserie

60 King Street
Knutsford
Cheshire
WA16 6DT

Tel: 01565 633060
Fax: 01565 634150
E-mail: belleepoque@csi.com

Nerys, Keith and
David Mooney

Not for wimps, but those who like their opulence laced with bonhomie will love this quirky restaurant with rooms. The Mooneys came here 25 years ago and, as if to revenge its past as a temperance hall, they have lavished rich colour and Victorian wonder throughout. At night, you could almost be in 1920s Paris, with waiters weaving past packed tables, the hum of conversation rising to the rafters. You are escorted to your table across the mosaic floor, past huge marble plinths, erupting ferns, statues and smouldering fires. Three-foot high vases stand on tables and, in the middle of one dining room, a brass goddess thrusts flower-filled arms skyward. On the walls, maybe a swathe of green silk or an acre of thick purple curtain and tucked up in one corner a romantic table lies hidden, guarded by two Doric columns. After a fabulous meal (*escargots*, quail, lamb's liver), the shallow steps of old wooden stairs take you up to very homely, very comfy bedrooms; they're not grand, but just right and great value for money. A bohemian dreamscape.

Rooms: 6: 5 doubles and 1 twin.
Room price: £60; singles £50.
Breakfast: Flexible. Continental included;
Full English £5.
Meals: Lunch, 2 courses, £6.95. Dinner,
3 courses, from £23.50.
Closed: Christmas & Bank Holidays.
Rooms available Monday-Friday only.

Directions: M6, junction 19, then follow
signs to Knutsford. Right at roundabout,
then left at second set of lights (both signed Macclesfield). Down hill and first left
into King Street.

Entry no: 120   Map no: 6

Oak Tree Farm

Hints Road
Hopwas, nr. Tamworth
Staffordshire
B78 3AA

Tel: 01827 56807
Fax: 01827 56807

Sue Purkis

Porcelain Chinese temple dogs in the dining room to ward off evil spirits, Bougainvillaea and terracotta pots in the conservatory swimming pool and cherry, apple and pear trees in a garden that runs down to the river Tame... it's hardly surprising that businessman and pleasure seeker alike spurn the centre of Birmingham (13 miles away) for Sue's creeper-clad, farmhouse B&B hotel — an oasis of peace in the middle of motorway-country. Sue is a great hostess, easy to talk to, kind and gentle. She has thought of all the little things: piles of papers for lazy Sunday breakfasts, bowls of organic fruit to raid, bottle openers, glasses and buckets of ice for sundowners (Oak Tree Farm is not licensed), backgammon in the bedrooms and Wellington boots for countryside forays. Big, generous bedrooms in the converted red-brick barn have oak furniture, sofas, pure cotton linen, floods of light and country views — peace and quiet, too. Bring your bikes and ride along the canal footpath into the heart of the city. The NEC is 30 minutes away, there's golf at The Belfry and you can eat at the pub at the end of the road.

Rooms: 5: 1 four-poster, 2 twins and 2 doubles.
Room price: £70; singles £52.
Breakfast: 7-10am weekdays; 8-10.30am weekends.
Meals: Available locally.
Closed: Christmas & New Year.

Directions: M42, junction 10. A5 west to A51 for Tamworth, then Lichfield. Cross bridge into Hopwas and left before Tame Otter pub. Last house on left.

Old Beams

Leek Road
Waterhouses
Staffordshire
ST10 3HW

Tel: 01538 308254
Fax: 01538 308157
Web: www.oldbeams.co.uk

Nigel, Ann, Simon and Sarah Wallis

There is only one Michelin star in Staffordshire and this is it. Nigel and Ann came here 20 years ago, started by renovating the place (the eponymous old beams were rubbed to a polish by their hands), then Nigel cooked up a reputation for superb food and now their children, Simon and Sarah, have joined the firm, while a team of chefs labours night and day (well, nearly) for your delectation. Everything possible is home-made: chocolates, soups, sorbets and pasta — even the biscuits in your bedroom come from the kitchen. Lots of plants, low ceilings, rich lighting, a stone fireplace and an open-plan feel that flows through to the muralled conservatory where fans hang from the ceiling and doors open out onto the pretty garden — you can eat here in summer. Bedrooms across the road (it is quiet at night) keep the clutter to a minimum and the comforts rolling: handmade Heal's of London beds, marble bathrooms, sunshine colours, good linen, fresh fruit, Roberts radios, a sofa if there's room. You don't make tea or coffee in your room — they bring it to you. Perfect.

Rooms: 5: 1 four-poster and 4 doubles.
Room price: £75-£90; four-poster £120; singles £65.
Breakfast: 7.30-9.30am weekdays; 8.30-9.30am weekends. Continental included; Full English £6.50.
Meals: Lunch (Fridays and Sundays only), 2 courses, £16.95. Dinner (Tuesday-Saturday), 3 courses, about £30
Closed: January.

Directions: Waterhouses is on the A523, about 5 miles north-west of Ashbourne. House in middle of village and signed.

Entry no: 122

Map no: 6

Riber Hall

Matlock
Derbyshire
DE4 5JU

Tel: 01629 582795
Fax: 01629 580475
E-mail: info@riber-hall.co.uk
Web: www.riber-hall.co.uk

Alex Biggin

Alex is wonderfully 'old school', very much his own man, and he runs this 14th-century Elizabethan manor house with one foot in the past. The sitting room and dining room fires smoulder all year round making the house feel grand, warm and intimate. The bedrooms are great fun, the majority with antique four-posters; expect timber-framed walls, mullioned windows, rich thick fabrics, beams and good furniture. There are lots of perfect touches, too: beds are turned down discreetly, there are carafes of bubble bath in super bathrooms and each room has umbrellas, fresh fruit and home-made shortbread. There's a tucked-away conservatory, full of colour and scent all year, and a walled orchard garden for pure tranquillity with long views. The food is excellent and Alex is a gentle host. He is easy to talk to and speaks with passion about Spain, New World wines and local wildlife. Chatsworth House is close by. *Children over ten welcome.*

Rooms: 14: 9 four-posters, 2 twins and 3 doubles.
Room price: £92-£162; singles £73-£107.
Breakfast: 7-9.30am. Full English £8; Continental included.
Meals: Lunch from £13. Dinner from £27.
Closed: Never.
Directions: A615 west from Matlock to Tansley. In village, turn right by petrol station (Alders Lane). Wind up hill for 1 mile to hotel.

Map no: 6   Entry no: 123

Biggin Hall

Biggin-by-Hartington
Buxton
Derbyshire
SK17 0DH

Tel: 01298 84451
Fax: 01298 84681
E-mail: bigginhall@compuserve.com
Web: www.bigginhall.co.uk

James Moffett

Biggin Hall, a 17th-century Grade II* listed farmhouse, is knee-deep in the country. A path from the house leads you out past the geese hut and stables to fields, hills, woods, rivers and waterfalls. Not far away is the 1831 Cromford and High Peak railway — one of the first in the world — now the preserve of cyclists and walkers. James, gently-spoken and humorous, knows his patch of England well and will guide you to its many secrets. He came here 24 years ago and started his labour of love, the restoration of Biggin Hall, keeping its fine old character — stone-flagged floors, old beams, the original fireplace, mullioned windows and leaded lights — while adding contemporary comforts. The bedrooms in the old house have bags of character and there's also a pretty dining room for good wholesome home-cooked English food. The view through its big window is a seamless transition from garden to paddock, then country beyond. Not surprising, then, that guests go away gleamingly happy. *Children over 11 welcome and pets by arrangement.*

Rooms: 17: 8 in main house and 9 in outbuildings.
Room price: £49-£110.
Breakfast: Until 8-9am. Continental included; Full English £3.50.
Meals: Dinner at 7pm, 4 courses, £14.50. Teas and packed lunches also available.
Closed: Never.

Directions: From A515 take turning to Biggin between Ashbourne and Buxton. Turn right just after Waterloo pub up drive to Biggin Hall.

Entry no: 124   **Map no: 6**

The North of England

Lancashire
Yorkshire
Cumbria
Co. Durham

"Trust in Allah, but tie your camel."
– Old Muslim Proverb

The White Hart Inn

51 Stockport Road
Lydgate, nr. Oldham
Greater Manchester
OL4 4JJ

Tel: 01457 872566
Fax: 01457 875190
E-mail: charles@thewhitehart.co.uk
Web: www.thewhitehart.co.uk

John Rudden and Charles Brierley

They've won just about every award going here both for the food and for the rooms — all deserved, though that hasn't stopped them hatching plans. The new extension is superb, the stone and slate all 200 years old to keep it historically accurate — this is a conservation village. Charles has renovated well, giving the place an airy feel while keeping all the nice old bits — the stone walls, the open fires, the odd beam, the wooden floors. Upstairs, in the bedrooms, part of the building's antiquity *has* been removed — the shackles to which they tied prisoners when the house was a prison. In their place, old radiators, big beds, lace bedcovers, compact bathrooms, Georgian colours for authenticity, maybe timber frames in a vaulted ceiling. All are extremely comfortable — good value for money — with views across churchyard and open country towards Manchester. Exceptional food comes either in the pub and its brasserie (more traditional meals), or in the smart, contemporary restaurant (more complex fare). They even have their own sausage factory, so take home a pack as a souvenir. The Moors are close.

Rooms: 12: 8 doubles and 4 twins.
Room price: £90; singles £62.50.
Breakfast: 7-9.30am weekdays; 7-10am weekends.
Meals: Brasserie lunch and dinner from £10. Dinner, 3 courses, £25.
Closed: Never.

Directions: Leave Oldham for Grasscroft on A669. Go through Grotton, climb hill into Lydgate and turn right at top of hill. Inn on left.

Entry no: 125   Map no: 6

The Inn at Whitewell

Whitewell   **Tel:** 01200 448222
Forest of Bowland, Nr. Clitheroe   **Fax:** 01200 448298
Lancashire
BB7 3AT

Richard Bowman

Richard, the Bowman of Bowland, wears an MCC tie and peers over half-moon glasses with a soft, slightly mischievous smile constantly on his face. "All those years ago" he was advised not to touch this inn with a bargepole, which must qualify as some of the worst advice ever given. You'll be hard-pressed to find anywhere — hotel or inn — as good as this — it's pure informal bliss. Peat fires, sofas, music systems, great art, a square piano... and that's only the bedrooms. They are a triumph of style, warm and fun (you're encouraged to scruff them up), some with fabulous Victorian brass-piped power showers others with deep cast-iron baths — superb. The inn sits just above the river Hodder with views at the back across parkland; the long restaurant drinks it in or there's a terrace if you want to be outside. Wander around inside and you'll come across old sporting memorabilia hanging in a corridor, settles, rugs, beams in the terracotta-walled bar, wood floors, open fires... the works. But, be warned: book early; weekends can be booked up months in advance. Fabulous.

Rooms: 15: 4 four-posters, 1 suite,
10 twin/doubles.
Room price: £82-£94; singles £57-£68;
suite £114.
Breakfast: 7.30-9.30am.
Meals: Lunch and dinner in bar from
£5.50. Dinner, à la carte, from £23.50.
Closed: Never.

Directions: M6, junction 31a, then B6243
east. Leaving Longridge for Clitheroe, turn
left, signed Whitewell and Chipping. Follow Whitewell signs for 9 miles to inn.

Map no: 6   **Entry no: 126**

Weaver's

15 West Lane
Haworth
Yorkshire
BD22 8DU

Tel: 01535 643822
Fax: 01535 644832
E-mail: colinjane@aol.com
Web: www.weaversmallhotel.co.uk

Colin and Jane Rushworth

If you don't know what a Clun or a Lonk is, use it as an excuse to make a trip to this unusual restaurant with rooms — the answer is somewhere on the walls. There's a rambling eccentricity downstairs, where nothing has a place, but everything is exactly where it should be. The front bar is intimate and has the feel of an old French café with heavy wood, marble-topped tables, atmospheric lighting and comfy chairs. The lively restaurant at the back is where Jane, who cooks, serves the best and most unpretentious food imaginable; maybe smoked haddock soup, Pennine meat and potato pie and home-made ice cream. The value is outstanding and people come back time and again. Bedrooms upstairs are just as surprising and ooze more understated originality: French beds, dashes of bright colour, the odd bust and antique furniture — everything seems just right. Rooms at the back overlook the Brontë Parsonage. Colin runs the front of house and is a real Yorkshire character: straight-talking, down-to-earth and with a good sense of humour. Worth a long detour.

Rooms: 3: 1 twin, 1 double and 1 single, all with private bathrooms.
Room price: £75; singles £50.
Breakfast: Until 9am.
Meals: Set menus £13.50; à la carte up to £25; bar suppers about £10. Restaurant closed Sundays and Mondays.
Closed: Two weeks after Christmas and one week in June.

Directions: From A629 take B6142 to Haworth. Follow Brontë Parsonage Museum signs. Use their car park; Weaver's backs onto it. Ignore signs for Brontë village.

Entry no: 127   **Map no: 6**

The Weavers Shed Restaurant with Rooms

Knowl Road
Golcar, Huddersfield
Yorkshire, HD7 4AN
Tel: 01484 654284
Fax: 01484 650980
E-mail: stephen@weavers-shed.demon.co.uk

Stephen and Tracy Jackson

Stephen's reputation for producing sublime food goes from strength to strength at The Weavers Shed, a restaurant with rooms firmly fixed on the wish lists of foodies all over the country. His passion stretches as far as planting a one-acre, kitchen garden; it now provides most of his vegetables, herbs and fruit. You may get warm mousse of scallops, Lunesdale duckling and warm tartlet of rhubarb, the latter home-grown, of course. The old mill owner's house sits at the top of the hill, with cobbles in the courtyard and its own lamp post by the door. Inside, whitewashed walls are speckled with menus from famous restaurants, a small garden basks beyond the windows and at the bar, malts and *eaux de vie* stand behind a piece of wood that look as if it came from an ancient church, but actually came from the Co-op. Earthy stone arches and plinths in the Sardinian-tiled restaurant at the back give the feel of a Tuscan farmhouse. Elsewhere, gilt mirrors, comfy sofas and big, bright, brilliantly priced bedrooms that hit the spot with complimentary sherry, dried flowers, bath robes and wicker chairs.

Rooms: 5: 1 four-poster, 3 doubles and 1 twin/double.
Room price: £55-£65; singles from £40.
Breakfast: 7-9am weekdays; 8-10am weekends.
Meals: Lunch (Tuesday-Friday) from £13.95. Dinner (Tuesday-Saturday) about £25.
Closed: Christmas & New Year.

Directions: West from Huddersfield on A62 for 2 miles, then right signed Milnsbridge and Golcar. Left at Kwiksave, and signed on right at top of hill.

Map no: 6   Entry no: **128**

The Grange Hotel

1 Clifton
York
Yorkshire
YO30 6AA

Tel: 01904 644744
Fax: 01904 612453
E-mail: reservations@grangehotel.co.uk
Web: www.grangehotel.co.uk

Jeremy and Vivien Cassel   **Manager: Shara Ross**

Half a mile from the city wall where the ancient Minster stands, The Grange is everything a big town house hotel should be — gracious and elegant with a sumptuously warm grandeur that unwinds you immediately. Stone floors and Doric columns greet you in the hall, flowers erupt from urns and there's a leather sofa to sink into in the corner. The same effortless style runs throughout the hotel: back-to-back, plump-cushioned sofas and green Regency-striped wallpaper in the morning room; murals and a small gallery of equine 'greats' in the dining rooms; a vaulted-brick roof in the brasserie down in the cellars — it's all spot-on. Bedrooms are full of the same flair: bold greens and reds, a silky purple four-poster, writing paper on the desks, rich fabrics and rugs — you'll find everything you need to spoil yourself. Jeremy rescued the building from neglect and has worked a gentle magic making it a great place to linger, especially on racing days — it is here that the optimists gather. York, brimming with history, starts outside the front door, so don't linger too long.

Rooms: 30: 1 suite, 2 four-posters, 24 twin/doubles and 3 singles.
Room price: £125-£185; suites £215; singles £99.
Breakfast: 7-10am; 8-10am on Sunday.
Meals: Dinner, 3 courses, £25. Light meals from £7.95.
Closed: Never.

Directions: From ring road, A19 south into York. The Grange is on the right after 2.5 miles, 400 yards from the city walls.

Entry no: 129   **Map no: 6**

The Hawnby Hotel

Hilltop
Hawnby, Helmsley
Yorkshire
YO6 5QS

Tel: 01439 798202
Fax: 01439 798344
E-mail: info@hawnbyhotel.co.uk
Web: www.hawnbyhotel.co.uk

Kathryn and Dave Young

Leave your alarm clock at home and wake to the sound of birdsong. This is fabulous country, a very pretty village hidden away deep in the North York Moors. Tied cottages stretch lazily up the side of the hill, the river Rye rambles through at the bottom and from the hotel you get superb views down the valley, of woodland, of fields, of snaking river glinting in the morning sun. You can set off on intrepid walks, following ancient footpaths along the river to Rievaulx Abbey, five miles away. And where better to return after a day lost in the hills? The Hawnby is everything it should be: honest, comfortable, welcoming, peaceful. A flat cap on the hat stand in the local's bar, a small coal fire, smart red carpets, a crisp and elegant dining room, fine home-cooked food and Laura Ashley-style bedrooms that give surprising levels of comfort for their price. Kathryn and Dave are young and easy-going. They bought the place on a whim and are perfect for it, bringing new ideas, masses of energy and an easy *laissez faire* spirit. Horse riding and fishing can both be arranged. A great spot.

Rooms: 6: 4 twins and 2 doubles.
Room price: £60; singles £45.
Breakfast: 8.15-9.15am.
Meals: Lunch from £6. Dinner, 3 courses, about £18.
Closed: Never.

Directions: From Thirsk, A170 west over A19, then left signed Felixkirk and Boltby. Straight ahead 8 miles to Hawnby. There, right up hill and signed.

Crab Manor at The Crab and Lobster

Asenby
Thirsk
Yorkshire
YO7 3QL

Tel: 01845 577286
Fax: 01845 577109
E-mail: reservations@crabandlobster.co.uk
Web: www.crabandlobster.co.uk

David and Jackie Barnard

An exceptional place, original in every way, full of thrills and surprises. At the Manor there are deep leather armchairs in the lavish sitting room, a secret beer tap in the hall, and upstairs, past the eight-foot tall yeti on the landing (he can talk), inspirational bedrooms that will take you round the world in 12 nights (each room is influenced by a famous hotel from around the globe). They are all superb, with maybe free-standing baths in Italian-tiled bathrooms, wood carvings, cherubs on the walls, massive wooden antique beds, elephant hats, crushed-velvet cushions, mosquito nets; three in the tropical beach house have saunas and hot tubs. You can eat in the conservatory amid terracotta pots, plinths and busts, but a gentle stroll through the garden, along lantern-lit gravel paths, brings you to The Crab and Lobster. Here you can eat sumptuous food in equally quirky rooms: bookshelf bars, ceilings dripping with memorabilia, a small tucked-away panelled room. The locals flock here in droves. There's a one-hole golf course, too, and an oasis is on the way.

Rooms: 12: 9 four-posters and 3 doubles.
Room price: £120-£140; singles from £80. Dinner, B&B from £70 p.p.
Breakfast: 8-10am.
Meals: Lunch from £10. Dinner, 3 courses, about £25.
Closed: Never.

Directions: A1(M), junction 41, then A168 for Thirsk. After 2 miles: left, signed Topcliff; left again, signed Asenby; left, signed 'village only'; first right and house on right.

Entry no: 131　　　　　　　　　　　　**Map no: 6**

The General Tarleton

Ferrensby
Knaresborough
Yorkshire
HG5 0QB

Tel: 01423 340284
Fax: 01423 340288
E-mail: gti@generaltarleton.co.uk
Web: www.generaltarleton.co.uk

Denis Watkins and John Topham

The first thing you notice here is how friendly and helpful the staff are, all local, all proud of their lovely slice of England. After about five minutes a newspaper had been found for me, my coffee and home-made biscuits had arrived and I knew the exact dates of the Harrogate flower festival (last week of April — don't miss it!), all delivered with gentle smiles. Then came Denis and you could see where they got it from. The easy style and elegance of his hotel and the tiptop service are a reflection of his natural friendliness. As we wandered round, he moved effortlessly from story (this is a patronage pub, opened originally by a soldier who fought for General Tarleton) to straightforward facts ("the bedrooms are simple with very good basics"). Spot on. Rooms at the front have views of rolling country; all are spotless, with lots of colour, padded headboards and power showers. You'll also find a smart, crisp restaurant with stone walls, comfy sofas in reception, a warm and traditional, beamed bar and a conservatory for excellent brasserie food. A lovely place, run by equally lovely people.

Rooms: 15: 1 four-poster, 8 doubles and 6 twins.
Room price: £60-£85. Dinner, B&B from £55 p.p.
Breakfast: 7.30-10am.
Meals: Lunch and dinner in brasserie from £7. Dinner, 3 courses, £25.
Closed: Christmas Day.

Directions: The inn is on A6055, either 2 miles north of Knaresborough or 3 miles south of A1(M), junction 48.

Map no: 6

Entry no: 132

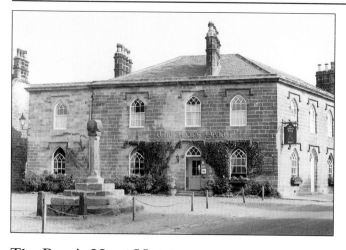

The Boar's Head Hotel

Ripley Castle Estate
Harrogate
Yorkshire
HG3 3AY

Tel: 01423 771888
Fax: 01423 771509
E-mail: boarshead@ripleycastle.co.uk
Web: www.ripleycastle.co.uk

Sir Thomas and Lady Emma Ingilby

When the Ingilbys decided to re-open The Boar's Head, the attic at the castle got a shakedown and the spare furniture was sent round. The vicar even came to bless the beer taps — you'll find them in Boris's bar, Boris being the eponymous head. Elegant fun is the net result and there's something for everyone. The décor has been brilliantly created by Lady Ingilby. The sitting rooms and hall have crisp yellow Regency wallpaper, big old oils, roaring fires and gilt mirrors. The restaurant is a deep, moody crimson, candle-lit at night, and you drink from blue, smoked-glass. There are games, newspapers to peruse, menus to drool over and a parasolled garden for summer drinks. Up the staircase, past more ancestors, bright bedrooms have delicate floral fabrics, flowers and maybe a sofa, some antique furniture, tumbling crowns above big beds or a rag-rolled bathroom. In the coachman's loft in the courtyard, you'll find the odd beam and pretty pine panelling. You can visit the castle gardens as a guest of the hotel; there are umbrellas and wellies for rainy days, too.

Rooms: 25: 21 twin/king doubles and 4 doubles.
Room price: £115-£135; singles £95-£115. Dinner, B&B £75 p.p. (minimum 2 night stay).
Breakfast: 7.30-9.30am.
Meals: Dinner, 3 courses, £27.50-£35. Bistro main courses from £6.95.
Closed: Never.

Directions: North from Harrogate on A61. Ripley signed left at roundabout after 3 miles.

Entry no: 133

Map no: 6

The Red Lion

By the Bridge at Burnsall
Nr. Skipton
Yorkshire
BD23 6BU

Tel: 01756 720204
Fax: 01756 720292
E-mail: redlion@daelnet.co.uk
Web: www.redlion.co.uk

Elizabeth and Andrew Grayshon

Although an old-fashioned inn with lots of old-world charm, the place is fun too; even the ghost in the 12th-century cellars has a sense of humour, occasionally turning the beer taps off! This is an inn for all ages; the sitting room, strewn with both guide books and children's books, is cosy with old armchairs, sofas and woodburning stove. The family are all involved. Son-in-law Jim cooks seriously good food — the rest of the family eat it — while Elizabeth keeps a matriarchal eye on things. The net result is a cosy, unpretentious inn that is thoroughly comfortable. The bar hums with happy locals; upstairs, bedrooms have beams and slanting, low ceilings. In the next door annexe the rooms are larger: one has an open fire and a big brass bed. Family rooms have highchairs and baby listeners, too. Originally it was a ferryman's inn. Now the river runs wide and shallow under the bridge, through an English landscape of great beauty and past a deeply sleepy village. The Burnsall fell race in August (eight minutes up, four minutes down!) starts outside the front door. *Pets by arrangement.*

Rooms: 11: 1 family, 1 single,
4 twin/doubles and 5 doubles.
Room price: £95-£120; singles from
£47.50. Dinner, B&B from £70 p.p.
Breakfast: Until 9.30am.
Meals: Dinner in restaurant, £24.95.
Bar food from £7.50.
Closed: Never.

Directions: A59 west from Harrogate,
then B6160 at Bolton Bridge. Continue to
Burnsall. Hotel next to bridge.

Waterford House

19 Kirkgate
Middleham
Yorkshire
DL8 4PG

Tel: 01969 622090
Fax: 01969 624020

Everyl and Brian Madell

Richard III lived in Middleham's now ruined castle and locals will tell you that history has been unkind to his memory; he was, they say, not such a bad fellow after all. What is beyond dispute is the excellence of Waterford House. Is it a restaurant with rooms? More like a home with restaurant, and Brian and Everyl assume that their job is to make all guests happy. Thus their galaxy of 1,000 wines is, remarkably, available by the glass and there are mountains of glorious Everyl-cooked food that will keep you going for a week. It's full of pretty antiques and knick-knacks — everywhere there is something — but the clutter is magnificent and thoroughly under control. The bedrooms are hard to fault. You are treated to sherry and old transistor radios — an unusual touch — and they range from delightfully cosy to grand four-poster. If you sleep at the front, you will hear racehorses from local stables ambling past in the morning on their way to the Moor. You can even get married here. But, all this would be blossom in the wind without Everyl's unflagging dedication and kindness.

Rooms: 5: 2 four-posters, 1 twin/double and 2 doubles.
Room price: £75-£95; singles £50-£60.
Breakfast: Until 10am.
Meals: Dinner from £24.50. Lunch from £22.50. Booking essential.
Closed: Never.

Directions: Southbound from A1 at Scotch Corner via Richmond and Leyburn. Northbound from A1 on B6267 via Masham. House in right-hand corner of square.

The Blue Lion

East Witton
Nr. Leyburn
Yorkshire
DL8 4SN

Tel: 01969 624273
Fax: 01969 624189
E-mail: bluelion@breathemail.net
Web: www.bluelion.co.uk

Paul and Helen Klein

The Blue Lion is one of those names that follow you round a county, with everyone asking if you've been there. There's good reason for this — superlative food served up in this dreamy inn have made it a favourite with locals. Paul and Helen came here ten years ago and have mixed the traditions of a country pub with the elegance of a country house. Aproned staff, polished beer taps, stone flagged floors and smouldering fires. In the bar, newspapers hang on poles and there are big settles to sit at, while huge bunches of dried flowers hang from beams and splashes of flowers erupt from vases. The two restaurants offer boarded floors and shuttered Georgian windows, two coal fires, gilt mirrors and candles everywhere. Bedrooms are split between the main house (comfortable rather than luxurious, with dashes of colour, big padded headboards and wooden beds) and the stables (exposed beams, old pine furniture, regal colours and maybe a brass bed). A place to come for a spot of indulgence. Jerveaulx Abbey is a mile away.

Rooms: 12: 9 doubles, 2 twins and 1 family.
Room price: £69-£89; singles £54.
Breakfast: 8-10am.
Meals: Lunch and dinner in bar from £7. Dinner, 3 courses, about £25.
Closed: Never.

Directions: East Witton is 3 miles south of Leyburn on the A6108. The inn is in the village.

The Burgoyne Hotel

On the Green
Reeth, Richmond
Yorkshire
DL11 6SN

Tel: 01748 884292
Fax: 01748 884292

Derek Hickson and Peter Carwardine

Standing at the top of the village green with sweeping views of Swaledale, The Burgoyne has a dignified and august air. Peter and Derek have created a crisp and comfortable interior with lots of old-fashioned elegance and contemporary warmth: cool mints, bold greens, delicate lighting, dramatic displays of fresh flowers and cushions as plump as Christmas geese. Big bedrooms upstairs are full of colour and have everything you could possibly need: bathrobes, sewing kits, shoe polish, even slippers. There are cushioned-window seats — you need them for the view — the original shutters and rich fabrics. You've come here to eat, too. Peter cooks superbly (he's the one in kitchen whites) using fresh, local ingredients, and Derek's careful choice of wine guarantees an excellent evening. There's also a small garden at the back with more good views across stone walls to sheep grazing on rising fells.

Rooms: 8: 4 doubles and 1 twin; 2 twins and 1 double, with private bathrooms.
Room price: £80-£140; singles from £70.
Breakfast: Until 9.30am.
Meals: Dinner, 3 courses, £24.50.
Closed: 2nd January for 6 weeks.

Directions: From Richmond, A6108, then B6270 to Reeth. House on village green.

Entry no: 137   **Map no: 6**

Simonstone Hall

Hawes
Yorkshire
DL8 3LY

Tel: 01969 667255
Fax: 01969 667741
E-mail: e-mail@simonstonehall.demon.co.uk
Web: www.simonstonehall.com

Manager: Jill Peterson

As you drool over the picture of Simonstone, do know that it's just as good inside. This is a glorious country house, built in the 1770s as a shooting lodge for the Earl of Wharncliffe. The drawing room is magnificent — gracious and elegant — with a wildly ornate fireplace, painted panelled walls and a flurry of antiques. Its triumph is the huge stone-mullioned window through which Wensleydale unravels — a place to stand rooted to the spot. Elsewhere you'll find stone-flagged floors, stained-glass windows and old oils and trophies on the walls. There's a big warm traditional bar — almost a pub — with fishing nets hanging from the ceilings, clocks and mirrors on the walls, and if you don't want to eat in the panelled dining room you can have excellent bar meals here. Bedrooms are superb. It's well worth splashing out and going for the grander ones — they indulge you completely: four-posters, mullioned windows, stone fireplaces, oils — the full aristocratic Monty. You can even have breakfast on the terrace with those fabulous views.

Rooms: 18: 5 four-posters, 2 suites,
7 doubles and 4 twin/doubles.
Room price: £90-£180; four-posters £200;
singles from £60. Dinner,
B&B £55-£105 p.p.
Breakfast: 8.30-10am.
Meals: Lunch and dinner £5-£25.
Closed: Never.

Directions: From Hawes, follow signs
north for Muker for about 2 miles. The
hotel is on the left, at the foot of Buttertubs Pass.

Hipping Hall
Cowan Bridge
Kirkby Lonsdale
Cumbria
LA6 2JJ

Tel: 015242 71187
Fax: 015242 72452
E-mail: hippinghal@aol.com
Web: www.dedicate.co.uk/hipping-hall

Richard, Jean, Martin and Tamara Skelton

The house is a remnant of a 15th-century hamlet; outside you'll come across an old stone wash-house, a stream and a spring-fed pond, while the ancient well is now in the stone-flagged conservatory. The Skeltons took over recently and have kept things much as they always were: informal, stylish, relaxing. You can still dine in true house-party style at one table in the Great Hall, surrounded by old oak floors, rugs, candles and beams, not far from the school attended by the Brontë sisters. Jean cooks and there is a separate dining room if you want to be on your own. The style is 'country house': bedrooms are warm and homely, there are bookshelves all over the place, bathrooms are spotless and there's lots of good furniture. There are three acres of garden, majestic countryside (Hipping Hall is in a perfect position with the Yorkshire Dales to the east, the Lakes to the west) and sleep-inducing comfort to come home to. Perfect for private parties or self-indulgent walkers; a footpath leads out over Leck Fell to Barbondale. Ingleton Waterfalls are close by and worth a visit.

Rooms: 6: 2 twins, 2 doubles and 2 cottage suites.
Room price: £92-£106; singles £74.
Breakfast: 8.30-9.30am.
Meals: Dinner, 3 courses, from £18. Light lunches by arrangement.
Closed: 1 November — 28 February (private parties by arrangement).

Directions: M6, junction 36, then A65 east, 2.5 miles beyond Kirkby Lonsdale. House is on left 8.5 miles from M6.

Entry no: 139   **Map no: 6**

Aynsome Manor Hotel

Cartmel
Nr. Grange-over-Sands
Cumbria
LA11 6HH

Tel: 015395 36653
Fax: 015395 36016
E-mail: info@aynsomemanorhotel.co.uk
Web: www.aynsomemanorhotel.co.uk

Christopher and Andrea Varley

Stand at the front door and look away from the house. Three-quarters of a mile across ancient meadows Cartmel Priory stands, magnificent after 800 years, still the heart of a small, thriving community. The view is almost medieval. You can strike out across fields to the village and discover its gentle secrets. The house, too, echoes with history — it was the home of the descendants of the Earl of Pembroke and, in 1930, it gave up a long-held secret when a suit of chain armour dating back to 1335 was found behind a wall in an attic bedroom. There's a tongue-and-ball ceiling in the panelled dining room and, in the hall, a melodious grandfather clock, a wood and coal fire and carved-oak panels, the gift of an 1839 storm. A cantilevered spiral staircase with cupola-domed window leads up to the first-floor sitting room where newspapers hang from poles and there's an Adams-style marble fireplace. The bedrooms vary in size and are simple and comfortable, some with gently sloping floors. Racegoers will love the National Hunt racecourse. *No under fives in the restaurant.*

Rooms: 12: 4 twins, 5 doubles,
1 four-poster and 2 family rooms.
Room price: £69-£80; singles from £39.
Dinner, B&B £48-£58 p.p.
Breakfast: 8.30-9.30am.
Meals: Dinner, 4 courses, £22.
Closed: January.

Directions: Leave A590 (M6 — Barrow road) at top of Lindale Hill. Follow signs left to Cartmel. Hotel on right 3 miles from A590.

The Old Vicarage

Church Road
Witherslack
Cumbria
LA11 6RS

Tel: 015395 52381
Fax: 015395 52373
E-mail: hotel@oldvicarage.com
Web: www.oldvicarage.com

Jill and Roger Brown and Irene and Stanley Reeve

Thank goodness for the Browns and the Reeves! The potted history of these four effervescent souls is that 20 years ago they escaped the rat race 'down south', swapped suits, first for overalls (the house needed a major make-over), then, liberated, aprons. They have been indulging their passions ever since, number one on the list being food. Everyone I spoke to in the area had eaten here and thoroughly recommended it; the TV cameras have, of course, paid a visit. The baton has been passed to the next generation with James, Jill's and Roger's son, now in the kitchen. Add to this rooms of simple, stylish luxury and you have guests as happy as the owners. Rooms in the main house look out over the garden and are closer to the fun; those in Orchard house are bigger, better and utterly secluded, so stroll through the damson trees and past the tennis court on your way up. Maps and routes for walkers, high teas and chairs for children, and Yewbarrow Fell ('The Noddle') is just behind. A ten-minute walk to the top brings spectacular views. Quite simply, heaven-sent and down-to-earth.

Rooms: 12: 1 four-poster, 1 family,
6 doubles and 4 twins.
Room price: £98-£138; four-poster £158;
singles from £65. Dinner, B&B
£60-£100 p.p.
Breakfast: 8-9.30am.
Meals: Dinner, à la carte, 3 courses from
£25. Sunday lunch £15.50. Packed lunches
also available.
Closed: Never.

Directions: M6, junction 36, then A590 towards Barrow. After 6 miles, right signed Witherslack. In village, left after phone box. House on left just before church.

Entry no: 141   Map no: 5

White Moss House
Rydal Water
Grasmere
Cumbria
LA22 9SE

Tel: 015394 35295
Fax: 015394 35516
E-mail: sue@whitemoss.com
Web: www.whitemoss.com

Susan and Peter Dixon

This is the epicentre of Wordsworth country; walk north a mile to his home at Dove Cottage or west to his somewhat more salubrious house at Rydal Mount. The paths are old and you can follow his footsteps up fell and through wood. He knew White Moss, too — he bought it for his son and came here to escape. The Dixons have lived here for 18 years — they took over from Susan's parents — and they have kept the feel of a home: flowers everywhere, a wood burning stove, pretty floral fabrics and lots of comfy sofas and chairs. There's a small bar in an old linen cupboard, and after-dinner coffee in the sitting room brings out the house-party feel. Upstairs, bedrooms range in size, but not comfort. All are different, with maybe a glazed-pine panelled bay window, old wooden beds and a sprinkling of books and magazines. All have good views, and bathrooms have Radox to soothe fell-fallen feet. There's also the small matter of the food, all cooked by Peter. Five courses of famed indulgence await — expect to have your taste buds tickled. *Pets by arrangement.*

Rooms: 9: 3 doubles, 2 twin/doubles and 2 twins; 1 cottage (let to same party only) comprising 1 four-poster and 1 twin, with shower-room and bathroom.
Room price: Dinner, B&B £65-£90 p.p.
Breakfast: 8.30-9.30am.
Meals: Dinner, 5 courses, included in price. Packed lunches £5. Restaurant closed Sunday nights.
Closed: 1 December — mid-February.

Directions: North from Ambleside on A591. House signed on right at north end of Rydal Water.

Map no: 5

Entry no: 142

Michaels Nook

Grasmere
Ambleside
Cumbria
LA22 9RP

Tel: 015394 35496
Fax: 015394 35645
E-mail: m-nook@wordsworth-grasmere.co.uk
Web: www.grasmere-hotels.co.uk

Reg and Elizabeth Gifford

The immense luxury of Michaels Nook is offered in the most understated way, making it easy to understand why it is one of Britain's finest country house hotels. You can expect the best of everything: a Michelin-starred restaurant, a treasure trove of antique furniture, Honduran mahogany staircase and panelling, sumptuously rich fabrics and bold décor. Bedrooms are superb. There are high four-posters, drapes, armoires, maybe an aubergine-coloured *chaise longue* or a big old cast-iron bath with the equivalent of a Victorian power shower — marvellous. The suite has some lovely Chinese lacquer furniture and a big window to frame the lakeland view. Reg has been here for 30 years and presides over it all with gentle good humour and an unpretentious Cumbrian warmth. You'll meet his Great Danes, too — they're as friendly as they are big. He won best of breed at Crufts in 1997 and 2000, yet still has a soft spot for Scruffs. There are three acres of landscaped gardens, 10 acres of hillside and you can walk into the fells from the front door.

Rooms: 14: 2 suites, 1 four-poster and 11 twin/doubles.
Room price: Dinner, B&B £85-£137.50 p.p.; suites £160 p.p.; singles from £135.
Breakfast: 8.30-9.30am.
Meals: Dinner, 5 courses, included.
Closed: Never.

Directions: A591 north from Windermere. At the Swan on A591 at Grasmere, turn right between the pub and its car park. Hotel signed on right.

Entry no: 143   **Map no: 5**

Old Dungeon Ghyll

Great Langdale
Ambleside
Cumbria
LA22 9JY

Tel: 015394 37272
Fax: 015394 37272
E-mail: neil.odg@lineone.net
Web: www.odg.co.uk

Neil and Jane Walmsley

This is an old favourite of those hardy mountaineers and it comes as no surprise to learn that Tenzing and Hillary stayed here. The hotel is at the head of the valley, surrounded by spectacular peaks, a hikers' and climbers' heaven and a place to escape to. The scenery is breathtaking, and this is a solid and genuine base... as unpretentious as can be. The bedrooms are eclectically decorated with the odd brass bed, patchwork quilts, maybe floral wallpaper and patterned carpets. They are also blissfully free of phones and TVs — you wouldn't want them here, not when you can go downstairs. In winter, the fire crackles comfortably in the sitting room, the food is all home-cooked (fresh bread, teacakes and flapjacks every day) and there's a small snug residents' bar. Best of all is the famed hikers' bar (hotel wedding parties always seem to end up here). Guitars and fiddles appear (do they carry them over the mountain?), *ceilidhs* break out, laughter is the main language and it's all overseen by Neil, Jane and a great staff. Come to walk and to leave the city far behind.

Rooms: 14: 4 twin/doubles; 1 twin,
2 family, 3 singles and 4 doubles, all
sharing 4 baths and 1 shower.
Room price: £64-£75.
Breakfast: 8.30-9.30am.
Meals: Dinner, 3 courses, £18.50.
Bar snacks from £6. Packed lunches £3.95.
Closed: 24-26 December.

Directions: On A593, from Ambleside
towards Coniston, turn right onto B5343.
Hotel signed after 5 miles on right, just after Great Langdale campsite.

Map no: 5   **Entry no: 144**

The Wasdale Head Inn

Wasdale Head
Gosforth
Cumbria
CA20 1EX

Tel: 01946 726229
Fax: 019467 26334
E-mail: wasdaleheadinn@msn.com
Web: www.wasdale.com

Howard Christie

Wasdale Head is incomparable, perfect and unique. The vastness of the scenery is staggering, its remoteness is second-to-none. No great surprise, then, to discover that this inn is the home and birth place of world mountain climbing, the resident's bar being its 'holy of holies'. On the walls hang original photos taken by the Abrahams brothers, the pioneers of climbing photography, and they, too, are staggering. Nowhere, either inside or out, is there a trace of commercialism; Wasdale remains blissfully free of the outside world. The inn is warm and intimate, lively and fun. There's a hiker's bar where blackboards tell of the weather as well as the food, a restaurant dripping in old climbing memorabilia and, outside, a beer garden with views off to Kirk Fell, Great Gable and Scafell — England's highest mountain. Bedrooms are split between the main house (simple chalet style) and the cottages (more luxurious). Howard is part of the mountain rescue team, so expect the best advice. He's also 'the Biggest Liar in the World' — a competition the inn has hosted for 118 years.

Rooms: 12: 3 suites, 5 doubles, 1 twin, 1 triple and 2 singles.
Room price: £70-£90; singles £35-£45.
Breakfast: 7.30-9am.
Meals: Bar meals, lunch and dinner, from £3. Dinner, 4 courses, £22.
Closed: Never.

Directions: From Gosforth (A595) head east through Wellington and follow signs to Wasdale Head; from Windermere (1.5 hours), weather permitting, cross Wrynose and Hardknott passes: after Great Langdale it's 'first right' every time... literally, and maybe the best drive in England.

Entry no: 145   **Map no: 5**

Swinside Lodge

Grange Road
Newlands, Keswick
Cumbria
CA12 5UE

Tel: 017687 72948
Fax: 017687 72948
E-mail: stay@swinside.fsbusiness.co.uk

Kevin and Susan Kniveton

A short stroll takes you to the edge of Derwentwater — the Queen of the lakes. Immediately behind, the fells rise and spirits soar. At Swinside — a small-scale model of English country house elegance — reception rooms are crisp and fresh with fine period furniture offset by pastel blues and yellows. In the bold dining room, deep reds combine with candle-lamps burning oil... formal, yet very relaxed. There are lots of books in the sitting rooms, maps for walkers, bowls of fruit, fresh flowers and no clutter. Every tiny detail has been well thought out, not least in the bedrooms where sensitivity and forethought have pulled off a maestro's touch: the rooms have been furnished with cream furniture to make them feel bigger than they are — it works a treat. The bedrooms are all good and two are huge. You'll find drapes, more crisp materials and uplifting views — you can watch the weather change. The food is honest and delicious: perhaps asparagus and herb risotto, celery and apple soup, lamb, warm chocolate mousse. *Children over ten welcome.*

Rooms: 7: 2 twins and 5 doubles.
Room price: Dinner, B&B, £87-£95 p.p.; singles from £90.
Breakfast: 8.30-9.30am.
Meals: Dinner, 4 courses, included in price. Non-residents £28. Booking essential.
Closed: Never.

Directions: M6, junction 40, then A66 west past Keswick. Over roundabout, then second left, signed Portiscale and Grange. Follow signs to Grange for 2 miles. House signed on right.

Map no: 5

Entry no: 146

The Pheasant

Bassenthwaite Lake
Nr. Cockermouth
Cumbria
CA13 9YE

Tel: 017687 76234
Fax: 017687 76002
E-mail: pheasant@easynet.co.uk
Web: www.the-pheasant.co.uk

Matthew Wylie

The snug bar at The Pheasant — a treasured relic of its days as a coaching inn — is tremendous, the walls a shiny combination of 300 years of nicotine and polish. It's wonderful! There's also a low-slung wooden bar where the barman guards his 28 malts. The inn, however, has turned into a hotel and drinks are usually served in one of the sitting rooms, where elegance is piled upon elegance in an utterly understated way: gilt mirrors, sprays of garden flowers, trim carpets, rugs and fresh yellow walls, fine furniture and a beam or two — everything is just right, immaculate yet immediately relaxing. The bedrooms have been beautifully refurbished this year; the odd hidden beam has been revealed, mellow lighting added, warm colours put on the walls and a rug or two thrown in for good measure. All are elegant and you still come across Housekeeping armed with feather dusters — perfect. There's a kennel for visiting dogs, Skiddaw to be scaled and Bassenthwaite lake to be paddled. *Children over eight welcome.*

Rooms: 16: 11 twin/doubles and
2 singles; 2 doubles and 1 single in garden lodge.
Room price: £80-£130; singles from £59.
Dinner, B&B from £59 p.p.
Breakfast: 7.30-9.30am.
Meals: Lunch from £5. Dinner, 3 courses,
£21.50-£28.
Closed: Christmas Day.

Directions: The hotel is signed left on the A66, 7 miles north-west of Keswick.

The Old Church Hotel

Watermillock
Penrith
Cumbria
CA11 0JN

Tel: 017684 86204
Fax: 017684 86368
E-mail: info@oldchurch.co.uk
Web: www.oldchurch.co.uk

Kevin Whitemore

This is the sort of country house you search high and low for. The drive drops down through fields, past a 1200 year-old yew tree, to lawns that hug Lake Ullswater. You are on a tiny peninsular, bounded on three sides by water, and once in the house, the view just follows you around. You enter into a small but lovely hall, with obligatory roaring fire, old oak furniture, deep scarlet walls and thick, red velvet curtains to keep the draught out (they do). The friendliest of local staff come out to greet you and take you up to lovely rooms. Typically, these have polished wood furniture, shuttered windows, bright colours and an airy feel; all are super-comfortable, as warm as toast, as is the whole house. Creaking stairs, leather armchairs on the landing, wonderfully wild floral wallpaper in the double-aspect sitting room, a snug bar, games, books, magazines, maps for walkers and a letter box in the hall. A very romantic pace in all weather: when the wind whips up, it can come in across the water at 90 miles an hour! A great place to be snowed in. You can bring your boat and sail, too.

Rooms: 10: 9 doubles and 1 twin.
Room price: £85-£135; singles £59-£99.
Breakfast: 9-9.30am.
Meals: Dinner, 3 courses, £25.
Closed: Mid-November — mid-March.

Directions: M6, junction 40, A66 west (to Ullswater) for 0.5 miles, then left onto A592. South 5 miles, through Watermillock, and hotel signed left down private drive.

The Mill Hotel

Mungrisdale   **Tel:** 017687 79659
Nr. Penrith   **Fax:** 017687 79155
Cumbria
CA11 0XR

Richard and Eleanor Quinlan

A small, eclectic bolt hole, this 1651 mill house on the northern border of the lakes
has a stream racing past that is fed by fells that rise behind. Richard and Eleanor
belong to that band of innkeepers who do their own thing instinctively and
immaculately — this is the very antithesis of a big, impersonal hotel. Richard comes
out to greet you at the car, to help with the bags, to show you up to your room, and
finally, invites you down for drinks "whenever you're ready". Downstairs you'll find
a tiny library and a homely sitting room with rocking chair, ancient stone fireplace,
wood carvings and piles of reference books on every subject under the sun. All the
while, Eleanor has been cooking up five courses of heaven for your supper, all home-
made (and organic where possible), from the olive bread to the watercress soup;
breakfasts, too, are first class. Bedrooms range in size, but not style. The old mill,
wrapped in clematis Montana, has its own sitting room, and you can fall asleep here
to the sound of the river. In the main house, beams, bowls of fruit, African art, fresh
flowers and good linen.

Rooms: 9: 4 doubles and 3 twins;
1 double and 1 twin with shared bath.
Room price: Dinner, B&B £59-£74 p.p.
Breakfast: 8.30-9.15am.
Meals: Dinner, 5 courses, included in
price.
Closed: 1 November — 1 March.

Directions: Mungrisdale is signed north
from A66, 7 miles west of Penrith. The
hotel is bang next door to the Mill Inn.

Entry no: 149   Map no: 9

Crosby Lodge

High Crosby
Crosby-on-Eden, nr. Carlisle
Cumbria
CA6 4QZ

Tel: 01228 573618
Fax: 01228 573428
E-mail: crosbylodge@crosby-eden.demon.co.uk
Web: www.crosbylodge.co.uk

Michael and Patricia Sedgwick

Come to elope — Gretna is close — or just to escape. Patricia never seems to stop, though she wasn't in a hurry. Walking round outside, we came across the blacksmith, the donkey and a Shetland pony — and there could be grandchildren out there! Not that you'd mind. Crosby Lodge is relaxed and unpretentious enough to thrive on its 'take-us-as-you-find-us' approach. It's very much a family affair. Michael and Patricia came here 28 years ago and now their children, James and Pippa, have both joined the firm. Inside is warm and cosy with the odd *chaise longue*, fenders round open fires, lots of rugs and oak furniture. Bedrooms are fun. Pat won't have "square corners", so you get arches and alcoves instead. They're big and bright with good fabrics and colours, and you might get arrow slits or a lovely gnarled half-tester as well. The food is all home-made — soups, breads and ice-creams — and you can eat out on the terrace in summer. Wild flowers grow in the garden, the fabulous Eden valley starts over the fence and Hadrian's wall is less than ten miles away.

Rooms: 11: 2 half-testers, 3 family,
5 twin/doubles and 1 single.
Room price: £110-£140; singles £82.
Breakfast: 7.30-9.30am.
Meals: Dinner, 4 courses, £29; à la carte,
£13-£30. Lunches from £5.
Closed: 24 December — 21 January.

Directions: M6, junction 44, then A689
east for 3.5 miles. Turn right to Low
Crosby, go through village and house
signed right in less than 1 mile.

Lovelady Shield

Nenthead Road
Nr. Alston
Cumbria
CA9 3LF

Tel: 01434 381203
Fax: 01434 381515
E-mail: enquiries@lovelady.co.uk
Web: www.lovelady.co.uk

Peter and Marie Haynes

This area of the High Pennines is remote and utterly unspoilt. You can walk straight out from Lovelady — the river Nent runs through the garden and at the bridge, four footpaths meet. The house, hidden away down a long and suitably bumpy drive, was rebuilt in 1832. The cellars date from 1690, the foundations from the 14th century when a convent stood here. No noise, but antiphonic sheep bleat in the fields and if you sleep with your window open, you can hear the river. Peter and Marie have been here three years and run the place with a hint of eccentricity and a lot of good-natured charm. A small rag-rolled bar and pretty sitting rooms give a low key, country house feel. Long windows in all rooms bring the views inside and French windows open up in summer for Pimms on the lawn. The food is wonderful; you eat in the very pretty dining room surrounded by gilt mirrors, sash windows and fresh flowers. Upstairs, dark hallways lead through old pine doors to bright bedrooms with cushioned window seats, maybe a sofa, good furniture and Scrabble; most have gorgeous views.

Rooms: 10: 1 four-poster, 7 doubles and 2 twins.
Room price: Dinner, B&B £57.50-£107.50 p.p.
Breakfast: 8.30-9.30am.
Meals: Dinner, 4 courses, included in price. Non-residents £29.50. Lunch by arrangement.
Closed: Never.

Directions: West from Alston on A689. House signed left after 2 miles, at junction with B6294.

Entry no: 151

Map no: 10

Rose and Crown

Romaldkirk
Barnard Castle
Co. Durham
DL12 9EB

Tel: 01833 650213
Fax: 01833 650828
E-mail: hotel@rose-and-crown.co.uk
Web: www.rose-and-crown.co.uk

Christopher and Alison Davy

In the small locals' bar, you can sit at settles in front of the fire and read the *Stockton Times* or the *Teesdale Mercury*, while a few trophies peer down on you from the walls. This inn is dreamy, superbly comfortable and traditional, and built in the 1750s when Romaldkirk's famous son, Captain Bligh, was still young. The mood is softly elegant, gently informal, utterly unpretentious, warmed by smart red carpets, stone walls, beams, and a bright, panelled dining room. Alison and Christopher are easy-going and — they may not know this — perfectionists; their hard work has made the Rose and Crown the place to stay, the place to eat. You can expect vibrant rooms, with slanting eaves and window seats as well as fun contemporary colours and fabrics. The food, too, is excellent — another example of the fantastic value-for-money this place represents. Outside, the village green is surrounded by church and untouched stone cottages; further afield, countryside, as good as any in Britain, and Barnard Castle (Barney to the locals) wait to be explored.

Rooms: 12: 5 doubles and 7 twins.
Room price: £86; suites £100; singles £62.
Breakfast: 7.30-9.30am.
Meals: Bar lunch and dinner £5-£11.
Dinner, 4 courses, £25.
Closed: 24-26 December.

Directions: B6277 north from Barnard Castle for 6 miles. In village, turn right towards green and hotel on left.

The Pheasant Inn

Stannersburn
Kielder Water
Northumberland
NE48 1DD

Tel: 01434 240382
Fax: 01434 240382
E-mail: thepheasantinn@kielderwater.demon.co.uk

Walter, Irene and Robin Kershaw

A really super little inn, the kind you hope to chance upon. It is not grand, not scruffy, just right. The Kershaws run it with huge passion and an instinctive understanding of its traditions. The stone walls hold 100-year old photos of the local community; from colliery to smithy, a vital record of their past heritage remains — special indeed. The bars are wonderful; brass beer taps glow, anything wooden — ceiling, beams and tables — has been polished to perfection with varnish and the clock above the fire keeps perfect time. The attention to detail is staggering. Robin and Irene cook with relish, again nothing fancy, but more than enough to keep a smile on your face: game pies, salmon and local lamb as well as wonderful Northumbrian cheeses. Bedrooms, all next door in the old hay barn, are as you'd expect: simple and cosy, super value for money. You are in the Northumberland National Park here; you can hire bikes and cycle round the lake, sail on it or go horse riding. No traffic jams, no too-much-hurry and wonderful Northumbrian hospitality — they really are the nicest people.

Rooms: 8: 4 doubles, 3 twins and 1 family.
Room price: £60; singles £40. Dinner, B&B from £46 p.p.
Breakfast: 8-9am.
Meals: Bar meals, lunch and dinner, from £6. Dinner, 3 courses, £15-£20.
Closed: Never.

Directions: From Bellingham, follow signs west to Kielder Water and Falstone for 7 miles. Hotel on left, 1 mile short of Kielder Water.

Scotland

"Unusual travel suggestions are dancing lessons from God."
– Kurt Vonnegut

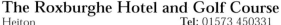

The Roxburghe Hotel and Golf Course

Heiton
Nr. Kelso
Borders
TD5 8JZ

Tel: 01573 450331
Fax: 01573 450611
E-mail: hotel@roxburghe.net
Web: www.roxburghe.net

The Duke of Roxburghe   **Manager: Stephen Browning**

Not quite a castle, but a big, old pile none the less. Bonnie Prince Charlie came here in 1745, but the house that stood then was rebuilt in the same Jacobean style after a 1770 fire. It is now a grand country house hotel with all the trimmings: the richest of fabrics in opulent bedrooms; the most intricate of carved fireplaces in the sitting room; the deepest of sofas into which to sink in the grand drawing room. High ceilings, roaring fires, an ocean of floor to cross in reception, marble bathrooms, the best linen... tremendous stuff. Noble pursuits include, archery, falconry, fishing... and golf. The course here is one of Scotland's finest — unknown to most, thrilling to all. For golfers, cavernous bunkers, huge undulating greens and, of course, the odd moment of terror. But, you do not have to be a golfer to enjoy it. The course cuts through glorious country, rolls down through parkland to the river Teviot and passes by a 19th-century viaduct railway bridge — a breathtaking sight. Nearby, Floors Castle, the Duke's family seat and the oldest inhabited castle in Scotland, is open to the public.

Rooms: 22: 2 suites, 4 four-posters, 7 doubles, 7 twins and 2 singles.
Room price: £120-£205; suites £255; singles £120.
Breakfast: 7.30-9.30am, 8-10am on Sundays.
Meals: Lunch from £5.50. Dinner, 3 courses, £25-£35.
Closed: 24-29 December.

Directions: Leave Kelso to the south on A698. The hotel is signed right after 2 miles, at the southern end of Heiton village.

Entry no: 154   **Map no: 10**

The Traquair Arms

Traquair Road
Innerleithen
Borders
EH44 6PD

Tel: 01896 830229
Fax: 01896 830260

Gig and Dianne Johnston

Travel along the glorious Tweed valley and you pass the market towns of Kelso, Selkirk, Galashiels — names that carry a fine Scottish resonance. Glimpse the river itself and, almost inevitably, you spy a fisherman up to his waist in water, the flick of his line glistening in the sun. The Borders have great beauty; hills roll down to mature woodlands that cling to the river while mansions stand grandly back from the water, a reminder of the wealth that came here in the 19th century. The Traquair was part of that prosperity, bequeathed by the eponymous Earl in 1875. It still echoes a sense of solid duty and tradition — don't come in search of anything too fancy. You'll find plush tartan fabrics, log fires in the well-stocked bar, gilt mirrors, good food and a pretty country-cottage breakfast room. Sit out front in summer flanked by blazing window boxes and watch thirsty walkers tumble in — the Southern Upland Way passes close by. Bedrooms (one is in a turret) are warm and simple, cosy, with lashings of hot water and rooftop views. Traquair House is close by and the golf in this area is superb.

Rooms: 10: 2 doubles, 2 twins, 3 family and 3 singles.
Room price: £58-£80; singles £45.
Breakfast: 8-9am weekdays; 8.30-9.30am weekends.
Meals: Lunch and dinner in bar from £5. Dinner, 3 courses, £18.
Closed: 25-26 December; 1-2 January.

Directions: From Peebles, A72 east to Innerleithen. In village, right, signed Traquair, and hotel on left.

Map no: 9

Entry no: 155

Knockinaam Lodge

Portpatrick
Wigtownshire
Dumfries and Galloway
DG9 9AD

Tel: 01776 810471
Fax: 01776 810435

Michael Bricker and Pauline Ashworth

The writer, John Buchan, knew this 1869 shooting lodge and describes it in *The 39 Steps* as the house to which Hannay flees. It's a good place to hide out, hunkered down with hills on three sides and the sea at the end of the vast lawn. In spring the grounds turn lilac as hundreds of thousands of bluebells appear and sunsets can be awesome with the Irish Sea streaked red. Knockinaam is as good as its setting — this is a supremely comfortable country house. A Michelin star in the dining room, breakfasts fit for kings, a wine list for the gods and 144 malts in the panelled bar. Everywhere, a crisp, uncluttered elegance. Big windows flood gracious rooms with light, an open fire smoulders in the panelled drawing room, an antique Queen Anne sofa takes the strain. Bedrooms have the best fabrics, big beds, pillows and cushions piled high; two have sea views. Michael and Pauline, easy-going perfectionists, came over from Canada to make this peaceful land of Galloway their home and, as Michael will tell you, the weather here is much better than you'd think. His daily log reveals 130 days of summer sunshine.

Rooms: 10: 8 doubles and 2 twins.
Room price: Dinner, B&B £85-£165 p.p.; singles from £140.
Breakfast: 8.15-9.30am.
Meals: Bar lunches from £3.50. Lunch, 3 courses, £29. Dinner, 4 courses, included in price.
Closed: Never.

Directions: From A77 or A75, follow signs for Portpatrick. 2 miles west of Lochans, left at smokehouse, then first left, first right and straight on — all signed 'Knockinaam.'

Entry no: 156   Map no: 8

Culzean Castle

The National Trust for Scotland
Maybole
Ayrshire
KA19 8LE

Tel: 01655 884455
Fax: 01655 884503

Jonathan Cardale

Culzean Castle, by Robert Adam, is awe-inspiring by any castle standards. The top floor, with six double bedrooms, is probably the most interesting hotel address in Scotland, especially loved by Americans because it was presented to General Eisenhower for his lifetime use. The rooms are exquisitely decorated in elegant country house (rather than castle) style with inimitable views of the wild coast to the Isle of Arran and Ailsa Craig. The sitting room is spectacular, oval in shape and jutting out above the cliffs with a sheer drop down to breaking rollers. But to single one room out for praise is unfair; Culzean (pronounced Cullane) is a thrilling architectural masterpiece, both inside and out, and you can expect the very best of everything. Jonathan gives a superb tour of the castle and there are 560 acres of country park to delve into (with deer park, swan pond, orangery, exotic stone pagoda and cliff walks). You'll find fresh flowers from the walled garden everywhere and *Cordon Bleu* cooking from Susan Cardale. A showpiece of the National Trust for Scotland.

Rooms: 6: 1 four-poster, 3 twin/doubles and 1 twin; 1 twin/double with private bath.
Room price: £200-£375; singles from £140.
Breakfast: Flexible.
Meals: Dinner, 4 courses, £45 including house wine, by arrangement.
Closed: 1 November — 31 March.
Directions: From A77 in Maybole take A719 for 4 miles following signs for Culzean Castle.

Babbity Bowster

16/18 Blackfriars Street
Glasgow
G1 1PE

Tel: 0141 552 5055
Fax: 0141 552 7774

Fraser Laurie

A place to "drop anchor for a blether (a chat)," says Fraser of his spirited café/brasserie, a favourite of free-thinkers, in the heart of the Merchant City (Glasgow's blossoming equivalent of Covent Garden). No TV, no piped music, but you may get some foot-stomping, live folk music instead — the best acts play here. The big and breezy ground-floor bar has stripped wooden floors, a peat fire and high Georgian windows, with Art Deco touches and superb black and white photos of Glasgow on the walls. Stovies (delicious Scottish meat and potato pies) and home-made soups in the bar, or upstairs to the first-floor restaurant (a good buffer zone between bar and bedroom) for more serious food. Fraser (Billy Connolly with an eye patch) is a francophile through and through, a man dedicated to bringing conviviality and conversation to Glasgow. Bedrooms on the second floor are simple and spotless and fit the mood perfectly — just don't expect *The Ritz*. You can play *pétanque* in the back yard or stroll through this beautiful city to the Modern Art Gallery close by.

Rooms: 7: 2 doubles, 2 twins, 2 singles
and 1 apartment.
Room price: £70; singles £50.
Breakfast: 8-10.30am.
Meals: Bar food all day from £5. Dinner in
restaurant, 3 courses, about £17.50.
Restaurant closed Sundays.
Closed: Never.

Directions: M8, junction 15, and follow
signs to 'Glasgow Cross and Cathedral'.
Pass Cathedral on left, continue for half a mile and Blackfriars Street is on right.
Staff will show you to car park.

The Bonham
35 Drumsheugh Gardens
Edinburgh
EH3 7RN

Tel: 0131 226 6050
Fax: 0131 226 6080
E-mail: reserve@thebonham.com
Web: www.thebonham.com

Manager: Fiona Vernon

Old meets very new at The Bonham, a Victorian town house hotel with a strikingly contemporary interior: plush purple carpets, abstract paintings by up-and-coming local artists and a scarlet spiral sofa in reception — you have to see it to believe it. It's all fabulous — an aesthetic treat. You get dramatic displays of willow or cane instead of flowers, excellent halogen lighting to add to the mood and large, wood-framed mirrors. But 'the old' lives on, too. There are green, scarlet and brown leather armchairs and half-panelled walls within the original Victorian rooms. The bedrooms are no less impressive; every detail has been wonderfully thought out, from a three-poster bed (so you can watch TV), to a pioneering state-of-the-art home entertainment/computer/internet system in every room. The décor is just as dramatic as the reception rooms with lots of bold colours and impeccable bathrooms. In the restaurant, modern Scottish cooking is on offer, and, from the front door, the centre of Edinburgh is less than five minutes walk.

Rooms: 48: 2 suites, 36 twin/doubles and 10 singles.
Room price: £165-£225; suites £295; singles from £135.
Breakfast: Until 9.30am weekdays; 10am weekends. Continental included; Full Scottish £7.50.
Meals: Lunch £11.50-£15.50. Dinner £23-£25.
Closed: 24-28 December.

Directions: From the West End (Hope St), follow Queensferry St north-west. Turn left at the second set of lights, then first right into Drumsheugh Gardens. The hotel is at the end on the right.

Channings

12-16 South Learmonth Gardens
Edinburgh
EH4 1EZ

Tel: 0131 315 2226
Fax: 0131 332 9631
E-mail: reserve@channings.co.uk
Web: www.channings.co.uk

Manager: Marco Truffelli

Channings is Edwardian through and through. The cobbled street, the gardens it overlooks, and the five town houses that make up the hotel are all part of the turn-of-the-century expansion of residential Edinburgh. Everywhere inside, the period feel lives on with the colours, fabrics and furniture all chosen to fit the Edwardian bill: prints and cartoons on the walls, plaster-moulded ceilings, ornately tiled fireplaces and the rich wood panelling of the library. Upstairs, bedrooms typically have high ceilings, thick carpets, good linen and chintzy curtains. But, there is variety. Some are smaller than others (bathrooms likewise) while others have views across rooftops to the Firth of Forth and the Fife hills beyond. The common thread is excellent basics and pretty colours. In the basement, you'll find the 'odd room out'. The wine bar is a contemporary feast of brightly polished pine floor, chrome stools and shiny beer taps — a popular haunt of locals. Once a month, they host live jazz here, the bar snacks are fabulous (you can also eat in the restaurant), the staff friendly and helpful.

Rooms: 46: 3 suites, 1 four-poster,
37 twin/doubles and 5 singles.
Room price: £150-£198; suite £255-
£260; singles from £125.
Breakfast: 7.30-9.30am; 8-10am on
Sundays.
Meals: Lunch £12-£15. Dinner £19.50-
£23.50.
Closed: 24-28 December.

Directions: From the West End (Hope St),
turn north-west into Queensferry St, then branch right onto Dean Bridge. Curve left, then third right (South Learmonth Ave); right at bottom (South Learmouth Gdns).

Entry no: 160   **Map no: 9**

The Peat Inn

Peat Inn
by Cupar
Fife
KY15 5LH

Tel: 01334 840206
Fax: 01334 840530
E-mail: reception@thepeatinn.co.uk
Web: www.peatinn.co.uk

David and Patricia Wilson

You'll find the home of golf just up the road at St Andrews, while here you get the home of modern Scottish cooking. David came here 28 years ago and in that time he has not only put The Peat Inn on the gastronomic *Mappa Mundi*, but he has also inspired a whole generation of Scottish chefs to follow his lead and to cook brilliantly. He is irrepressible, too, and when I arrived at nine o'clock one morning, I found him making pastry in the kitchen, his passion as strong today as it ever has been. You can take it as read that his restaurant is the perfect place for a feast, that his bedrooms bring a fine night's sleep. You eat amid gilt mirrors, sprays of fresh flowers, stone walls, the odd four-foot high statue, tapestries on the walls. In the snug bar at the front, a fire burns in an ancient fireplace and smart sofas are piled high with cushions, so sit down with a glass of champagne while your table is prepared. Bedrooms are just as good. All are split-level suites with sleigh beds, four-posters, marble bathrooms, home-made biscuits, bowls of fruit. Expect to be spoiled in every way.

Rooms: 8 suites.
Room price: £145; singles £95.
Breakfast: 8-10am.
Meals: Lunch, 3 courses, £19.50.
Dinner, 3 courses, £28-£35.
Closed: Rooms and restaurant both closed Sundays and Mondays.

Directions: A90 north from Edinburgh, then A92 for Dundee. Right onto A91 and into Cupar. There, take B940 for Crail into Peat Inn.

Creagan House

Strathyre
Callander
Perthshire
FK18 8ND

Tel: 01877 384638
Fax: 01877 384319
E-mail: mail@creaganhouse.fsnet.co.uk

Gordon and Cherry Gunn

Cosy, convivial and occasionally quirky... with a breakfast menu to beat all others. There is something very special about sitting at a long, polished slab of oak in a baronial dining room and reading a small treatise entitled *The Iconography of the Creagan Toast Rack* while waiting for your bacon and eggs. Cherry and Gordon have ploughed great reserves of dedication into their restaurant with rooms, making it warm and friendly with exceptional food and a remarkable homely simplicity — a great place to be. The bedrooms up in the eaves have Sanderson wallpaper and bed covers, old wood furniture and no TVs — "you don't come to Creagan to watch a box", says Cherry quite rightly. Downstairs there's a small bar with brass hangings and a beam 'acquired' from the Oban railway line; better still, it's stocked with 42 malts and a good whisky guide to help you choose. There are no airs and graces, just the sort of attention you'll only get when it's small and owner-run. You can also 'bag a Munro' — walking sticks at the front door will help you up Ben Shean.

Rooms: 5: 4 doubles and 1 twin.
Room price: £85; singles £52.50.
Breakfast: 8-9.30am.
Meals: Dinner, 3 courses, £23.50.
Closed: February.

Directions: A84 north from Stirling, through Callander and on to Strathyre. Hotel 0.25 miles north of village on right and signed.

Entry no: 162   **Map no: 9**

Monachyle Mhor

Balquhidder
Lochearnhead
Perthshire
FK19 8PQ

Tel: 01877 384622
Fax: 01877 384305
www.monachylemhor.com

Rob, Jean, Tom and Angela Lewis

They started here as farmers, went on to do B&B and ended up with a hotel. It's a warm, friendly and eclectic place, full of music that scales the heights from jazz to opera, and it's packed with interest too. It's run by a very spirited family: son Tom cooks fabulously, a fabric-designer daughter accounts for the dramatic and innovative bedrooms and Rob and Jean chat, serve and greet. Rob and another son still run the farm too, so walk as much as you like. The place seems to evolve at it's own pace — a vegetable garden has just been put in — and it's restful. You're nearly at the end of the road, yet it's dynamic and interesting; huge bedrooms in the barns make bold use of space and colour. There's a snug, traditional bar with open fire too. Outside, hills rise on one side while Loch Voil stretches out on the other; you can either walk round it or go boating on it. The truly lazy can slump into a chair on the parasolled terrace and contemplate it glass in hand.

Rooms: 10: 5 doubles, 2 twins, 3 suites.
Room price: £70-£90; singles from £45.
Breakfast: Until 9.30am.
Meals: Dinner, 3 courses, £29. Sunday lunch £17.50. Packed lunches by arrangement.
Closed: Never.

Directions: Turn off A84 at Kings House Hotel, following signs to Balquhidder. Continue beyond Balquhidder along Loch Voil. Monachyle (pink) is up drive on right and signed.

The Four Seasons Hotel

St. Fillans
Perthshire
PH6 2NF

Tel: 01764 685333
Fax: 01764 685444
E-mail: info@thefourseasonshotel.co.uk
Web: www.thefourseasonshotel.co.uk

Andrew Low

This is a great position with forest rising immediately behind and Loch Earn stretching out seven miles distant. It all comes into play; you can ski, sail, canoe or fish on the lake (you can even learn to fly on it) or simply take to the hills for fabulous walks. The hotel has simple chalets on the lower slopes and each has long views, through pine trees, across water. Andrew is a great traveller, a Scot born 'down south' who has now come home, and his love and enthusiasm for this heavenly spot are contagious. He has refurbished the interior completely, bringing bright colours to the walls, a gentle elegance to the rooms, superb food to the tables and a relaxed spirit to the whole place. Sit out on the small terrace underneath cherry trees for evening drinks and stare out across the lake or stay in front of the fire with a malt to warm you — The Four Seasons is well-named. Bedrooms in the house are excellent — smart, with plush carpets, huge beds and those at the front have lake views. Fish successfully and they'll cook your catch for supper. A super place.

Rooms: 18: 7 doubles, 5 twins and
6 family chalets.
Room price: £64-£88; singles from £32;
Dinner, B&B from £38 p.p.
Breakfast: 8-9.30am; 8.30-10.30am on
Sundays.
Meals: Lunch and dinner in bar from £8.
Dinner, 4 courses, £23.95.
Closed: January & February.

Directions: St. Fillans is on the eastern tip
of Loch Earn on A85, 12 miles west of Creiff, 25 miles north of Stirling.

Entry no: 164   **Map no: 9**

Killiecrankie Hotel

Pass of Killiecrankie
By Pitlochry
Perth and Kinross
PH16 5LG

Tel: 01796 473220
Fax: 01796 472451
E-mail: enquiries@killiecrankiehotel.co.uk
Web: www.killiecrankiehotel.co.uk

Colin and Carole Anderson

Pitlochry is known in Scotland as the gateway to the Highlands. Keep going north a couple of miles and you come to Killiecrankie, where, blissfully, nothing particular happens at all. The glorious glens here are home to castles and distilleries, fine lochs and mountain paths, a place to unwind with a dram or a rod. The Killiecrankie is the perfect base for such work. Colin and Carole have been here for 12 years and share their knowledge of the area with unhurried generosity, talking you through a walk or letting you know the best picnic spots on Loch Tummel. But the big idea here is that whatever exertions you get up to by day, by night you return to the cosseting luxuries of their hotel. Piping hot baths, drinks by the fire in the panelled bar, sublime food in the restaurant, scrabble in the sitting room, a final stroll around the four-acre garden and then upstairs to very pretty bedrooms for undisturbed sleep. On one side of their house, the hills that rise are an RSPB sanctuary, so you may see buzzard or falcon circling. Golf and fishing can also be arranged.

Rooms: 10: 6 twin/doubles, 2 doubles and 2 singles.
Room price: Dinner, B&B £60-£90 p.p.
Breakfast: 8-9.30am; 8.30-10am on Sundays.
Meals: Lunch from £8. Dinner, 4 courses, included in price. Non-residents £33.
Closed: January.

Directions: Leave A9 1 mile north of Pitlochry for B8079, signed Killiecrankie. Straight ahead for 1 mile and hotel signed left.

The Cross
Tweed Mill Brae
Kingussie
Highland
PH21 1TC

Tel: 01540 661166
Fax: 01540 661080
E-mail: relax@thecross.co.uk
Web: www.thecross.co.uk

Tony and Ruth Hadley

The position here may not be deep country, but it's very special all the same. Out on the terrace, as the river pours down the hill, you can see copper beech, hazel, willow, alder, and sycamore. The trees climb the hill and wrap the place in peace and quiet. They bring in the wildlife, too: dippers dive, heron and otters fish, red squirrel leap — they've even had roe deer on the terrace. Inside, whitewashed, stone walls meet cool, contemporary interiors. There are plush red carpets, old wooden beams, an open-plan feel and modern art scattered about the place. Upstairs, clean lines and light-flooded rooms give a Scandinavian feel, with skylights in eaved walls. Bedrooms have the same smart, minimalistic feel with halogen lights and excellent beds. Rooms on one side have the river right below them and one has a small balcony. But the heart of The Cross is the restaurant — one of the best in Scotland. Ruth's exceptional food has won stacks of awards, so climb that mountain in the afternoon and have no guilt at supper! *Children over 12 welcome.*

Rooms: 9: 7 doubles and 2 twins.
Room price: Dinner, B&B £115 p.p.
Breakfast: 8-10am. Health/Continental only.
Meals: Dinner, 5 courses, included in price. Restaurant closed Tuesdays.
Closed: 1 December — 28 February.

Directions: At the only traffic lights in Kingussie, turn right (if coming from north). Go up hill and signed left.

Entry no: 166

Map no: **12**

Minmore House

Glenlivet
Banffshire
AB37 9DB

Tel: 01807 590378
Fax: 01807 590472
E-mail: minmorehouse@ukonline.co.uk

Victor and Lynne Janssen

Driving up from Balmoral in the late afternoon sun, it struck me that the colour green had probably been created here. The east of Scotland often plays second fiddle to its 'other half', but this lush cattle-grazing land is every inch as beautiful as the west. I also had a preconceived idea that Minmore wouldn't be right... which was as far off the mark as I could possibly have been. This is a great wee pad run breezily by Victor and Lynne. They used to live in South Africa where they had a restaurant and they once cooked for Prince Philip. Their kingdom here stretches to ten spotless bedrooms, all cosy and warm, not grand, just downright comfortable; a pretty sitting room where guests swap highland tales and, best of all, a carved wood bar, half-panelled, with scarlet chairs, a resident Jack Russell, the odd trophy and oodles of Glenlivet light flooding in. Oh, and 104 malts! The garden has a good swimming pool, chickens range free and the famous Glenlivet distillery is just up the road. Hire bicycles locally and follow tracks deep into the Ladder Hills; you may see buzzard, falcon, even eagles.

Rooms: 10: 1 four-poster, 4 doubles, 3 twins and 2 singles.
Room price: £70-£100; singles £50. Dinner, B&B £50-£70 p.p.
Breakfast: 8-9.30am.
Meals: Dinner, 4 courses, £25. Light lunches £5-£10. Packed lunches available.
Closed: Limited opening in winter.

Directions: From Aviemore, A95 north to Bridge of Avon, then south on B9008 to Glenlivet. House at top of hill, 400 yards before the distillery.

Map no: 12

Entry no: 167

Clifton House

Nairn
Highland
IV12 4HW

Tel: 01667 453119
Fax: 01667 452836
E-mail: macintyre@clara.net
Web: www.macintyre.clara.net/clifton

J Gordon Macintyre

Inverness may be a touch far-flung, but Clifton House is worth a detour from just about anywhere in the world. Unique, powerful, magnetic — this is easily one of my favourite hotels — an artistic cauldron, yet, remarkably, without even the slightest hint of pretension. Gordon has fashioned his world over the years, keeping it beyond the designer's grasp. Everywhere there is something exceptional: Pugin wallpaper (of Lord Chancellor fame) in a drawing room stuffed with beautiful things; red silk on the walls of the long corridor; a handmade marbled table in the dining room; sprays of fresh flowers and wall-hugging art in the yellow sitting room. Gordon is gently passionate about opera, art and life and, in winter, there are plays, concerts and recitals. He cooks, too, sublime food — a symphony he orchestrates in tandem with his son, Charles. The bedrooms, some with views of the Moray Firth, are all different, all delightful, with Zoffany fabrics, Vogue prints, busts... you get the picture. If this all sounds a bit over-the-top, blame it on my exuberance, but Clifton House really is a very special place.

Rooms: 12: 4 singles, 4 doubles and 4 twins.
Room price: £85-£117; singles £60.
Breakfast: Until 11.30am.
Meals: Dinner, à la carte, about £25.
Closed: Christmas & New Year.

Directions: From Inverness, west on A96. In Nairn, left at only roundabout, signed to the beach. Continue along seafront (sea on right) and hotel signed on left.

The Albannach

Baddidarrach
Lochinver
Highland
IV27 4LP

Tel: 01571 844407
Fax: 01571 844285

Colin Craig and
Lesley Crosfield

Colin and Lesley would be anarchists if they took life seriously, which luckily they don't. Instead, they prefer to chew the cud, to drink good wine, to cook fine food — to live with just a little irreverence and a lot of laughter. Colin thinks Lochinver a touch metropolitan but manages to cope by sailing Lesley off to holidays on deserted islands to get away from it all. They spend their days on dry land hatching new plans for the table. Gillian, a friend, crofts the veg (you may get an impromptu herb tasting), the waitress's father catches the crayfish and Colin dives for scallops. Seriously good food is fabulously fresh — expect your supper to be divine... rather like their home. They've done it all themselves, brilliantly of course — renovated, extended, panelled the downstairs, built the terrace, designed the conservatory. Sink into wicker chairs amid rugs and erupting greenery and gaze out across water to Suilven rising majestically in the distance; or climb it instead. Bedrooms are just right, fit the mood perfectly, have heaps of comforts; but it's the indefatigable spirit of the place that makes it so special.

Rooms: 5: 3 doubles and 2 twins.
Room price: Dinner, B&B £72-£85 p.p.; singles from £105.
Breakfast: 8.30-9.45am.
Meals: Dinner, 5 courses, included in price. Non-residents £30.
Closed: 1 December — 15 March.

Directions: A837 for Lochinver. Approaching town, right over bridge for Baddidarrach. First left and house signed right after 100 metres.

Altnaharrie Inn

Ullapool
Highland
IV26 2SS

Tel: 01854 633230

Fred Brown and Gunn Eriksen

Some inn! I can think of few drover's cottages that put on a private launch to ferry you across the loch to be greeted by well-dressed porters on a jetty, waiting to carry your bags up to the house. Altnaharrie delivers exactly what its price suggests — the very best of everything. The position, amid Scots pines and rowan trees right in the lap of Loch Broom, is a highland dreamscape, the food a glorious Michelin-starred *tour de force* from Gunn, and the house a whitewashed paradise with a simplicity that takes your breath away. You'll find polished stone flagging, the heady scent of fresh flowers, candles and open fires, rugs and draped curtains. Bedrooms are superb, mixing antique and contemporary furniture. There are cushions tumbling off pillows, fresh fruit and carafes of spring water and torches by your bed — Altnaharrie is remote enough to need its own generator. There's a folly turret, paths lead up to the hills for heaven-sent, west coast views and there's a burn tumbling through the middle of the garden. *Children over eight welcome.*

Rooms: 8: 2 twins and 6 doubles.
Room price: Dinner, B&B £165-£205 p.p.
Breakfast: 8.30-9am.
Meals: Dinner, 5 courses, included in price.
Closed: Early November — Easter.

Directions: Directions. The hotel will ferry you across by launch from Ullapool harbour. They will advise on times as these depend on the tides. Private parking is arranged in Ullapool.

Entry no: **170**

Map no: **12**

Pool House Hotel

Poolewe
Wester Ross
IV22 2LD

Tel: 01445 781272
Fax: 01445 781403
E-mail: poolhouse@inverewe.co.uk
Web: www.poolhouse.com

Peter, Margaret and Elizabeth Harrison

At high tide, you can sit out with your sundowner as the waters of Loch Ewe lap ten feet away. In midsummer, sunsets blaze and the odd boat chugs by (maybe John, the cook's, as he goes in search of mussels for the pot). Across the bay, pine trees at Inverewe's unmissable gardens tower on rocky outcrops. The Harrisons came here to restore the hotel to its Victorian glory. Doors have been stripped, tassel lamps and fire screens bought and bold colours put on the walls. The expensive rooms are superb: one has a panelled bathroom where, as a fire smoulders, you can luxuriate in an 1865 power shower while gazing out to sea. There's also the Titanic suite (Margaret is related to the captain) with a seven-foot four-poster and a fire waiting to be lit in the sitting room, where binoculars will lead you to sea eagles, seals, maybe an otter. Less expensive rooms are smaller and simpler but most have loch views. Behind the hotel you can follow the river over the hill to Loch Maree — one of the prettiest lochs in Scotland. Great food, too, and fillet steaks for breakfast. *Children over 12 welcome.*

Rooms: 9: 1 four-poster, 1 suite, 3 doubles, 2 twins and 2 singles.
Room price: £90-£180; suite £200-£250; singles £45-£65.
Dinner, B&B from £60 p.p.
Breakfast: 8-9.45am.
Meals: Lunch and dinner in bar from £6. Dinner, 4 courses, £25-£35.
Closed: January & February.

Directions: Poolewe is on A832 south of Laide and north of Gairloch. The hotel is on Loch Ewe.

Map no: 11   **Entry no: 171**

Applecross Inn

Shore Street
Applecross
Wester Ross
IV54 8LR

Tel: 01520 744262
Fax: 01520 744400

Judith Fish

No Highland fling would be complete without a pint at the Applecross, firmly fixed on the west coast trail given its awesome position. There are two ways in: the spectacular coastal road and *Bealach-Na-Ba*, Britain's highest mountain pass. The latter is not for the light-hearted and is cut off by snow for much of the winter, but the view from the top across mountain peaks and Hebridean seas is stupendous. Down in the tiny village of Applecross, the inn sits on the bay with huge views off to Rassay and Skye. At low tide, acre upon acre of golden sand appears — a great place to walk. At her whitewashed inn, Judith is extending and refurbishing, rag-rolling walls, putting bathrooms in, stone-flagging the bar — generally giving the place a makeover. Traditionalists may not approve (the simplicity of the Applecross has always been its hallmark), but much simplicity remains: the peat fires, the half pints of fresh prawns, the accordion player in summer and the tiny single with its gigantic view. Lots of fish on the excellent menu, a family feel and one of the best views in Scotland.

Rooms: 7: 1 double, 1 twin and 1 family; 1 double, 1 twin and 2 singles sharing 2 bathrooms.
Room price: £50-£60; singles £25.
Breakfast: 7.30-9.30am weekdays; 8-10am weekends.
Meals: Lunch and dinner in bar from £5. Dinner, 3 courses, £20.
Closed: New Year's Day.

Directions: The best way into Applecross is over *Bealach-Na-Ba* pass, clearly signed west off A896 north of Loch Carron. In snow the pass closes. The road via Fearnmore is the other option.

Scarista House

Isle of Harris
Western Isles
HS3 3HX

Tel: 01859 550238
Fax: 01859 550277
E-mail: tnpmartin@ukgateway.net
Web: www.scaristahouse.com

Patricia and Tim Martin

For a book in which views count, Scarista takes the oatcake. The landscape here is nothing short of magnificent. The beach? Two or three miles of pure white sand, hidden from the rest of the world, and you will probably be the only person on it. Then there's the gentle curve of the crescent bay, ridges running down to a turquoise sea and sunsets to astound you. One of the most beautiful places I have ever visited — anywhere in the world. Patricia and Tim took over recently — the fulfilment of a dream. They have been coming to the island for many years (they can guide you to its secrets) and are absolutely committed to their new life here. Their house — an old manse — is a perfect island retreat: shuttered windows, peat fires, rugs on bare oak floors, whitewashed walls. Bedrooms are just right, too, with old oak beds, mahogany dressers, maybe a writing desk facing out to sea. The food is delicious; Tim and Patricia cook brilliantly. Kind island staff may speak in Gaelic, books wait to be read. There's golf, too — the view from the first tee is surely the best in the game. Worth every moment it takes to get here.

Rooms: 5: 3 doubles and 2 twins.
Room price: £116; singles from £58.
Breakfast: 8.30-9.30am.
Meals: Dinner, 4 courses, £27.50. Packed lunches £5.50.
Closed: Occasionally in winter.

Directions: From Tarbert take A859, signed Rodel. Scarista is 15 miles on the left, after the golf course.

Flodigarry Country House Hotel

Flodigarry   **Tel:** 01470 552203
Isle of Skye   **Fax:** 01470 552301
IV51 9HZ   **E-mail:** info@flodigarry.co.uk
                          Web: www.flodigarry.co.uk

Andrew Butler

Andrew was having a 'bad phone day', with BT doing its best (but inevitably failing) to remove the ever-present smile from his face. Tougher adversaries are needed to defeat this man! He'll tow you out of a ditch at sunset on your birthday, then bring you back for a celebratory drink, battle railway guards to make sure they don't lock you *in* the station, or, more commonly, just let you get on with falling in love with his easy-going hotel. It is, of course, in a stunningly beautiful spot, looking out across the Minch to the Torridon mountains with the towering columns of Quiraing behind (Victorians used to climb it and then play cricket). Staffin island, too, is close by. But don't stray too far. At night you can eat just about anything, just about anywhere; the conservatory, the restaurant, the locals' bar or the terrace, for food as rich or simple as you want — Andrew and his gentle, Gaelic-speaking staff want everyone to be happy. The hotel has an easy elegance, the bar is a must for Saturday night *ceilidhs* and the bedrooms are excellent; you can even sleep in Flora MacDonald's cottage.

Rooms: 19: 6 doubles, 9 twins, 3 family and 1 single.
Room price: £98-£178; singles from £55.
Breakfast: Flexible.
Meals: Dinner £32.50. Sunday lunch £17. Bar and conservatory meals also available.
Closed: Never.

Directions: From Skye Bridge, A87 to Portree, then A855 through Staffin to Flodigarry. The hotel is on the right.

Entry no: 174   Map no: 11

Stein Inn
Stein
Waternish
Isle of Skye
IV55 8GA

Tel: 01470 592362
Fax: 01470 592362
E-mail: angus.teresa@steininn.demon.co.uk
Web: www.steininn.demon.co.uk

Angus and Teresa McGhie

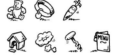

White cottages bob by the quay in the remote, tiny fishing village, sparkling in the salty breeze. If a thirsty appetite nags after your day's Hebridean adventures there is always the Stein — the oldest inn on Skye. At the beer-seasoned bar Angus stocks 70 single malts and real ale under the blackened joists of his rough hewn, fire-warmed hostelry. If the weather is good, sit out by the sea loch's shore. Across the water, the headland rises up dramatically, while to the north a few low-slung islands lie scattered about. It is a perfect place to lose yourself and I sat out with my pint watching the locals potter around in their boats while a truly blinding sun set. The food is really good too, and if cosiness comes from contrast and setting then the clean, closely eaved, blue-carpeted and pine-panelled rooms above are perfect. Watch from your window the catch landed, hauled from the sea to your plate, impossibly fresh. There are moorings for yachts, too, so — sailors, ring ahead and Angus will have your provisions waiting.

Rooms: 5: 4 doubles and 1 single.
Room price: £47-£57; singles £23.50-£28.50.
Breakfast: Until 9.30am.
Meals: Dinner, 3 courses, about £13. Bar lunches from £3.50.
Closed: 24 December — 1 January.

Directions: From Isle of Skye Bridge take A850 to Portree. There, follow sign to Uig for 4 miles. Then, left on A850 towards Dunvegan for 14 miles. Hard right turn to Waternish on B886. Stein is 3.5 miles along on loch side.

Map no: 11   Entry no: 175

Viewfield House

Portree
Isle of Skye
IV51 9EU

Tel: 01478 612217
Fax: 01478 613517
E-mail: info@viewfieldhouse.com
Web: www.viewfieldhouse.com

Hugh and Linda Macdonald

Viewfield may look a touch imposing but in fact it's gracious, relaxing and unstuffy with liberal helpings of laid-back grandeur all around. The big, bright sitting room of pure country-house elegance has huge windows and shutters, polished wooden floors and rugs, masses of lovely furniture and, according to Linda, "stuff" — the "stuff" being sculpture, crystal, and silver. It's a home, too, albeit quite a grand one, but Linda and Hugh remain delightfully unfazed by the magnificence that surrounds them. The effect is great: no hushed voices, no trembling guests wondering if it's OK to borrow a book; instead everyone dives in to enjoy it all. The dining room is superb with 1887 wallpaper, Hugh's ancestors on the walls and stained-glass windows. Eat dinner-party, Aga-cooked food either communally around the huge mahogany table, or separately at small tables at the side. Bedrooms are just as good, just as warm, just as fun. Climb through woods to Fingal's Seat for 360° views and a loch you can swim in. A great place run by great people and hard to beat for that house-party warmth.

Rooms: 12: 5 twins, 4 doubles and 1 single; 1 double and 1 single sharing bath and shower.
Room price: £80-£90; singles £35-£60. Dinner, B&B £55-£65 p.p.
Breakfast: 8.30-9am.
Meals: Dinner, 5 courses, £15. Packed lunches £4.
Closed: Mid-October — mid-April.

Directions: On A87, coming from south, drive entrance is on the outskirts of Portree, opposite BP garage.

Entry no: 176   Map no: 11

Hotel Eilean Iarmain

Isleornsay
Sleat
Isle of Skye
IV43 8QR

Tel: 01471 833332
Fax: 01471 833275
www.eileaniarmain.com

Sir Iain and Lady Lucilla Noble

For those seeking a Gaelic bolthole, this bastion of all things Hebridean is a must. Kind local staff speak gentle Gaelic, tartan carpets welcome you in the hall; on Thursday evenings a ceilidh breaks loose in the bar and fiddles fly. This is the end of the road — only the Sound of Sleat lies ahead — and you may see local fisherman land their catch at the small jetty. At low tide you can walk across to Robert Louis Stevenson's lighthouse which paddles in the water a few hundred yards away. The hotel is dreamy, a cross between gentleman's club and shooting lodge. Hessian cloth hangs on the walls, fires smoulder under the gaze of a trophy. Bedrooms are just right, country house in style, with half testers, an old four-poster, maybe big sofas if there's space. The rooms across in the old stables (now newly whitewashed) are fabulous with pretty fabrics and an indulging feel; sea views make them bright and airy. Sir Iain is keenly involved in the regeneration of Skye's woodland and is helping to bring back oak and birch to the island. There's an art gallery and a whisky company, too.

Rooms: 16: 4 suites, 6 doubles and 6 twins.
Room price: £110-£130; suites £160; singles from £80.
Breakfast: 8-9.30am.
Meals: Lunch and dinner in bar from £7. Dinner, 4 courses, £31.
Closed: Never.

Directions: A87 over Skye Bridge (toll £5.50), then, after 4 miles, left onto A851, signed Armdale. After 5 miles, Eilean Iarmain (Isleornsay) is signed left.

Glenelg Inn

Glenelg
By Kyle of Lochalsh
Highland
IV40 8JR

Tel: 01599 522273
Fax: 01599 522283
E-mail: christophermain@glenelg-inn.com
Web: www.glenelg-inn.com

Christopher Main

Why drive to the shops when you can skim across the water in your motor boat? Catch Christopher going your way and he may give you a lift. As for his inn — just perfect. The bedrooms are extremely good — Colefax and Fowler fabrics, bowls of fruit, great views — but splash out on the suite and you get an *enormous* room, beautifully decorated, where you can have breakfast in bed while gazing over the sea to Skye. There's also a restaurant, bar and sitting room. The latter is more 'country house drawing room', with leather sofas, an open fire and oils on the walls, but the epicentre of this lively place is the panelled bar: fishermen, farmers and sailors all come for the unpretentious atmosphere. Low beams and fires, and in one corner a pile of old fish boxes to sit on (which might sound awful, but they're perfect). Come here for excellent bar meals (steamed mussels, wild salmon, venison) and music, too: pipers, fiddlers and folk musicians all pass by. In summer, there's the garden with its awesome views and close by the tiny Kylerhea ferry will take you across to Skye.

Rooms: 9: 3 doubles, 3 twins and 3 family.
Room price: £86; master room £126. Dinner, B&B from £67.
Breakfast: 8-9.30am.
Meals: Bar lunches and dinner from £7. Dinner, 4 courses, £24.
Closed: Never.

Directions: West off A87 at Sheil Bridge. Keep left into village and inn on right. (The Kylerhea ferry from Skye is a beautiful alternative.)

Entry no: 178   **Map no: 11**

The Old Library
Arisaig
Highland
PH39 4NH

Tel: 01687 450651
Fax: 01687 450219
E-mail: reception@oldlibrary.co.uk
Web: www.oldlibrary.co.uk

Alan and Angela Broadhurst

Local Hero was filmed here and the beach where the helicopter lands is just up the road. Alan — a navy diver turned restaurateur — cooks wonderfully and whatever can be is home-made. Piping hot loaves of oregano and olive bread appear from the oven while mussel and fennel soup simmers in the pot. Scan the menu and you get the picture — simple food, simply cooked: goats cheese marinated in herbs and olive oil; fresh Mallaig cod with saffron mash; baked figs in honey and lemon. The restaurant is just across the road from the sea and in summer you can eat outside with views across to Eigg and Rum. Bedrooms are split between the main house and the garden rooms ten paces away. The latter are big, have their own terraces and you can chat to Alan while he harvests herbs for dinner. Rooms in the house are smaller but have sea views. All are irresistible value for money and prettily furnished. You may hear jazz (Alan has a show on local radio) or the sound of lapping waves. A super little place with a Mediterranean touch for both food and Angela's generous hospitality.

Rooms: 6: 5 doubles and 1 twin.
Room price: £76; singles £45.
Breakfast: 8.30-9.30am.
Meals: Lunch from £7. Dinner, £12.50-£24 (restaurant closed Tuesday lunchtimes).
Closed: 1 November — 31 March.

Directions: From Fort William, A830 west for Mallaig. Restaurant in Arisaig, next to post office.

Old Pines Restaurant with Rooms

Spean Bridge
By Fort William
Highland, PH34 4EG
Tel: 01397 712324
Fax: 01397 712433
E-mail: goodfood@oldpines.co.uk
Web: www.oldpines.co.uk

Sukie and Bill Barber

Old Pines is a must for anyone in search of that rare combination of relaxed informality and seriously good food. Sukie and Bill do things effortlessly, be it marshalling one of their children off to bed while greeting a guest or sitting down in the garden for a chat while chopping the herbs. In between, Sukie somehow finds time to prove her fast-growing reputation as one of Scotland's top chefs, cooking up truly ambrosial food that's eaten communally in the stone-flagged, chalet-style dining room. Bill readily shares his enthusiasm for local scenery, wildlife, history and culture; nothing at Old Pines is too much trouble. Pretty rooms, comfortable sofas, log fires, loads of books and family pics. Plants and flowers frame Ben Nevis in the conservatory. Guests' children can eat and play with the Barbers' (there's a fenced garden, a playroom, pool and table tennis). Bedrooms are chalet-style with stripped pine walls and duvets, all perfect, but it's the Barbers who make this place so special. They are kind, generous, fun and thoroughly down-to-earth. Don't miss it.

Rooms: 9: 2 family, 2 twins, 2 doubles and 2 singles; 1 single with private bathroom.
Room price: Dinner, B&B £60-£75 p.p.; singles from £60; children £7.50 plus food when sharing with parents.
Breakfast: Flexible.
Meals: Dinner, 5 courses, included. Non-residents £30. Lunch always available. Afternoon tea also included.
Closed: Rarely.

Directions: On A82, 1 mile north of Spean Bridge turn left just after Commando Memorial onto B8004 to Gairlochy. Old Pines is 300 yards down road on right.

Entry no: 180   **Map no: 12**

Kilcamb Lodge

Strontian
Highland
PH36 4HY

Tel: 01967 402257
Fax: 01967 402041
E-mail: kilcamblodge@aol.com
Web: www.kilcamblodge.com

Anne and Peter Blakeway

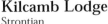

Peter, once a racing skipper (America's Cup), comes from a family with 10 generations of fishermen behind him, so the water is in his blood. It's also at the end of his garden — Loch Sunnart will take you out to Mull, Coll, Tiree, America! The position here is breathtaking with Glas Bheinn rising up across the loch and you can walk down to the shore along grass paths flanked by bluebells — just wonderful, a great place to be shipwrecked. In good weather they'll take you out in the boat in search of langoustine, lobster, crab, then cook it for your supper. The house is exquisite — small, relaxed, welcoming. Smart red carpets in the bar, cut-glass crystal in the richly green dining room, a crackling fire and comfy sofas in the drawing room. Bedrooms are excellent — fresh flowers, lovely fabrics and big, spoiling bath towels — and after a fabulous dinner (my spinach and parmesan tart the best first course of my year), you head for bed to find curtains drawn, the bed turned down. Drive west to the end of the road and you come to Ardnamurchan, the most westerly point in Scotland; it's further west than Land's End, or so they say!

Rooms: 11: 4 doubles and 7 twin/doubles.
Room price: £60-£100; suite £130.
Breakfast: 8.30-10am. Full Scottish £12.50. Continental £8.50.
Meals: Lunch from £6. Dinner, 2 courses, £20.50; 4 courses, £29.50.
Closed: January & February.

Directions: You can drive round, but the Corran ferry (£6), off A82 (10 miles south of Fort William) saves about an hour. Then, follow A861 to Strontian. Hotel signed left just west of village.

Map no: 8   Entry no: **181**

Ardsheal House

Kentallen of Appin   **Tel:** 01631 740227
Argyll   **Fax:** 01631 740342
PA38 4BX   **E-mail:** info@ardsheal.co.uk
    Web: www.ardsheal.co.uk

Neil and Philippa Sutherland

At the end of a two-mile, private, bumpy drive and just a stroll from Loch Linnhe, you'll find Ardsheal, a grand old Scottish mansion set in 11 acres of peaceful gardens and impressively ancient woodlands. The Sutherlands are relaxed and friendly and have kept the grandeur, while expunging any leftover stuffiness — if there was any. You can ask Neil — he grew up here. The hall is awesome, oak-panelled, with roaring fire, leather armchairs and a barrel window giving a porthole view of Loch Linnhe. Equally awesome is the billiard room; walls, floors, ceiling, all are wood, and there's a big bay window looking out to sea with an old naval telescope to scour the horizon. You shouldn't be too surprised to hear that the bedrooms are grand, too, in that old 'country house' style that is Ardsheal. There's a Javanese four-poster, lots of period furniture, and rooms at the front have 'the view'. There's also a conservatory dining room and Philippa, who is fun and bubbly, does most of the cooking. More home than hotel, it's terrific value and you can walk down to the loch for a swim.

Rooms: 8: 1 four-poster, 3 doubles, 3 twin/doubles and 1 single.
Room price: £90; singles £45.
Breakfast: 8.30-9.30am.
Meals: Dinner, 4 courses, £25.
Closed: Occasionally.

Directions: North from Oban on A85, then A828. Continue for about 25 miles to Kentallen and house drive signed left just after the town sign.

Calgary Farmhouse and Dovecote Restaurant

Calgary
Nr. Tobermory
Isle of Mull
PA75 6QW

Tel: 01688 400256
Fax: 01688 400256
E-mail: calgary.farmhouse@virgin.net
Web: www.calgary.co.uk

Julia and Matthew Reade

On a good day you could be in Italy or France, such is the Mediterranean feel of the place. Matthew and Julia, who have been here 11 years, have let their world evolve naturally and they do their own thing brilliantly: you'll find tea shop, restaurant, and art gallery, the occasional free-range child, a very relaxed atmosphere and absolutely tons of commitment. The restaurant is fabulous, with brick arches, whitewashed walls, polished wood floors and a simple, crisp, country elegance everywhere. Matthew, who renovated the entire place himself, makes huge wooden chairs in his work shop (they could pass for Balinese thrones); those in the restaurant get booked in advance by returning guests! In the courtyard, wrought-iron tables and terracotta pots are scattered around the fountain, and the gallery has fine local art and ceramics, all of which you can buy; a woodland sculpture walk is on the way. Bedrooms fit the mood perfectly: pretty fabrics, whitewashed walls, comfy beds — nothing to disappoint. Walk down to Calgary beach for wonderful sunsets. A truly inspiring place.

Rooms: 9: 4 doubles, 2 twins, 2 family and 1 single.
Room price: £64-£70; singles from £32.
Breakfast: 8.15-9am weekdays; 8.30-9.30am weekends.
Meals: Light lunches from £5. Dinner, 3 courses, about £18.
Closed: 1 November — Easter.

Directions: B8073 west from Dervaig for 5.5 miles and the house is signed right before Calgary Bay.

Assapol House Hotel

Bunessan   **Tel:** 01681 700258
Isle of Mull   **Fax:** 01681 700445
PA67 6DW   **E-mail:** alex@assapol.com
                                  Web: www.assapol.com

Thomas, Onny and Alex Robertson

Assapol is quiet all year round. The road that leads down is ignored by both tourists and map-makers alike, though you may come across the odd majestic stag. The garden of this gleamingly whitewashed 1780 manse runs down to its own loch. You can strike out to walk round it, row on it or fish from the boat if you like. The house has a soothing uncluttered simplicity to it. Trim carpets, light and airy rooms, a bank of CDs to raid (Mozart to Bob Dylan via Ella Fitzgerald) and an easy-going feel. Pick up a book and read all day or follow Alex's advice and head down to Kilvickeon beach. Bowls of fruit and terracotta Farrow and Ball paint in the dining room for superb Robertson-cooked delights. Alex and Onny indulge in a daily competition to see who can produce the best pudding and Thomas makes a mean bowl of porridge. Much of the meat is island-reared and local, free-range eggs for breakfast. Bedrooms are big, not grand, just warm, spotless and pretty and fit the mood perfectly. Boat trips can be arranged: Staffa and Fingals Cave or the Treshnish Isles and its bird sanctuary. *Children over ten welcome.*

Rooms: 5: 2 doubles and 2 twins; 1 single with private bath and shower.
Room price: Dinner, B&B £73 p.p.
Breakfast: 8.30-9.30am.
Meals: Dinner, 4 courses, included in price; packed lunches £6.50.
Closed: End of October -Easter.

Directions: West on A849 for Fionnphort. Turn left just before Bunessan village, 100 yards after the school. On right after 0.5 miles and signed.

Entry no: 184   **Map no: 8**

Argyll Hotel

Isle of Iona
PA76 6SJ

Tel: 01681 700334
Fax: 01681 700510
E-mail: reception@argyllhoteliona.co.uk
Web: www.argyllhoteliona.co.uk

Claire Bachellerie and Daniel Morgan

When the boat stops at six, the Argyll is a good spot to be marooned. Walk over to the west coast, about a mile away, for awesome sunsets — there's nothing between you and America. Daniel and Claire, who are young and gentle, took over last year, keen to preserve the old, cosy island feel — and keep the designers at bay. Quite right. The rooms are spot-on and full of simple, homely comforts: piles of old paperbacks, armchairs, comfy beds and boiling hot water bursting from bathroom taps; you won't for a minute think you're being deprived of a thing. Sitting rooms have open fires, the dining room has a lovely old fashioned feel and there's a pretty conservatory, too. Outside, Iona is magical, a mystical dreamscape, home to a hermit's cave, the Abbey and sandy beaches; St. Columba landed on one of them, bringing Christianity to Scotland in 563 AD. Mark, maintenance man, friend and sailor, will take you under sail to Fingal's cave, seal colonies and dolphins. A perfect place for those who want solitude to be fun.

Rooms: 15: 1 family, 3 doubles, 3 twins and 7 singles; 1 single with shared bath.
Room price: £70-£86; singles £35-£43. Dinner, B&B £54-£63 p.p.
Breakfast: 8.15-9am.
Meals: Dinner, 4 courses, usually included. Non-residents £19.50. Light lunches and cream teas also available.
Closed: 1 November — 1 April.

Directions: Oban ferry to Craignure on Mull, then west to Fionnphort for Iona ferry. Cars are not allowed on Iona but can be left safely at Fionnphort.

Tigh an Truish
Clachan   **Tel:** 01852 300242
Isle of Seil
Argyll
PA34 4QZ

Miranda and Gustl Brunner

There is nothing grand about this honest old inn, but it's fun, and just one card in the Brunner pack. Cross the 'Bridge over the Atlantic', and you enter their world: pub, petrol station, postbox and photo gallery — it's all theirs, all ten paces apart, a small enclave of engagingly odd, mild eccentricity. Miranda rules the inn with a rod of pure sponge. It's full of life, you may get a *ceilidh*, definitely a pint and good home-cooked food. Her brother farms oysters and may drop some off, fresh from the seabed; otherwise you'll have to settle for *moules marinières*, half a lobster or venison. There are two big, modestly comfy bedrooms, both with enough room for sofas and chairs. You also get a kitchen — tiny, tiled and functional. One of the quirks of Tigh an Truish is that your fridge is left stocked with porridge, cereals, bread, eggs and juice for you to cook up whenever you want. Look out for the Gustl-made furniture, especially the strange but remarkably comfortable bar bench. You can 'bag' another small island, Luing; Miranda will give you the best advice.

Rooms: 2: 1 double and 1 twin.
Room price: £40-£45.
Breakfast: Flexible.
Meals: Bar meals available (April-October only) from £5.
Closed: Christmas & New Year.

Directions: A816 south from Oban, then B844 towards Easdale. After 3 miles, cross bridge and house on right opposite petrol station.

Royal Hotel
Tighnabruaich
Argyll
PA21 2BE

Tel: 01700 811239
Fax: 01700 811300
E-mail: royalhotel@btinternet.com
Web: www.royalhotel.org.uk

Roger and Bea McKie

In that never-ending search for a tourist-free destination, Tighnabruaich is near the top of my list — an end-of-the-road village, lost to the world and without great need of it. The Royal is its relaxed and informal hub. Yachtsman tie up to the moorings and drop in for lunch, the shinty team pop down for a pint after a game and fishermen land fresh mussels and langoustine straight from the sea for Roger to cook. Roger and Bea — ex-pat Scots — came back up from Cheltenham with an eye to "buying something run-down so they could..." run it up? That's very much what they've done. There's a fresh, designer-feel downstairs, where Bea has rag-rolled a bold orange onto the walls. Wooden floors, rugs and jazz in the brasserie, a small locals' bar at the back and a big, bright restaurant with great views of the Kyles of Bute. Upstairs, the bedrooms are big, warm, comfy and homely — just what you'd hope for — and all but one with glorious sea views. There's a nearby tennis court where you can lose balls in the sea and Bute is a short ferry-ride away.

Rooms: 11: 10 doubles and 1 twin.
Room price: £74-£124. Dinner, B&B from £50 p.p.
Breakfast: 9-10.30am.
Meals: Dinner, 3 courses, £23.95. Meals in brasserie from £6.
Closed: Christmas Day.

Directions: From Glasgow, A82 north, A83 west, A815 south, A886 south, A8003 south, then B8000 north into village. The hotel is on the seafront.

Map no: 8   **Entry no: 187**

Wales

"Old men and far travellers may lie with authority."
– Anonymous

Gliffaes Country House Hotel

Crickhowell
Powys
NP8 1RH

Tel: 01874 730371
Fax: 01874 730463
E-mail: calls@gliffaeshotel.com
Web: www.gliffaeshotel.com

Nick and Peta Brabner and James and Susie Suter

Gliffaes is matchless — a perfect place — grand, yet as casual and warm as home. It's a house for all seasons — not even driving rain could mask its beauty. In summer you can stroll along the rhododendron-flanked drive and wander the 33 acres of stunning gardens and woodland or just bask in the sun on the high, buttressed terrace while the river Usk cuts through the valley 150 feet below. In winter, stay inside amid gleamingly polished floors, panelled walls and fires burning in extravagantly ornate fireplaces (one looks like the Acropolis), waiting for tea — a feast of scones and cakes laid out on a long table at one end of the sitting room. But the house could be a garden shed and you'd still love it — as long as the Brabners and Suters remained at the helm. They've been welcoming guests for 52 years (the fourth generation, aged two and four, are nearly ready for some rope-learning) and they run their home with instinctive generosity. Bedrooms are excellent, the cooking is British with a Mediterranean influence and a hint of the Orient, and you can fish seriously, too.

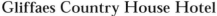

Rooms: 22: 16 twin/doubles and 6 singles.
Room price: £65-£130; singles from £51.
Breakfast: 8-9.30am.
Meals: Light lunches, from £2.50. Dinner, 3 courses, £24.
Closed: Never.

Directions: From Crickhowell take A40 west for 2.5 miles. Gliffaes is signed left. Wind up hill for exactly 1 mile.

Map no: 2   Entry no: 188

Three Cocks Hotel

Three Cocks   **Tel:** 01497 847215
Brecon   **Fax:** 01497 847339
Powys   **Web:** www.hay-on-wye.co.uk/3cocks
LD3 0SL

Michael, Marie-Jeanne and Thomas Winstone

"You don't have to walk through it; the house just creaks on its own", says Michael of this 500-year-old coaching inn built around a tree. Michael and Marie-Jeanne are exceptionally friendly and have brought much energy and experience over from Belgium, where they had a restaurant for ten years. They obviously know their Belgian onions. Michael (he's actually English, but Belgian by marriage) and his son Thomas produce incredible Belgian dishes (i.e. French without the portion control) in the stonewalled restaurant that's peppered with some fine old Dutch oils. The house is hugely welcoming with a bright red carpet, stone walls, a crackling fire, heavy rugs and lots of lovely Belgian beer. It's a very sociable place, too; the warm and simple bedrooms are TV-free, so people stay up late chatting in the limed-oak panelled drawing room downstairs. When you do make it up to bed, you can expect beams, sloping floors, timbered walls, thick old eiderdowns and comfy beds. At breakfast the feasting continues with home-baked bread that melts in the mouth.

Rooms: 7: 4 doubles and 2 twins; 1 twin with private bath.
Room price: £60-£67.
Breakfast: 8-9am weekdays; 8.30-9.30am weekends.
Meals: Dinner, 4 courses, £27.
Closed: 1 December — 14 February.

Directions: On A438 Brecon-Hereford road. 27 miles from Hereford, 11 miles from Brecon, 4 miles from Hay-on-Wye. Signed.

Entry no: 189   Map no: 2

The Lake Country House
Llangammarch Wells
Powys
LD4 4BS

Tel: 01591 620202
Fax: 01591 620457
E-mail: info@lakecountryhouse.com
Web: www.lakecountryhouse.com

Jean-Pierre Mifsud

The very essence of a real country house, not stuffy at all, but grand and cosseting nevertheless. Afternoon tea is served in the drawing room where seven beautiful rugs warm a brightly-polished wooden floor and five chandeliers hang from the ceiling. The hotel opened 100 years ago and the leather-bound fishing logs and visitor's books go back to 1894. A feel of the 1920s lingers. Fires come to life in front of your eyes, seemingly unaided by human hands, walking sticks wait at the door, grand pianos, antiques and grand father clocks lie about the place and snooker balls clink in the distance. The same grandeur marks the bedrooms, most of which are suites: *trompe l'oeil* wallpaper, rich fabrics, good lighting, stacks of antiques, crowns above the beds, a turndown service — the works. Jean-Pierre runs his home with gentle charm, happy to share his knowledge of this deeply rural slice of Wales. The grounds hold a lake to fish (you can hire rods), a nine-hole golf course, the river Ifron where kingfishers swoop and acres of peace and quiet. Horse riding can also be arranged.

Rooms: 18: 10 suites and 8 twin/doubles.
Room price: £125-£145; suites £175-£205; singles £90.
Breakfast: 9-10am.
Meals: Lunch, 3 courses, £17.50. Dinner, 3 courses, £30.
Closed: Never.

Directions: From Builth Wells A483 west for 7 miles to Garth. Hotel signed from Garth village.

Elan Valley Hotel

Elan Valley
Rhayader
Powys
LD6 5HN

Tel: 01597 810448
Fax: 01597 810448
E-mail: hotel@elanvalley.demon.co.uk
Web: www.elanvalleyhotel.co.uk

Louise Osborn and Pippa Boss

If you get the chance, arrive via the old Aberystwyth mountain road — one of the most beautiful in Britain. You drop down from Devil's Bridge to Cwmystwyth, then follow the river Elan through blistering countryside to the reservoirs and on to the village — a wonderful way in. Pippa, Louise, Richard and Anthony all come from a theatrical background and monthly events here include storytelling, music and theatre. The 'Farmer's Bar' — the real centre of the hotel — can host a colourful mix of actors, musicians and locals and the place acts as a sort of community/arts centre; the locals come here for quizzes, quilting, football training, films, Breton folk dancing — you name it, if they have an idea, they bring it here. Bedrooms are simple, pretty, colourful, but it's the mood of the place that is priceless. Don't come in search of fancy hotel luxury, but do come to escape the city, to eat good food, to wander ancient woods. Red Kites, buzzards and falcons glide and there are excellent cycle tracks round the lakes, so bring your bikes. They will carry luggage onwards for bikers and walkers. We salute them.

Rooms: 11: 4 doubles, 1 twin,
4 twin/family and 1 single; 1 single with
private bath.
Room price: £55-£70; singles £32.
Breakfast: 8-9.30am weekdays;
8.30-10am weekends.
Meals: A la carte dinner, 3 courses, about
£17.50. Bar meals £2.95-£7.95; toddler's
and children's menus £2.25-£4.95.
Closed: 2 weeks mid-January.

Directions: In Rhayader, take B4518 west up Elan Valley for 2.5 miles. Hotel signed. (Don't confuse with Elan Hotel.)

Entry no: 191

Map no: 5

The Cawdor Arms Hotel

Rhosmaen Street
Llandeilo
Carmarthenshire
SA19 6EN

Tel: 01558 823500
Fax: 01558 822399
E-mail: cawdor.arms@btinternet.com
Web: www.cawdor-arms.co.uk

John, Sylvia and Jane Silver

The Cawdor stands quietly on the High Street, much as it has for the past two hundred years. It is a smart hotel — the grandest place in town — and always has been. Local farmers cross its stone-flagged floors and the daughters of retired doctors honeymoon here. It is traditional in a rural sense, unmoved by passing fashions (just as it should be) and much prettier than its photos suggest. If you arrive in the early evening, the chances are that Sylvia or Jane will be playing the grand piano in the hall as guests sink into red leather armchairs in front of the fire, their martinis in hand. Waiters bring you olives, home-made crisps (the latter still warm) and menus, then return, first to take your order, later to escort you to your table for sublime food. Bedrooms lead off grand corridors. Expect country quilts, good linen, Victorian oak dressers, books and lots of old-fashioned warmth. This is beautiful country, too. Soft, rolling hills cradle the town, so come here to paint; they run the occasional course. There are murder mystery weekends, too.

Rooms: 16: 2 four-posters, 8 doubles, 5 twins and 1 family.
Room price: £60; four-posters £75; single occupancy £45.
Breakfast: 7.30-9.30am weekdays; 8-10am weekends.
Meals: Lunch, 2 courses, £11.95. Dinner, 3 courses, £21.
Closed: Never.

Directions: M4, junction 49, A48 north, then A476 to Llandeilo. Turn left into town, cross bridge and hotel on left.

Three Main Street

Fishguard
Pembrokeshire
SA65 9HG

Tel: 01348 874275
Fax: 01348 874017

Inez Ford and Marion Evans

A beautiful Georgian townhouse — a restaurant with rooms — less than a minute's walk from Fishguard's market square. Marion and Inez have made a bit of a splash in Wales building up a reputation for sublime food and for the style and generosity of spirit with which they serve it. Rugs and stripped wooden floors, candles, handwritten menus and classical music or jazz all combine to give a warm and relaxed, slightly bohemian feel to the place. Big bedrooms have a hint of Art Deco and are homely with fresh flowers, rugs, sofas, good furniture, maybe a walnut bed. The whole place is extremely comfortable — superb value for money — but the pounding heart of Three Main Street is the kitchen whence comes exceptional food. Inez makes the pastries and puddings while Marion looks after the starters and mains so expect maybe baked goats cheese on toasted *brioche*, sea-bass baked with garlic, chilled lemon and lime soufflé. Take to the nearby coastal path and walk off your sin amid divine Welsh landscape. Day trips to Dublin are also possible; it's only an hour and a half away by Sealynx.

Rooms: 3: 2 doubles and 1 twin.
Room price: £65-£75; singles £45.
Breakfast: 8-10am.
Meals: Lunch (Easter-October) £10.
Dinner, 3 courses, £28.
Closed: February. Restaurant closed
Sundays and Mondays.

Directions: Main Street runs off the town
square in the centre of town. All roads lead
to it.

Entry no: 193

Map no: 1

Cnapan

East Street
Newport
Pembrokeshire
SA42 0SY

Tel: 01239 820575
Fax: 01239 820878
E-mail: cnapan@online-holidays.net
Web: www.online-holidays.net/cnapan/

John and Elund Lloyd, Michael and Judith Cooper

The welcome is immediate and wonderful — you'll feel like an old friend by the time you've walked through the front door. Michael and Judith were on duty the Saturday afternoon I arrived. They were up to their eyeballs in the restaurant with a *cawl* lunch to raise money for the twinning committee, but they still made me feel my arrival was the best thing to happen all day. Michael answered the door with a big welcoming grin and, immediately, Judith pulled her hands out of a mixing bowl in the kitchen, gave them a wipe and came over to shake my hand as if this was the most normal thing in the world to do. The house has all you'll need to feel comfy and cosy: stone walls, pine dressers, fresh flowers, bright rooms and lots of books. Bedrooms are homely without a whisper of bad taste. When lunch finished, the rugby started — France v Wales in Paris. "When was the last time Wales won in France?" Michael asked. "Waterloo", joked a retired teacher at the lunch. And so, of course, Wales won — another slice of Cnapan magic. "It's only our house — you can take it or leave it," said Judith. Take it.

Rooms: 5: 1 family, 1 double and 3 twins.
Room price: £60; singles £37.
Breakfast: 8.30-9.30am.
Meals: Dinner, 3 courses, £19. Restaurant closed Tuesday nights, Easter-October. Lunches (high season only) from £6.50.
Closed: January & February.

Directions: Newport is on the A487 between Fishguard and Cardigan. Coming from the north, Cnapan is the first pink house on the right.

Penhelig Arms

Aberdyfi
Gwynedd
LL35 0LT

Tel: 01654 767215
Fax: 01654 767690
E-mail: penheligarms@saqnet.co.uk

Robert and Sally Hughes

The value at the 'little inn' is second to none — dinner, bed and breakfast from £50 in a perfect position on the Dyfi estuary (all but one room has long views across it) with friendly folk and an easy elegance all around. Yet you'd trade all of that just for the welcome you get here. Within minutes of arriving I was involved in a coffee tasting with Robert while he waved to people passing outside and greeted friends coming in — the Penhelig is a vibrant part of the local community. I played fantasy food with the menu — fish soup followed by Mediterranean fish stew — then moved on to the wine list where bottle after bottle costs less than £15, underlying how fair and generous the place is. When Robert was called to the phone, Glyn happily deputised and showed me round. Sea-grass and rugs, long views, cool colours and light flooding in. The bar of wood and stone is hugely intimate and cosy: settles, fire, good ales and a gallery for pictures of the locals' boats. Bedrooms match the mood perfectly, some big, some small, and not a nasty thing in sight.

Rooms: 10: 4 twin/doubles, 5 doubles and 1 single.
Room price: £69-£79; singles £39.50.
Dinner, B&B, £51-£59 p.p.
Breakfast: Until 9.30am.
Meals: Lunch and dinner, in bar or restaurant, £2.25-£20.
Closed: Christmas Day & Boxing Day.

Directions: The Penhelig Arms is on the main road in Aberdyfi.

Penmaenuchaf Hall

Penmaenpool
Dolgellau
Gwynedd
LL40 1YB

Tel: 01341 422129
Fax: 01341 422787
E-mail: relax@penhall.co.uk

Mark Watson and Lorraine Fielding

The track that leads up to the Hall is bumpy, but it's worth it for the views. You can stand at the front of the house, on the Victorian stone balustrade, and gaze down on the tidal ebb and flow of the Mawddach estuary, or walk around to the back to blazing banks of rhododendrons, azaleas and camellias, a rising forest behind. When you manage to reach the front door, you'll be equally delighted. The house is pristine. There are rugs, wooden floors and oak panelling, flowers erupting from jugs and bowls, leather sofas and armchairs, open fires and sea-grass, and, everywhere, those views. Some of the rooms have cushioned window seats, a sort of aesthetic pre-emptive strike! Upstairs, the bedrooms (more views, of course) come in different shapes and sizes, the big being *huge*, the small being warm and cosy. One room up in the eaves has a fine bergère bed. You can also fish — they have 13 miles of river — and, back in the garden, they grow as much as they can. There's Mark's sense of humour, too. *Children over six welcome and pets by arrangement.*

Rooms: 14: 1 four-poster, 5 twins and 8 doubles.
Room price: £110-£170; singles from £70.
Breakfast: Until 9.30am weekdays; 10am weekends.
Meals: Dinner, 4 courses, £27.50. Lunch, £3.50-£15.50.
Closed: Ten days in early January.

Directions: Take A493 west from Dolgellau. After about 1.5 miles, house signed left.

Borthwnog Hall

Bontddu   **Tel:** 01341 430271
Dolgellau   **Fax:** 01341 430682
Gwynedd   **E-mail:** borthwnoghall@enterprise.net
LL40 2TT   **Web:** homepages.enterprise.net/borthwnoghall

Derek and Vicki Hawes

The hills behind the house are full of gold. Bontddu's mine has provided for Royal wedding rings and you can pan the streams that feed the Mawddach estuary. The blue-shuttered house dates back to the late 17th century and to a shoemaker who made his money making shoes for cattle — they needed them to get over the mountains and to market. Later, it became the Manor house of the Borthwnog estate before the Victorians added the balcony that runs along the front; two light-flooded bedrooms open onto to it. The bedrooms are good. There's a suite at the back with antique mahogany beds and crimson bedspreads, but you really want to try for the balcony rooms. One is enormous with three sets of French windows, the other is snugger with a big brass bed and compact en suite shower. Vicki and Derek have continued the spirit of evolution by opening a small art gallery (you can buy paintings, books and pottery) and a small restaurant. As for the view... it needs no description.

Rooms: 3: 1 suite, 1 twin/double and 1 double.
Room price: £70-£115. Dinner, B&B £52.50-£70 p.p.
Breakfast: Until 9am.
Meals: Dinner, 3 courses, £19.50. Packed lunches by arrangement.
Closed: 23-27 December.

Directions: A470 north through Dolgellau, then west for 2 miles on A496. House on left and signed.

Entry no: 197   **Map no: 5**

Llwyndû Farmhouse and Restaurant

Llanaber
Barmouth
Gwynedd
LL42 1RR

Tel: 01341 280144
Fax: 01341 281236
E-mail: intouch@llwyndu-farmhouse.co.uk
Web: www.llwyndu-farmhouse.co.uk

Peter and Paula Thompson

It's a good mile down the steepish hill to the gracious sweep of Cardigan Bay, but it looks as though you could hurdle the wall and jump straight into it. An old stone wall frames the view perfectly. The beach is long and wide, a good place to walk, as are the Rhinog mountains which take to the skies behind. And walkers will love Llwyndû. It's warm and earthy, generously simple, with bold colours on ancient stone walls, spiral stone stairways that lead nowhere, a woodburner in the big inglenook and a priest's hole cupboard (maybe). Peter, a historian turned cook, has brought life to the simple, everyday story of the house and its past owners; you can read up on it. Old wills hang on the walls, the proof of fables. Bedrooms are split between the main house and the converted granary; there are two four-posters, beams, bold Peter-painted stone walls, good bathrooms and bunk beds for children. All this in four pretty acres, with great views both up and down, cats, dogs and a horse that comes home for the holidays.

Rooms: 7: 2 four-posters, 2 doubles, 2 family and 1 twin.
Room price: £58-£70.
Breakfast: 8.30-9.30am.
Meals: Dinner, 3 courses, £17.95-£21.95. Packed lunches £4-£5. Restaurant closed Sunday nights.
Closed: Christmas Day & Boxing Day.

Directions: From Barmouth, A496 north. Pass through Llanaber. Llwyndû farmhouse is signed right where the street lights and the 40 m.p.h limit end.

Map no: 5   Entry no: 198

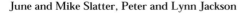

Hotel Maes-y-Neuadd

Talsarnau
Nr. Harlech
Gwynedd
LL47 6YA

Tel: 01766 780200
Fax: 01766 780211
E-mail: maes@neuadd.com
Web: www.neuadd.com

June and Mike Slatter, Peter and Lynn Jackson

Peter, who cooks, was busy the day I visited, but he still found time to take me on a lazy tour. He understated everything: the snug bar was "simple", with rich leather sofas, thick rugs and warming woodburner; the bedrooms were "comfortable", with home-baked biscuits, fresh flowers everywhere and complementary sloe gin, not to mention the musty scent of furniture polish, the bathrobes and the fabulous views. The truth, however, will out: Maes-Y-Neuadd is grand, yet it doesn't try to be. The mood is of an old country house with good furniture and warm colours, but it's not stick-in-the-mud country house — it has a nice contemporary feel and even on a dullish February afternoon the rooms seemed flooded with light. This may have something to do with its setting on wooded mountain foothills with long views off to Snowdon. Nearer to hand, there's a kitchen garden where they grow nearly all their fruit and veg (the gardeners rightly get a mention on the menu) and they also bottle oils, vinegars and dressings under their own label, so take home a souvenir.

Rooms: 16: 1 four-poster,
14 twin/doubles and 1 single.
Room price: £127-£177; singles from
£90. Dinner, B&B £89.50-£115 p.p.
Breakfast: Until 9.30am.
Meals: Lunch from £5. Dinner, 5 courses,
£27-£34.
Closed: Never.

Directions: A496 south through
Talsarnau, then left (straight on) onto
B4573. Left, signed hotel, after 0.25 miles,
then wind along for 2 miles. Hotel on
right.

Entry no: 199

Map no: 5

The Hotel Portmeirion

Portmeirion
Gwynedd
LL48 6ET

Tel: 01766 770000
Fax: 01766 771331
E-mail: hotel@portmeirion-village.com
Web: www.portmeirion-village.com

Robin Llywellen   **Manager: Meic Williams**

Portmeirion is unique, an accolade rare these days. It is also extraordinarily beautiful, challenging and memorable — a very special place. Clough Williams-Ellis designed and built it in the 1920s — a passionate statement of his belief that architecture could *and should* enhance, not destroy, its environment. Such foresight naturally included a hotel, built right on the tidal estuary with towering subtropical woodland behind. You can walk straight out into his Italianate village of pastel-coloured houses, a masterpiece in town planning. It was here in the '60s that *The Prisoner* was filmed. The hotel is equally fabulous: a restaurant that could double as a ballroom, a light blue, mirrored salon, the elephant bar with high-backed Indian chairs and candles. Bedrooms are inspirational, full of bold colours, rich fabrics and gorgeous antiques. Portmeirion is run in trust by Clough's grandchildren, their commitment to its future no less ardent than their grandfather's. The staff, too, love their world, and it shows.

Rooms: 40: 10 twins, 14 doubles,
2 four-posters, 3 family and 11 suites.
Room price: £110-£220; singles from
£90. Dinner, B&B £88-£134 p.p.
Breakfast: Until 10am.
Meals: Lunch, £11- £15. Dinner, 3
courses, £33.
Closed: 9 January — 4 February.

Directions: A487 west towards
Porthmadog. Portmeirion is signed left in
Minffordd.

Map no: 5   Entry no: 200

Plas Bodegroes
Pwllheli
Gwynedd
LL53 5TH

Tel: 01758 612363
Fax: 01758 701247
E-mail: gunna@bodegroes.co.uk
Web: www.bodegroes.co.uk

Chris and Gunna Chown

Close to the end of the world and worth every single second it takes to get here. Chris and Gunna are inspirational, their home a temple of cool elegance, the food possibly the best in Wales. Fronted by an avenue of two-hundred year old beech trees, this Georgian manor house is wrapped in climbing roses, wildly roaming wisteria and ferns. The veranda circles the house as do the long French windows that lighten every room, so open one up, grab a chair and sit out all day reading a book. Not a formal place, but instead come to relax and to be yourself. Bedrooms are wonderful, the courtyard rooms especially good; exposed wooden ceilings and a crisp clean style give the feel of a smart Scandinavian forest hideaway. Best of all is the dining room, almost a work of art in itself, cool and crisp with modern art and Venetian carnival masks on the walls — a great place to eat Chris's ambrosial food. Elsewhere (if you can tear yourself away) the Llyn peninsula is worth exploring: sandy beaches, towering sea cliffs, country walks. Snowdon is close, too. Gunna and Chris will tell you where.

Rooms: 11: 1 four-poster, 7 doubles,
2 twins and 1 single.
Room price: £70-£120; singles £35-£80.
Dinner, B&B from £55 p.p.
Breakfast: 8-9.30am weekdays; 8-10am
weekends.
Meals: Sunday lunch £13.50. Dinner,
3 courses, £25-£30.
Closed: 1 December — 1 March. Rooms
and restaurant closed Mondays.

Directions: Through Pwllheli on A497 towards Nefyn and house signed on left after 1 mile

Entry no: 201   **Map no: 5**

The Groes Inn
Ty'n-y-Groes
Nr. Conwy
Conwy
LL32 8TN

Tel: 01492 650545
Fax: 01492 650855
Web:
www.btinternet.com/~thegroesinn

Dawn, Tony and
Justin Humphreys

This 15th-century coaching inn — the first to be licensed in Wales — flourished in the 18th century, the high period of coach travel. With the 19th century came better roads and the traffic dried up, The Groes reverting to its "ancient role of serving the agricultural community of the lower valley". It is an exceptionally comfortable place in exceptionally beautiful country — the walking alone is reason to come. Views from the front stretch off across a wide sweep of the Conwy estuary while, behind, the Carneddau mountains start to rise. Come back after a day's adventure and rest up for an hour or so in wonderfully plush bedrooms. The sparkling white bathrooms are quite superb, with baths that fill in seconds, huge fluffy white towels and smart halogen lighting. Refreshed, walk across to the pub (the bedrooms are in a pretty whitewashed annexe) and enjoy the rambling beams, the smart red carpets, the nooks and crannies, the busts, the books, the fires, the hearty home-cooked food. Inn-lovers will be in heaven. At breakfast in winter the fire smoulders while in summer you can eat in the garden. Perfect.

Rooms: 14: 1 four-poster,
12 twin/doubles and 1 family.
Room price: £81-£115; singles from £64.
Dinner, B&B from £46 p.p.
Breakfast: 7.30am-9.30am weekdays;
8-10am weekends.
Meals: Bar meals from £7. Dinner,
3 courses, £25.
Closed: Never.

Directions: A55 to Conwy, then B5106
south for 1.5 miles and hotel on right.

Lake Vyrnwy Hotel
Llanwddyn
Montgomeryshire
SY10 0LY

Tel: 01691 870692
Fax: 01691 870259
E-mail: res@lakevyrnwy.com
Web: www.lakevyrnwy.com

The Bisiker Family

This little pocket of Wales is wonderfully remote. Pine forests and ancient grazing land meet on the hills and run down to the lake, man-made in 1890 to provide Liverpool's water. Victorian tourists flocked here to see the dam, then the biggest in Europe. The hotel started life as a shooting and fishing lodge, and tales of the 1930s echo. Ruth, aged 85, who ran it then, still comes in to do the flowers. The view is stupendous, the lake stretching away five miles distant, a playground for rolling mists and sunburst. You can walk or cycle round it, canoe, sail or fish on it. Bedrooms are excellent, only a few don't have a lake view, but the long light restaurant, the yellow drawing room, the leather-armchaired library and the terraced bar all amply make up for that. Over the years the Bisikers have given it back its old glory, with wood floors, a grand piano, heavy oak furniture, even a postbox in the entrance hall; and staff who care, too. A place to return to again and again.

Rooms: 35: 2 four-posters, 1 suite and 32 twin/doubles.
Room price: £110-£182; singles from £80. Dinner, B&B £73-£103 p.p.
Breakfast: 8.30-10am.
Meals: Lunch, 3 courses, £15.95. Dinner, 3 courses, £27.50-£35. Bar meals also available.
Closed: Never.

Directions: A490 from Welshpool, then B4393 to Lake Vyrnwy. The route is signed with brown signs from A5 at Shrewsbury as well.

Entry no: 203   **Map no: 5**

Quick Reference Index

GREAT VALUE

These are places where the room price based on 2 people sharing is £80 or under.

England

Bath & N.E. Somerset
38 • 39

Cheshire
119 • 120

Cornwall
2 • 3 • 5 • 6 • 7 • 8 • • 12 • 14

Cumbria
140 • 144 • 145 • 147 • 149

Derbyshire
124

Devon
17 • 18 • 19 • 20 • 21• 25• 28

Dorset
42

Gloucestershire
103 • 104 • 107 • 110

Hampshire
48

Herefordshire
111 • 112

Isle of Wight
53 • 54

Kent
65 • 66 • 67 • 70

London
74

Norfolk
82

Northumberland
153

Oxfordshire
96 • 97

Shropshire
116 • 118

Somerset
29 • 36

Staffordshire
121 • 122

Suffolk
75 • 76 • 79 • 80 • 81

Sussex
59 • 61 • 63 • 64

Warwickshire
114

Wiltshire
44 • 46

Yorkshire
127 • 128 • 130 • 132 • 136 • 137

Scotland

155 • 158 • 163 • 164 • 165 • 167 • 172 • 175 • 176 • 179 • 181 • 183 • 185 • 186 • 187

Wales

188 • 189 • 191 • 192 • 193 • 194 • 195 • 197 • 198 • 201

WHEELCHAIR

These owners have told us that they have facilities suitable for people in wheelchairs. It is essential that you confirm on the telephone what is available before arrival.

England

36 • 43 • 56 • 78• 89 • 90 • 94 • 101 • 129 • 133

Scotland

157 • 159 • 161 • 174 • 176 • 180

Wales

199 • 202

Quick Reference Index

ACCESS

These houses have bedrooms or bathrooms that are accessible for people of limited mobility. Please phone beforehand to confirm details and special needs.

England

Bath & N.E. Somerset
37 • 38

Bristol
40

Cambridgeshire
88

Channel Islands
1

Cornwall
4 • 5 • 6 • 13

Co. Durham
152

Cumbria
141 • 147 • 149 • 150

Devon
15

Dorset
41

Gloucestershire
100 • 102

Hampshire
49 • 50

Herefordshire
112

Isle of Wight
54

Kent
66 • 69 • 70

Lancashire
126

London
71 • 72 • 73

Norfolk
83 • 84

Northumberland
153

Nottinghamshire
86

Oxfordshire
91 • 92 • 93 • 95 • 97 • 98 • 99

Rutland
87

Shropshire
118

Somerset
31 • 35

Staffordshire
121 • 122

Suffolk
79

Sussex
57 • 58 • 60 • 61

Worcestershire
113

Yorkshire
128 • 131 • 132 • 134 • 136 • 137 • 138

Scotland
154 • 162 • 163 • 164 • 165 • 177 • 178 • 183

Wales
190 • 200

ORGANIC FOOD

These owners use mostly organic ingredients, chemical-free, home-grown or locally-grown produce.

England

Bath & N.E. Somerset
37

Channel Islands
1

Cheshire
119 • 120

Quick Reference Index

Cornwall
2 • 9 • 12

Cumbria
142

Devon
15 • 17 • 20 • 23 • 25

Gloucestershire
101 • 102 • 103 • 105 • 110

Herefordshire
111 • 112

Kent
67

Norfolk
85

Nottinghamshire
86

Oxfordshire
91 • 94 • 97

Shropshire
116 • 118

Somerset
29 • 30 • 35

Suffolk
81

Sussex
59

Yorkshire
127 • 128 • 133

Scotland
161 • 162 • 163 • 168 • 169 • 171 • 173 • 177 • 180 • 181 • 185

Wales
193 • 199 • 201 • 203

SWIMMING POOL

A swimming pool is available on the premises for guests.

England

Cornwall
11 • 12 • 13

Devon
19 • 23 • 25

Dorset
41

Isle of Wight
55

Kent
67

London
71

Norfolk
82

Rutland
87

Somerset
31 • 35

Staffordshire
121

Sussex
58

Worcestershire
113

Scotland
167

Wales
200

A short history of the company

Perhaps the best clue as to why these books have their own very particular style and 'bent' lies in Alastair's history.

After a law degree, a stint as a teacher in Voluntary Service Overseas led to a change in direction. He became a teacher (French and Spanish) and then a refugee worker, then spent several years in overseas development work before settling into environmental campaigning, and even green politics. Meanwhile, he was able to dabble - just once a year - in an old interest, taking clients on tours of special places all over Europe. This grew, eventually, into a travel company (it still exists as Alastair Sawday's Tours, operating, inter alia, walking and biking tours all over Europe).

Trying to take his clients to eat and sleep in places that were not owned by corporations and assorted bandits he found dozens of very special places in France - farms, châteaux etc - a list that grew into the first book, *French Bed and Breakfast*. It was a celebration of 'real' places to stay and the remarkable people who run them.

So, this publishing company is based on the success of that first and rather whimsical French book. It started as mild crusade, and there it stays. For we still celebrate the unusual, the beautiful, the highly individual. We have no rules for owners; they do things their own way. We are passionate about rejecting the ugly, the cold, the banal and the indifferent. And we are still passionate about promoting the use of 'real' food. Alastair is a trustee of the Soil Association and keen to promote organic growing especially.

It is a source of huge pleasure to us that we seem to have pressed the right button: there are thousands and thousands of people who, clearly, share our views and take up our ideas. We are by no means alone in trumpeting the virtues of standing up to the monstrous uniformity of so much of our culture.

The greatest accolade we have had was in *The Bookseller* magazine, which described us as 'head and shoulders above the rest'. That meant a lot. But even more satisfying is that we are building a company in which people matter. We are delighted to hear of new friendships between those in the book and those using it and to know that there are many people - among them artists, farmers, champions of the countryside - who have been enabled to pursue their unusual lives thanks to the extra income the book brings them.

Of course we want the company to flourish, but this isn't just about money; it is about people, too.

Alastair Sawday
Special Places to Stay series

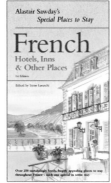

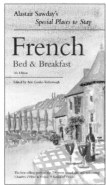

Tel: 01275 464891 Fax: 01275 464887
www.sawdays.co.uk

The Little Earth Book

The Little Earth Book

Alastair Sawday, the publisher of this (wonderful) guide-book, is also an environmentalist. For over 25 years he has campaigned, not only against the worst excesses of modern tourism and its hotels, but against environmental 'looniness' of other kinds. He has fought for systems and policies that might enable our beautiful planet - simply - to survive. He founded and ran Avon Friends of the Earth, has run for Parliament, and has led numerous local campaigns. He is now a trustee of the Soil Association, experience upon which he draws in this remarkable new book.

Researched and written by an eminent Bristol architect, James Bruges, *The Little Earth Book* is a clarion call to action, a mind-boggling collection of mini-essays on today's most important environmental concerns, from global warming and poisoned food to economic growth, Third World debt, genes and 'superbugs'. Undogmatic but sure-footed, the style is light, explaining complex issues with easy language, illustrations and cartoons. Ideas are developed chapter by chapter, yet each one stands alone. It is an easy browse.

The Little Earth Book provides hope, with new ideas and examples of people swimming against the current, of bold ideas that work in practice. It is a book as important as it is original. One has been sent to every M.P. Now you, too, can learn about the issues and join the most important debate of this century.

Oh - one last thing: *The Little Earth Book* is a damned good read! Note what Johnathon Porritt says about it:

"Be refreshed! *The Little Earth Book* is different. And instructive. And even fun."

Did you know.....

- If everyone adopted the Western lifestyle we would need five earths to support us

- 60% of infections picked up in hospitals are now drug-resistant

- Environmental diasters have already created 80 MILLION refugees

Order Form UK

All these books are available in major bookshops or you may order them direct. Post and packaging are FREE.

	Price	No. copies
Special Places to Stay: **British Bed & Breakfast**		
Edition 5	£12.95	
Special Places to Stay: **French Hotels, Inns** and other places		
Edition 1	£11.95	
Special Places to Stay: **Italy** (from Rome to the Alps)		
Edition 1	£9.95	
Special Places to Stay: **French Bed & Breakfast**		
Edition 6	£13.95	
Special Places to Stay: **British Hotels, Inns** and other places		
Edition 2	£10.95	
Special Places to Stay in Spain & Portugal		
Edition 3	£11.95	
Special Places to Stay in Ireland		
Edition 2	£10.95	
Special Places to Stay: **Paris Hotels**		
Edition 2	£8.95	
The Little Earth Book	£4.99	

Please make cheques payable to: **Alastair Sawday Publishing** **Total** | |

Please send cheques to: Alastair Sawday Publishing, The Home Farm, Barrow Gurney, Bristol BS48 3RW. **For credit card orders call 01275 464891 or order directly from our website www.sawdays.co.uk**

Name:

Address:

Postcode:

Tel: Fax:

If you do not wish to receive mail from other companies, please tick the box ❏

GBH2

Order Form USA

All these books are available at your local bookstore, or you may order direct. Allow two to three weeks for delivery.

Special Places to Stay: British Bed & Breakfast

	Price	No. copies
Edition 5	$19.95	

Special Places to Stay: French Hotels, Inns and other places

Edition 1	$19.95	

Special Places to Stay: French Bed & Breakfast

Edition 6	$19.95	

Special Places to Stay: Paris Hotels

Edition 2	$14.95	

Special Places to Stay in Ireland

Edition 2	$19.95	

Special Places to Stay in Spain & Portugal

Edition 3	$19.95	

Special Places to Stay: Italy (from Rome to the Alps)

Edition 1	$14.95	

Shipping in the continental USA: $3.95 for one book,
$4.95 for two books, $5.95 for three or more books.
Outside continental USA, call (800) 243-0495 for prices.
For delivery to AK, CA, CO, CT, FL, GA, IL, IN, KS, MI, MN, MO, NE, NM, NC, OK, SC, TN, TX, VA, and WA, please add appropriate sales tax

Please make checks payable to: The Globe Pequot Press   **Total**

To order by phone with MasterCard or Visa: (800) 243-0495. 9 a.m. to 5 p.m. EST; by fax: (800) 820-2329, 24 hours; through our Website: www.globe-pequot.com; or by mail: The Globe Pequot Press, P.O. Box 480, Guilford, CT 06437.

Name: _____ Date: _____

Address: _____

Town: _____

State: _____ Zip code: _____

Tel: _____ Fax: _____

Report Form

Comments on existing entries and new discoveries.

If you have any comments on entries in this guide, please let us have them. If you have a favourite house, hotel, inn or other new discovery, please let us know about it.

Report on:

Entry no: Edition:

New Recommendation:

Name of property:

Address:

                    Postcode:

Tel:

Comments:

From:

Address:

                    Postcode:

Tel:

Please send the completed form to: **Alastair Sawday Publishing, The Home Farm, Barrow Gurney, Bristol BS48 3RW, UK**

Thank you.

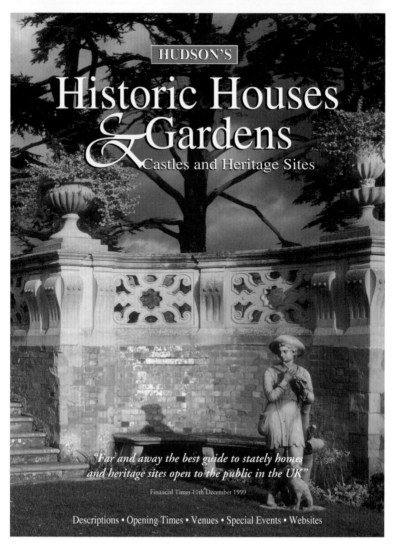

Index of Names

	Entry No.
Acorn Inn	42
The Albannach	169
Altnaharrie Inn	170
Applecross Inn	172
Apsley House	39
Ardsheal House	182
Argyll Hotel	185
Arundell Arms	15
Assapol House Hotel	184
Aynsome Manor Hotel	140
Babbity Bowster	158
Bailiffscourt Hotel	58
Bark House Hotel	28
Bath Place	92
The Beaufort	71
Belle Epoque Brasserie	120
Biggin Hall	124
Bindon Country House Hotel	31
Biskra Beach Hotel & Restaurant	53
Blackaller	20
Blue Lion	136
Boar's Head Hotel	133
The Bonham	159
Borthwnog Hall	197
Broomhill Art Hotel & Sculpture Gardens	25
Burford House	98
Burgoyne Hotel	137
Calgary Farmhouse & Dovecote Restaurant	183
Cawdor Arms Hotel	192
Channings	160
Churchill Inn	104
Clifton House	168
Cnapan	194
Combe House at Gittisham	22
Compasses Inn	44
Cormorant Hotel	12
Cornwallis Country Hotel & Restaurant	78
Crab Manor at The Crab and Lobster	131
Creagan House	162
Crosby Lodge	150
The Cross	166
The Crown	81
Culzean Castle	157
The Dolphin	80
Elan Valley Hotel	191
Elderton Lodge & Langtry Restaurant	83
Falcon Hotel	89
Falkland Arms	96
Feathers Hotel	95
Fingals	19
Flodigarry Country House Hotel	174
Four Seasons Hotel	164
Fowey Hall	11
Fox and Goose	115
Frogg Manor	119
General Tarleton	132
The George	34
George Hotel at Yarmouth	52
Glencot House	33
Glenelg Inn	178
Glewstone Court Hotel	111
Gliffaes Country House Hotel	188
Grange Hotel	129
Great House	76
Griffin Inn	61
Groes Inn	202
Gunfield Hotel	18
Halfway House Inn	14

Index of Names

Halmpstone Manor 24
Hambleton Hall 87
Hawnby Hotel 130
Hazelwood House 17
Heavens Above at The Mad Hatters Restaurant 110
Hipping Hall 139
Hoste Arms 84
Hotel du Vin & Bistro, Bristol 40
Hotel du Vin & Bistro, Royal Tunbridge Wells 70
Hotel du Vin & Bistro, Winchester 49
Hotel Eilean Iarmain 177
Hotel Maes-y-Neuadd 199
Hotel on the Park 108
Hotel Portmeirion 200
Howard Arms 114
Howard's House 45
Hundred House Hotel 117
Hunstrete House 35
Huntsham Court 27
Inn at Whitewell 126
Jeake's House 64
Kennel Holt Hotel 69
Kilcamb Lodge 181
Killiecrankie Hotel 165
Kings Arms 21
Knockinaam Lodge 156
La Sablonnerie 1
Lake Country House 190
Lake Vyrnwy Hotel 203
Lamb Inn 99
Langar Hall 86
Langley House Hotel & Restaurant 30
Lewtrenchard Manor 16
Little Barwick House 32
Little Hemingfold Hotel 63
Llwyndû Farmhouse & Restaurant 198
Lords of the Manor 102
Lovelady Shield 151
Lower Brook House 103
Malt House 106
Manor Cottage 8
Master Builder's House Hotel .50
Michaels Nook 143
Mill at Harvington 113
Mill Hotel 149
Millstream Hotel & Restaurant 56
Minmore House 167
Monachyle Mhor 163
Mr Underhill's at Dinham Weir 116
New Inn at Coln 100
Norfolk Mead Hotel 82
Number 6 9
Number Ten 73
Oak Tree Farm 121
Ockenden Manor 60
Old Bank 94
Old Beams 122
Old Bridge Hotel 88
Old Church Hotel 148
Old Dungeon Ghyll 144
Old Library 179
Old Parsonage Hotel 93
Old Pines Restaurant with Rooms 180
Old Railway Station 57
Old Rectory 79
Old Trout Hotel 91
Old Vicarage 141

Index of Names

Ounce House 77
Painswick Hotel 109
Paradise House 38
Peat Inn 161
Pen-y-Dyffryn Country Hotel 118
Penhelig Arms 195
Penmaenuchaf Hall 196
Penrhos Court Hotel 112
Penzance Arts Club 2
The Pheasant 147
Pheasant Inn 153
Plas Bodegroes 201
Plumber Manor 43
Polsue Manor 7
Pool House Hotel 171
Porlock Vale House 29
Portobello Gold 74
Priory Bay Hotel 55
Queensberry Hotel & Olive Tree Restaurant 37
Red Lion, Lacock 46
Red Lion, Skipton 134
Riber Hall 123
Ringlestone Inn 68
Rising Sun Hotel 26
Romney Bay House 65
Rose and Crown 152
Roxburghe Hotel & Golf Course 154
Royal Hotel 187
Royal Oak Hotel 47
Sandgate Hotel & La Terrasse Restaurant 66
Scarista House 173
Seaview Hotel 54
Simonstone Hall 138
St. Mawes Hotel 6
Stein Inn 175
Stone House 62
Stonor Arms 90
Strattons 85
Summer House Restaurant with Rooms 3
Summer Lodge 41
Sussex Arts Club 59
Swan Hotel at Bibury 101
Swinside Lodge 146
Talland Bay Hotel 13
Three Cocks Hotel 189
Three Main Street 193
Tigh an Truish 186
Tollgate Inn & Restaurant 97
Traquair Arms 155
Trebrea Lodge 10
Tregildry Hotel 4
Trengilly Wartha Inn 5
Two Hyde Park Square 72
Viewfield House 176
Wallett's Court Country House Hotel 67
Wasdale Head Inn 145
Waterford House 135
Weaver's 127
Weavers Shed Restaurant with rooms 128
Wesley House 107
Westover Hall 51
White Hart Inn, Nayland 75
White Hart Inn, Oldham 125
White Moss House 142
Wigham 23
Winford Manor Retreat 36
Wykeham Arms 48

Index of Places

	Entry No.
Aberdyfi	195
Aldeburgh	80
Alston	151
Applecross	172
Arisaig	179
Armscote	115
Asenby	131
Balquhidder	163
Bampton	28
Barnstaple	24, 25
Bassenthwaite Lake	147
Bath	37-39
Battle	63
Beaulieu	50
Bibury	101
Biggin-by-Hartington	124
Bosham	56
Bourton-on-the-Water	102
Brecon	189
Brighton	59
Bristol	40
Broad Campden	106
Bunessan	184
Burford	98, 99
Burnham Market	84
Bury St. Edmunds	77
Calgary	183
Callander	162
Campsea Ashe	79
Carlisle	150
Cartmel	140
Castle Ashby	89
Cawsand Bay	14
Cheltenham	108
Climping	58
Coln St-Aldwyns	100
Constantine	5
Conwy	202
Cranbrook	69
Crickhowell	188
Cuckfield	60
Cupar	161
Dartmouth	18, 19
Dolgellau	196, 197
Dover	67
East Witton	136
Edinburgh	159, 160
Elan Valley	191
Evershot	41, 42
Evesham	113
Eye	78
Fishguard	193
Flodigarry	174
Folkestone	66
Fort William	180
Fowey	11, 12
Fullers Moor	119
Glasgow	158
Glenlivet	167
Grasmere	142, 143
Great Langdale	144
Great Tew	96
Harlech	199
Harrietsham	68
Hawes	138
Hawnby	130

Index of Places

Haworth .127
Heathfield .62
Honiton .21, 22
Huddersfield .128
Huntingdon .88
Huntsham .27
Huntstrete .35
Ilmington .114
Innerleithen .155
Isle of Harris .173
Isle of Iona .185
Isle of Seil .186
Isle of Wight .52-55
Kelso .154
Kentallen of Appin .182
Keswick .146
Kielder Water .153
Kingham .97
Kingsbridge .17
Kington .112
Kingussie .166
Kirkby Lonsdale .139
Knaresborough .132
Knutsford .120
Kyle of Lochalsh .178
Lacock .46
Langar .86
Langford Budville .31
Lavenham .76
Lifton .15
Llanaber .198
Llandeilo .192
Llangammarch Wells .190
Llanwddyn .203
Lochinver .169
London .71-74
Looe .13
Lower Chicksgrove .44
Ludlow .116
Lymington .51
Lynmouth .26
Manaccan .4
Matlock .123
Maybole .157
Middleham .135
Morchard Bishop .23
Moreton-in-Marsh .103
Moretonhampstead .20
Mungrisdale .149
Nailsworth .110
Nairn .168
Nayland .75
New Romney .65
Newport .194
Norton St. Philip .34
Norwich .82
Oakfordbridge .28
Oakham .87
Okehampton .16
Oldham .125
Oswestry .118
Oxford .92-94
Padstow .9
Painswick .109
Paxford .104
Penzance .2, 3
Petworth .57

Index of Places

Pitlochry 165
Poolewe 171
Porlock Weir 29
Portmeirion 200
Portpatrick 156
Portree 176
Pwllheli 201
Richmond 137
Ripley 133
Romaldkirk 152
Ross-on-Wye 111
Royal Tunbridge Wells 70
Ruanhighlanes 7
Rye 64
Salisbury 45
Sark 1
Shifnal 117
Skipton 134
Sleat 177
Southwold 81
St. Fillans 164
St. Mawes 6
Stonor 90
Strontian 181
Sturminster Newton 43
Swaffham 85
Tamworth 121
Taunton 30
Thame 91
Thorpe Market 83
Tighnabruaich 187
Tintagel 10
Tresillian 8
Uckfield 61
Ullapool 170
Wasdale Head 145
Waterhouses 122
Watermillock 148
Waternish 175
Wells 33
Whitewell 126
Winchcombe 107
Winchester 48, 49
Winford 36
Witherslack 141
Woodstock 95
Yattendon 47
Yeovil 32
York 129

Exchange rate table

£sterling	US$
1	1.49
5	7.45
7	10.43
10	14.90
15	22.35
17	25.33
20	29.80
25	37.25
30	44.70
35	52.15
40	59.60
45	67.05
50	74.50

US$	£sterling
1	0.67
5	3.35
7	4.69
10	6.70
15	10.05
20	13.40
25	16.75

Rates correct at time of going to press August 2000

Spoofs

All our books have the odd spoof hidden away within their pages. Sunken boats, telephone boxes and ruined castles have all featured. Some of you have written in with your own ideas. As such, we have decided to hold a competition for spoof writing every year.

The rules are simple: send us your own spoofs, include the photos, and let us know which book it is intended for. We will publish the winning entries in the following edition of each book. We will also send a complete set of our guides to each winner.

Please send your entries to:

Alastair Sawday Publishing, Spoofs competition,
The Home Farm, Barrow Gurney, Bristol, BS48 3RW.
Winners will be notified by post.

Symbols

Symbols

Treat each one as a guide rather than a statement of fact and check important points when booking:

 Children of all ages are positively welcomed but cots, highchairs, etc are not necessarily available.

 Pets are welcome. There may be a supplement to pay or size restrictions.

 Vegetarians catered for with advance warning.

 Most, but not necessarily all, ingredients are organic, organically grown, home-grown or locally grown.

 Owners use only certified organic produce.

 Basic ground-floor access for people of limited mobility and at least one bedroom accessible without steps.

 Indicates full and approved wheelchair facilities for at least one bedroom and access to all ground-floor common areas.

 Swimming pool on the premises.

 Smoking restrictions exist, usually, but not always in the dining room and some bedrooms. For full restrictions, check when booking.

 A tennis court is available for guests on, or near, the premises.

 This house has pets of its own in the house: dog, cat, parrot...

 Payment by cash or cheques only.

 The premises are licensed.

 Restaurant open to non-residents and guests.